POWERFUL
Writing Strategies
FOR ALL Students

POWERFUL
Writing Strategies
FOR ALL Students

by

Karen R. Harris, Ed.D.
and
Steve Graham, Ed.D.
Vanderbilt University

Linda H. Mason, Ph.D.
Pennsylvania State University

Barbara Friedlander, M.A.
Montgomery County Public Schools

·P A U L·H·
BROOKES
PUBLISHING CO.®

Baltimore • London • Sydney

Paul H. Brookes Publishing Co.
Post Office Box 10624
Baltimore, Maryland 21285-0624
USA

www.brookespublishing.com

Typeset by Integrated Publishing Solutions, Grand Rapids, Michigan.
Manufactured in the United States by
Versa Press, Inc., East Peoria, Illinois.

The names of the children in Barbara Friedlander's class have been changed
to protect their privacy.

Readers of *Powerful Writing Strategies for All Students* may make copies
of the various materials in the book for educational purposes only.

Cover image © Masterfile.

Seventh printing, May 2016.

Library of Congress Cataloging-in-Publication Data
Powerful writing strategies for all students / by Karen R. Harris . . . [et al.].
    p.   cm.
    Includes bibliographical references and index.
    ISBN-10: 1-55766-705-5
    ISBN-13: 978-1-55766-705-2 (alk. paper)
    1. English language—Composition and exercises—Study and teaching.
2. Report writing—Study and teaching.   3. Learning disabled children—
Education.   I. Harris, Karen R.   II. Title.
    LB1576.P686 2008
    808'.042071—dc22
                                                    2007035843

Contents

V Strategy for a Writing Competency Test

VI Strategy for Reading and Writing Informational Text

About the Authors

Karen R. Harris, Ed.D., Currey-Ingram Professor of Special Education and Literacy, Peabody College of Education, Vanderbilt University, Nashville, Tennessee 37203

Dr. Harris has worked in the field of education for more than 30 years. She has taught kindergarten and fourth grade, as well as elementary and secondary students with attention-deficit/hyperactivity disorder and with learning and behavioral/emotional difficulties. Dr. Harris' research focuses on theoretical and intervention issues in the development of academic and self-regulation strategies among students who are at risk and those with severe learning challenges. She is currently editor of the *Journal of Educational Psychology* and has coauthored several books including *Writing Better: Effective Strategies for Teaching Students with Learning Difficulties* (Paul H. Brookes Publishing Co., 2005), *Making the Writing Process Work: Strategies for Composition and Self-Regulation* (Brookline Books, 1996), and *Handbook of Learning Disabilities* (Guilford Press, 2003).

Steve Graham, Ed.D., Currey-Ingram Professor of Special Education and Literacy, Peabody College of Education, Vanderbilt University, Nashville, Tennessee 37203

Steve Graham's research focuses on identifying the factors that contribute to writing development and writing difficulties, developing and validating effective instructional procedures for teaching writing, and the use of technology to enhance writing performance. He is the current editor of *Exceptional Children* and the past editor of *Contemporary Educational Psychology*. He is coauthor of *Best Practices in Writing Instruction* (Guilford Press, 2007), *Handbook of Writing Research* (Guilford Press, 2006), *Writing Better: Effective Strategies for Teaching Students with Learning Difficulties* (Paul H. Brookes Publishing Co., 2005), *Handbook of Learning Disabilities* (Guilford Press, 2003), and *Making the Writing Process Work: Strategies for Composition and Self-Regulation* (Brookline Books, 1996).

Linda H. Mason, Ph.D., Assistant Professor, Department of Educational and School Psychology and Special Education, College of Education, 20 Cedar, Pennsylvania State University, University Park, Pennsylvania 16802

Dr. Mason has a joint appointment in the Department of Educational and School Psychology and Special Education, and the Children, Youth, and Families Consortium at Pennsylvania State University. Prior to earning her Ph.D., she taught elementary special education in Maryland public schools for 6 years. Dr. Mason conducts research on self-regulated strategy instruction for reading comprehension and writing for students with high-incidence disabilities in public elementary and middle schools. Her U.S. Department of Education-funded work has been published in both scholarly and research-to-practice journals. Dr. Mason serves on the editorial boards of *Journal of Educational Psychology, Exceptional Children, Journal of Special Education, Learning Disabilities Research and Practice, Learning Disabilities Quarterly,* and *Intervention in School and Clinic.* She currently teaches special education methods courses and graduate seminars on reading and writing instruction and content learning at Pennsylvania State University.

Barbara Friedlander, M.A., Nationally Board Certified Special Education Teacher, Montgomery County Public Schools, Beverly Farms Elementary, 8501 Post Oak Road, Potomac, Maryland 20854

Barbara Friedlander has taught special needs and at-risk students since 1986 in an inclusive elementary classroom environment. She has been involved in a variety of written language research studies in the areas of learning disabilities and has coauthored a number of publications including *Summer of Learning: The Effects of Summer Tutoring for Students with Learning Disabilities* (*Division of Learning Disabilities Times*, 1997) and *Incorporating Strategy Instruction within the Writing Process in the Regular Classroom: Effects on the Writing of Students with and without Leaning Disabilities* (*Journal of Reading Behavior*, 1993). Ms. Friedlander has received numerous awards including the Shaklee Outstanding Special Educator Award, the Council for Exceptional Children Allyn Bacon Exemplary Program Award and Grant, the Baltimore Area Committee on Student Teaching Outstanding Cooperative Teacher Award, the Montgomery County Public Schools Educational Foundation Grant for Parent Training, the University of Maryland Alumni Award, and the Maryland Association of Supervision and Curriculum Development Judith Ruchkin Research Award.

Foreword

Anyone who has worked in our schools for long is well aware that there is a problem with written expression in this country. Put simply, our kids don't know how to write. And all of the evidence suggests that the problem is pervasive. The results of the National Assessment of Educational Progress found that three out of every four 4th-, 8th-, and 12th-grade students exhibited only partial mastery of the necessary writing skills and knowledge at their respective grade levels (Persky, Danne, & Jin, 2003). Moreover, only one in 100 students demonstrated "advanced" writing skills. Problems with written language are even more common for students with special needs or disabilities (e.g., Graham, Harris, & Larsen, 2001; Harris & Graham, 1999). These students' papers contain fewer ideas and are more poorly organized and of lower quality when compared with papers written by their typically achieving peers (Graham & Harris, 2002).

There are many reasons why students have problems with writing. One of the most obvious is simply that they've never been taught how to write. In my experience, I cannot recall ever receiving any formal instruction at any level (e.g., elementary, high school, or college) in the craft of writing. I can recall learning writing mechanics such as parts of speech, various types of sentences, and even how to diagram sentences, but never once can I recall a lesson on how to write that provided me with a strategy that would help me accomplish a writing task. There is good evidence suggesting that my experience was not unusual. In a national survey, classroom teachers have reported spending much more time on mechanics than on skills related to actual composition (such as how to plan a paper). Luckily the situation is improving thanks in part to increased attention. For example, the National Commission on Writing (2003) has increased awareness at both the public and policy levels about the importance of writing and has gone so far as to recommend that writing become a central focus of school-reform efforts because writing skills are crucial to students' educational and occupational success. Still, the success of reform efforts in writing depends on the application of effective instructional practices that improve the writing skills of students of all abilities and at all levels. It is especially critical to identify effective instructional practices for young beginning writers, particularly those students at risk for writing difficulties and students with special needs.

Another reason for writing problems is that writing is tough. Even some of the most accomplished writers find writing to be a difficult and demanding task. Kellogg (1993) wrote that writing literally is "the mental equivalent of digging ditches" (p. 17). Skilled writing is not like riding a bicycle; it is not automatic and natural and does not become effortless with practice. For anything much more involved than a grocery list, writing demands that students plan, create necessary content, and translate the content into written language. Of course, that's just for the first draft. Next they must revise and improve their initial draft (Graham & Harris, 2003). If we could magically look inside the head of a skilled writer in the act of writing, she or he would look very much like a busy switchboard operator trying to simultaneously juggle demands to plan, draw ideas from memory, develop new ideas, and consider the reader's reaction to the final product (Hayes & Flower, 1980). But that's not all that's needed. Writing also involves a high degree of self-regulation (Graham & Harris, 2003). And because writing is so demanding, many students (even at the most advanced levels) develop sophisticated strategies to avoid doing it. I know of one accomplished professor who admits that her house is at its cleanest when she has a writing task. And I confess that as I compose this foreword, I have a distinct desire to escape to the golf course. The sheer stick-to-it-iveness needed for successful writing can't be underestimated. Unfortunately, many children are not equipped with appropriate strategies to overcome these "writing avoidance behaviors" (Graham & Harris, 2003).

So what's a good way to address problems with written expression? Well, for a start, we should remember that the No Child Left Behind law stresses that schools employ methods that have been proven to be effective. It would also be nice if we could find a practical program that teachers could employ, and if kids liked it, that would be the icing on the cake. Fortunately, there is an approach to written expression that meets all of these criteria: Self-Regulated Strategy Development (SRSD). SRSD was developed by two of the preeminent written language researchers: Karen Harris and Steve Graham. SRSD is not a strategy itself; rather, it is a model for teaching strategies. It isn't a "flash in the pan" strategy. It has been *thoroughly researched and its effectiveness validated*. In fact, more than 25 years of research and more than 30 studies have demonstrated that SRSD is effective for a broad range of students. SRSD also fits the bill in terms of practicality: It has been verified in the real-world classroom with general education, at-risk, and special education students. Teachers with whom I have worked have enthusiastically adopted SRSD because it is practical and easy to use in the classroom. What do students think of SRSD? They love it because it helps them learn *how* to do a task. There's even an added bonus: As the name implies, SRSD includes the development of self-regulation strategies, which are powerful and simple to use and can have dramatic effects on motivation and performance. These strategies help to give students the perseverance they need to get through demanding tasks such as writing an essay.

There is absolutely no doubt that SRSD is a powerful tool for educators. A tool, however, is only as good as its user. This brings us to the purpose of this book. In this volume, Harris and Graham have refined three decades of research and practical classroom experience and created a practical step-by-step guide to SRSD instruction for the teachers. They take the user through the "how" and "why" of SRSD and offer insights gleaned from more than 25 years of experience in the classroom. Moreover, the material is presented in a reader-friendly style that the classroom teacher can easily relate to and gives practical examples of how it can be used. This is tremendously beneficial—but that's not all. The authors also provide detailed, step-by-step lesson plans. These lesson plans have been developed and polished to make them simple to use, and, best of all, they enable the teacher to use SRSD to teach effective strategies for common writing tasks such as narratives, opinion essays, and revising.

In summary, Harris and Graham have created a gem. For any teacher interested in improving their students' writing, this book is a must.

Robert Reid, Ph.D.
Professor
Department of Special Education
University of Nebraska

REFERENCES

Graham, S., & Harris, K.R. (2002). Prevention and intervention for struggling writers. In M. Shinn, G. Stoner, & H. Walker (Eds.), *Interventions for academic and behavior problems II: Preventive and remedial techniques* (pp. 589–610). Washington, DC: National Association of School Psychologists.

Graham, S., & Harris, K.R. (2003). Students with learning disabilities and the process of writing: A meta-analysis of SRSD studies. In H.L. Swanson, K.R. Harris, & S. Graham (Eds.), *Handbook of learning disabilities*. New York: Guilford Press.

Graham, S., & Harris, K.R. (2005). Improving the writing performance of young struggling writers: Theoretical and programmatic research from the Center on Accelerated Student Learning. *Journal of Special Education*, 39, 19–33.

Graham, S., Harris, K.R., & Larsen, L. (2001). Prevention and intervention of writing difficulties with students with learning disabilities. *Learning Disabilities Research and Practice, 16,* 74–84.

Harris, K.R., & Graham, S. (1999). Programmatic intervention research: Illustrations from the evolution of self-regulated strategy development. *Learning Disability Quarterly, 22,* 251–262.

Hayes, J., & Flower, L. (1980). Identifying the organization of writing processes. In L. Gregg & E. Steinberg (Eds.), *Cognitive processes in writing* (pp. 3–30). Hillsdale, NJ: Lawrence Erlbaum Associates.

Kellogg, R. (1993). *The psychology of writing* (p. 17). New York: Oxford University Press.

National Commission on Writing. (2003). *The neglected "R."* College Entrance Examination Board. Available at: http://www.writingcommission.org/prod_downloads/writingcom/neglectedr.pdf

Persky, H., Daane, M., & Jin, Y. (2003). *The nation's report card: Writing.* Washington, DC: U.S. Department of Education.

*This book is dedicated to the many students, teachers, and principals
who have worked with us over the past 25 years
and who have made this book possible.*

Part 1

Chapter 1

Welcome to Self-Regulated Strategy Development in Writing

As teachers, parents, and school personnel know, writing is a highly complex, demanding process. Difficulties with narrative, expository, and informative writing have been well-documented among students in our schools. National and state writing assessments indicate that we have yet to become highly effective at developing this critical competency among our students, as the majority of children in American schools demonstrate significant difficulties with writing. Five areas of competence have been identified as particularly difficult when students are learning to write: 1) generation of content, 2) creation of an organizing structure for compositions, 3) formulation of goals and higher-level plans, 4) quick and efficient execution of the mechanical aspects of writing, and 5) revision of text and reformulation of goals.

Although children typically begin school with a positive attitude toward writing, this attitude frequently becomes more and more negative during the elementary school years (Applebee, Langer, Mullis, Latham, & Gentile, 1994). Students who struggle with writing often lack important knowledge of the writing process, experience difficulties generating ideas and selecting topics, do little or no advance planning, engage in knowledge-telling (i.e., simply writing down what they think they know about certain topics without confirming the accuracy of their information), do not employ strategies for producing and organizing text, have difficulties with mechanics that interfere with the writing process, and engage in little or no revision of their content. As a result, these students frequently experience failure with writing, which leads to self-doubt, negative expectations and attributions, and low motivation.

The effective writer must negotiate the rules and mechanics of writing while maintaining a focus on factors such as organization, form and features, purposes and goals, audience needs and perspectives, and evaluation of the communication between author and reader. In addition, writing requires extensive self-regulation and attention control. For skilled writers, the process of writing is a flexible, goal-directed activity supported by a rich knowledge of cognitive processes and strategies for planning, text production, and revision. Skilled writers engage in purposeful and active self-direction of these processes and strategies. Self-regulation of the writing process is critical; the writer must be goal-oriented, resourceful, and reflective.

WHAT IS SRSD?

Self-regulated strategy development (SRSD) is a writing strategies instruction approach developed over the past 2 decades by Karen Harris, Steve Graham, their research colleagues (including Linda Mason), and numerous teachers (including Barbara Friedlander) and their students. SRSD, which brings together powerful strategies for writing and critical strategies for self-regulation of the writing process, has been used in the elementary through high school grades. Extensive research has shown that this approach is proven to help students, especially those who struggle with writing, become more effective writers and develop more positive attitudes toward writing and themselves as writers. Strategies have been developed and used in classrooms across the genres of story writing, creative writing, narrative writing, expository writing, and persuasive writing.

Created in 1982, SRSD was initially designed to meet the needs of students with severe learning problems, including those with learning disabilities. However, over the past 2 decades, we learned that students who struggle with writing, even those without disabilities, share critical characteristics. Generally, students with writing problems produce writing that is less polished, expansive, coherent, and effective than that of their typically achieving peers. In addition to the writing problems already mentioned, many of these students have difficulty with self-regulation of organized, strategic behaviors. They may have difficulty comprehending task demands, producing effective task strategies, and using strategies to mediate performance. They may also experience reciprocal relationships among academic failure, self-doubt, learned helplessness, maladaptive attributions, unrealistic pretask expectancies, low self-efficacy, and low motivation. Impulsivity, difficulties with memory or other aspects of information processing, low task engagement and persistence, devaluation of learning, and low productivity are also among the problems with which these students and their teachers must contend.

Thus, SRSD was created to address not just students' difficulties with the writing process but also their attitudes and beliefs about writing, motivation, and self-efficacy. Furthermore, struggling writers often require more extensive, structured, and explicit instruction to develop skills, writing and self-regulation strategies, and understandings that are more easily formed by some of their peers. SRSD provides this structured, explicit instruction to meet these students' needs and can be modified to meet teachers' needs as well. In Chapter 2, we cover how SRSD instruction is done and demonstrate how SRSD combines instructional components to help students develop writing strategies and acquire knowledge about the writing process, self-regulation strategies, positive attitudes and beliefs about writing, and confidence in themselves as writers.

AN OVERVIEW OF THE RESEARCH EVIDENCE FOR SRSD

More than 40 studies using the SRSD model of instruction have been reported in the area of writing, involving students from the elementary grades through high school. Teachers have been able to implement SRSD and have found it to be beneficial in their classrooms. SRSD has resulted in significant and meaningful improvements in children's development of writing strategies across genres, self-regulation strategies, generating and organizing writing content, advanced planning, revising with their peers, and revising their writing for both substance and mechanics. (References for the research base are included at the end of this chapter.)

SRSD has resulted in improvements in four main aspects of student performance: quality of writing, knowledge of writing, approach to writing, and self-efficacy. Across a variety of strategies and genres, the quality, length, and structure of students' compositions have improved. Depending on the strategy taught, improvements have also been documented in planning, revising, content, and mechanics. The majority of students have maintained these improvements over time, with some students needing booster sessions for long-term maintenance. Students have shown generalization across settings, persons, and writing media. Meaningful improvements have been found with average-to-better writers, as well as students who score at or below the 25th percentile on writing measures and other struggling writers.

SRSD IN THE CLASSROOM

With the SRSD approach, students are explicitly taught strategies for specific writing genres (e.g., story writing, opinion essay writing, report writing), as well as general writing strategies (e.g., employing good word choice, creating interesting openings). In addition, they learn how to use self-regulation strategies, including goal setting, self-monitoring, self-reinforcement, and self-instructions, to help them manage the writing strategies and tasks and to obtain concrete and visible evidence of their progress. Students learn to use these writing and self-regulation strategies within the writing process.

SRSD has been used successfully with entire classes, small groups, individual students, and in tutoring settings. The instruction is designed to promote students' ownership and independent use of the writing and self-regulation strategies. Instruction is scaffolded so that responsibility for applying and recruiting the writing and self-regulation strategies gradually shifts from teacher to student. Children are active collaborators in the learning process. The role of effort in learning and using the writing and self-regulation strategies is emphasized and rewarded. The level and type of feedback and instructional support are individualized by the instructor to be responsive to the students' needs. Instruction is criterion-based rather than time-based, as children move through each instructional stage at their own pace and do not proceed to later stages of instruction until they have met initial criteria for doing so. Instructional stages are revisited and combined as necessary. Thus, each stage does not equal a preset number of lessons, as will be seen in the lesson plans laid out in this book.

Typically, there are six stages of instruction used to introduce and develop the writing and self-regulation strategies in the SRSD approach:

1. Develop Background Knowledge

2. Discuss It

3. Model It

4. Memorize It

5. Support It

6. Independent Performance

These stages are presented in Chapter 2 and also are used in the lesson plans. Throughout these stages, teachers and students collaborate on the acquisition, implementation, evaluation, and modification of the writing and self-regulation strategies. The stages are not meant to be followed in a cookbook fashion but instead provide a general format and guidelines. The stages can be reordered, combined, revisited, modified, or deleted to meet student and teacher needs. Furthermore, the stages are meant to be recursive so that students and teachers can revisit any stage as needed.

Depending on grade level and class schedules, lessons typically run anywhere from 20 to 60 minutes at least three times per week. In the elementary and middle grades, 8 to 12 lessons running 30 to 40 minutes each have typically helped struggling writers complete the stages and write independently. More competent writers may reach independent use of the strategies more quickly. Thus, SRSD instruction is not costly in terms of classroom time and provides great benefits to students.

SRSD instruction is easily differentiated to accommodate student needs. Some stages may not be needed by all students. For example, some students may already have the background knowledge needed to use the writing strategies and self-regulation processes. Thus, they may skip the Develop Background Knowledge stage or act as a resource for other students who need assistance during this stage. More competent writers may not need to spend as much time in the Support It stage or again may assist their peers. Advanced writers may not need SRSD in some genres, or teachers may adapt the strategy for these students, calling for more sophisticated writing products.

We emphasize that research clearly shows that as students' learning and behavioral challenges become more significant, strategy and self-regulation instruction must be more explicit. Struggling writers need all six stages to learn how to use the strategies independently. Research has shown that developing background knowledge, discussing the strategies, and modeling the strategies is not enough for these students—the Support It stage is critical.

Students must remember these strategies over time and be able to use them in different settings. Procedures for promoting maintenance and generalization are integrated throughout the stages of instruction in the SRSD model. These include identifying opportunities to use the writing and/or self-regulation strategies in other classes or settings, discussing attempts to use the strategies at other times, reminding students to use the strategies at appropriate times, analyzing how these processes might need to be modified with other tasks and in new settings, and evaluating the success of these processes during and after instruction. Writing should occur across the curriculum. It is helpful to involve others, including other teachers and parents, as they can prompt the use of the strategies at appropriate times in other settings. Booster sessions, where the strategies are reviewed, discussed, and supported again if necessary, are very important for most students in terms of maintaining the strategies.

SRSD AND THE WRITING CURRICULUM

SRSD is meant to supplement, not supplant, the larger writing curriculum. It does not represent a complete writing program. Although writing and self-regulation strategies are essential to writing development, they are not the only abilities students must develop to improve their writing skills. Furthermore, to profit from SRSD instruction, young students must be able to write complete sentences. It is therefore inappropriate to ask students to engage in these writing and self-regulation strategies before they can write sentences. For young students, a simple sentence (e.g., *The dog ran.*) is fine. Writing skills such as sentence construction and usage, spelling, and handwriting must also be developed. SRSD, while not a panacea, is an important tool for teachers' repertoires—one that makes a difference.

In this book we do not recommend a prescribed sequence for teaching the writing and self-regulation strategies. Also, the strategies are not arranged from most to least critical. Teachers and administrators must decide which strategies to use at what time and with whom within the larger context of the curriculum and in terms of their goals and their students' needs. This book includes strategies that have been validated through research; however, there is not a strategy for every genre at every grade level. The strategies presented can be scaled up or down to different appropriate grade levels through adaptations in expectations (a single paragraph versus a five-paragraph essay) and sophistication of the strategies. (For details on adapting strategies, please consult the book *Writing Better: Effective Strategies for Teaching Students with Learning Difficulties*, referenced at the end of this chapter.) In addition, for both writing stories and writing persuasive essays, we have developed multiple writing strategies and sets of lesson plans. Some plans are aimed at younger or less proficient writers, while others are aimed at older or more sophisticated writers. Teachers should look at each set of strategies and the lesson plans that go with them to determine which is best for their students.

THIS BOOK

In Chapter 2, the stages of SRSD instruction are explained, with an example given from Barbara Friedlander's classroom. The characteristics of effective SRSD instruction are also discussed. In Chapter 3, more is explained about the development of self-regulation strategies. Chapter 4 includes advice on getting started with SRSD, as well as guidelines that teachers have helped develop for the evaluation of SRSD instruction. Complete lesson plans are included for each of the writing strategies that have been researched. Support materials that teachers may want to implement instruction are also included, such as strategy mnemonics and graphic organizers, strategy prompt sheets, self-instruction sheets, goal-setting materials, and progress-graphing sheets. These can be copied for the students and used to make overheads.

WANT TO KNOW MORE?

All of the stages of instruction can be seen in both elementary and middle-school classrooms in the video *Teaching Students with Learning Disabilities: Using Learning Strategies* (Association for Supervision and Curriculum Development, 2002). A free, on-line interactive tutorial on SRSD is available through Vanderbilt University at http://iris .peabody.vanderbilt.edu/index.html. The tutorial includes all stages of instruction and video clips from the ASCD video. From the IRIS homepage, select Resources, and then select Star Legacy Modules. Click on "Using Learning Strategies: Instruction to Enhance Learning." There is also a module on persuasive writing with the POW+TREE strategy for elementary students. Go to the heading "Differentiated Instruction" and then click on the module "Improving Writing Performance: A Strategy for Writing Expository Essays."

The book, *Writing Better: Effective Strategies for Teaching Students with Learning Difficulties*, by Steve Graham and Karen Harris (Brookes, 2005), includes more detail about each of the writing strategies, the research base, adaptations of these strategies across grade levels and student needs, and samples of student writing before and after instruction. An earlier book by Karen Harris and Steve Graham, *Making the Writing Process Work: Strategies for Composition and Self-Regulation* (Brookline Books, 1996), includes greater detail on the development of self-regulation in the classroom and on SRSD within the writing process or Writers' Workshop. Finally, there is a web site dedicated to strategies instruction at www.unl.edu/csi.

RESEARCH REFERENCES

A list of references is supplied here for those who would like to access the database on writing and SRSD.

Applebee, A., Langer, J., Mullis, I., Latham, A., & Gentile, C. (1994). *NAEP 1992: Writing report card.* Washington, DC: U.S. Government Printing Office.

Association for Supervision and Curriculum Development. (2002). *Teaching students with learning disabilities: Using learning strategies* [videotape]. Retrieved August 15, 2000, from http://shop.ascd.org/productdisplay.cfm?productid=402086

Bereiter, C., & Scardamalia, M. (1982). From conversation to composition: The role of instruction in a developmental process. In R. Glaser (Ed.), *Advances in instructional psychology* (Vol. 2, pp. 1–64). Mahwah, NJ: Lawrence Erlbaum Associates.

De La Paz, S. (1999). Teaching writing strategies and self-regulation procedures to middle school students with learning disabilities. *Focus on Exceptional Children, 31*, 1–16.

De La Paz, S., & Graham, S. (2002). Explicitly teaching strategies, skills, and knowledge: Writing instruction in middle school classrooms. *Journal of Educational Psychology, 94*, 687–698.

De La Paz, S., Owen, B., Harris, K.R., & Graham, S. (2000). Riding Elvis' motorcycle: Using self-regulated strategy development to PLAN and WRITE for a state exam. *Learning Disabilities Research and Practice, 15*(2), 101–109.

Graham, S., & Harris, K.R. (2003). Students with learning disabilities and the process of writing: A meta-analysis of SRSD studies. In H.L. Swanson, K.R. Harris, & S. Graham (Eds.), *Handbook of learning disabilities* (pp. 323–344). New York: Guilford Press.

Graham, S., Harris, K.R., & Zito, J. (2005). Promoting internal and external validity: A synergism of laboratory experiments and classroom-based research. In G. Phye, D.H. Robinson, & J. Levin (Eds.), *Experimental methods for educational intervention* (pp. 235–265). New York: Elsevier.

Greenwald, E., Persky, H., Ambell, J., & Mazzeo, J. (1999). *National assessment of educational progress: 1998 report card for the nation and the states.* Washington, DC: U.S. Department of Education.

Harris, K.R., & Graham, S. (1992). Self-regulated strategy development: A part of the writing process. In M. Pressley, K.R. Harris, & J.T. Guthrie (Eds.), *Promoting academic competence and literacy in school* (pp. 277–309). San Diego: Academic Press.

Harris, K.R., Reid, R., & Graham, S. (2004). Self-regulation among students with LD and ADHD. In B. Wong (Ed.), *Learning about learning disabilities* (3rd ed., pp. 167–195). San Diego: Academic Press.

Mason, L.H., Snyder, K.H., Sukhram, D.P., & Kedem, Y. (2006). TWA + PLANS strategies for expository reading and writing: Effects for nine fourth-grade students. *Exceptional Children, 73,* 69–89.

National Commission on Writing (2003). *The neglected "R."* College Entrance Examination Board.

Pressley, M., & Harris, K.R. (2006). Cognitive strategies instruction: From basic research to classroom instruction. In P.A. Alexander & P. Winne (Eds.), *Handbook of educational psychology* (2nd ed., pp. 265–286). New York: Macmillan.

Reid, R., & Lienemann, T.O. (2006). *Strategy instruction for students with learning disabilities.* New York: Guilford.

Chapter 1 Self-Test

1. True or False
   The majority of students in the United States are making adequate progress in writing and do not need to learn to self-regulate the use of writing strategies.

2. SRSD works best with
   a. Students with learning disabilities
   b. Struggling writers who do not have disabilities
   c. All students who struggle with writing

3. SRSD provides
   a. Extensive, explicit, structured instruction in writing and self-regulation strategies
   b. A way for students to discover on their own what skilled writers do
   c. A poor combination with Writers' Workshop

4. Evidence for the effectiveness of SRSD is provided by
   a. More than 40 research studies across the elementary to high school grades
   b. Significant and meaningful changes in students' writing quality, knowledge of writing, approach to writing, and self-efficacy
   c. Both a and b

5. True or False
   With SRSD, students progress through a preset number of lessons at an established pace.

6. True or False
   Teachers must be prepared to devote an extensive amount of time to SRSD.

Answers: 1. False   2. c   3. a   4. c   5. False   6. False

Chapter 2

SRSD for Writing

What, Why, and How

"Okay, students, begin writing."

The students look at their clean, white, lined paper, pick up their newly sharpened pencils, and begin to think. Some students start writing, while others continue to sit still, look around the room, and, after a few minutes, raise their hands. "What should I write about?" "How do I get started?" "I'm just no good at writing." With that informal assessment, the teacher decides on an approach that will provide the students with the keys to unlocking the strategies and skills that good writers use. The teacher is confident that these students can learn to use the same powerful writing and self-regulation strategies that good writers use.

In this chapter, the instructional model for teaching composing and self-regulation strategies, Self-Regulated Strategy Development (SRSD), is presented. The major goals of SRSD are threefold:

1. To assist students in mastering the higher-level cognitive processes involved in the planning, production, revising, and editing of written language

2. To help students further develop the ability to monitor and manage their own writing

3. To aid students in the development of positive attitudes and beliefs about writing and about themselves as writers

Many students have experienced a great deal of frustration, failure, or anxiety when faced with writing assignments. For these students, the development of positive attitudes and beliefs is essential. These attitudes and beliefs develop as the students learn powerful strategies that improve their writing. There is a great deal of truth in the old adage, "Nothing succeeds like success." To help students master writing strategies and use them effectively, the SRSD approach includes the development of skillful use of effective writing strategies, self-regulation of the writing process, and knowledge of one's own cognitive processes and other learning characteristics and an understanding of the potential and limitations of the strategies they learn.

Self-regulation of strategic performance and knowledge about the strategies are important in helping students

- Understand how and when to apply a strategy

- Independently produce, evaluate, and modify a strategy in an effective manner

- Recognize meaningful improvement in skills, processes, and products

- Gain new insights regarding strategies and their own strategic performance

- Improve their expectations of and attitudes regarding themselves as writers

- Maintain and generalize strategic performance

STAGES OF INSTRUCTION

In the SRSD approach, six basic stages of instruction are used to develop and integrate use of the strategy and self-regulation components. SRSD has been successfully used with entire classes, small groups, individual students, and in tutoring settings. Throughout these stages, teachers and students collaborate on the acquisition, implementation, evaluation, and modification of strategies. These stages are not meant to be followed in a "cookbook" fashion. Instead, they provide a general format and guidelines. The instructional stages are meant to be recursive, teachers may return to any stage at any time. The stages may be reordered, combined, or modified as needed to meet student and teacher needs. In fact, as will be seen in the lesson plans in this book, the first two stages (Develop Background Knowledge and Discuss It) are typically combined in the first lessons. Some stages may not be needed by all students. Some students may already have the background knowledge needed to use the writing strategy and self-regulation processes and may therefore skip this stage or act as a resource for other students who need this stage. Finally, lessons have typically run anywhere from 20 to 60 minutes (depending on grade level and class schedules) at least three times a week. Typically, in the elementary grades, 8 to 12 lessons running 30 to 40 minutes each have proven sufficient to allow students to complete the stages. More complex strategies may take longer in middle or high school.

Generalization and Maintenance

Procedures for promoting maintenance and generalization are integrated throughout the stages of instruction in the SRSD model. These include

- Identifying opportunities to use the writing and/or self-regulation strategies in other classes or settings

- Discussing attempts to use the strategies at other times

- Reminding students to use the strategies at appropriate times

- Analyzing how these processes may be modified with other tasks and in new settings

- Evaluating the success of these processes during and after instruction

It is helpful to involve others (e.g., other teachers, parents) as they can prompt the use of the strategies at appropriate times in other settings. Booster sessions in which the strategies are reviewed, discussed, and supported are very important for most students in terms of maintaining the strategies.

Self-Efficacy

Students who have experienced significant learning problems frequently develop negative beliefs and expectations that result in low motivation, attitudinal problems, and lessened effort. Repeated failure can result in feelings of helplessness. These students believe that further effort will have little effect, even when the task is doable. Self-efficacy is believed to have a strong influence on performance as it affects a person's choice of activities, the amount of effort expended, and the degree of persistence one demonstrates in the face of difficulty. Students who believe they are capable of successful performance are likely to choose challenging activities, work hard, and persist when difficulties are encountered. Throughout SRSD, self-efficacy is supported and developed.

A brief overview of the six stages of instruction in SRSD is presented in Table 2.1.

Table 2.1. SRSD stages: An overview

Develop Background Knowledge
- Read works in the genre being addressed (e.g., stories, persuasive essays) to develop vocabulary ("What is an opinion?"), knowledge ("What are the parts of a persuasive essay?"), concepts ("How does the writer grab the reader's interest?"), and so on that are needed for instruction. Continue development through the next two stages as needed.
- Discuss and explore both the writing and self-regulation strategies to be learned; you may begin development of self-regulation, introducing goal setting and self-monitoring.

Discuss It
- Explore students' current writing and self-regulation abilities.
- Graphing (self-monitoring) may be introduced, using prior compositions; this may assist with goal setting.
- Further discuss strategies to be learned: purpose, benefits, how and when they can be used (begin generalization support).
- Establish students' commitment to learning strategies and acting as a collaborative partner; establish role of student effort.
- May identify and address current negative or ineffective self-talk, attitudes, or beliefs.

Model It
- Use teacher modeling and collaborative modeling of writing and self-regulation strategies, which will result in appropriate model compositions.
- Analyze and discuss strategies and model's performance; make changes as needed.
- Can model self-assessment and self-recording through graphing of model compositions.
- Continue student development of self-regulation strategies across composition and other tasks and situations; discuss use (continue generalization support).

Memorize It
- Though typically begun in earlier stages, require and confirm memorization of strategies, mnemonic(s), and self-instructions as appropriate.
- Continue to confirm and support memorization in the next stage, Support It.

Support It
- Teachers and students use writing and self-regulation strategies collaboratively to achieve success in composing.
- Challenging initial goals established collaboratively; criteria levels increased gradually until final goals are met.
- Prompts, guidance, and collaboration are faded individually until each student can compose successfully alone.
- Self-regulation components not yet introduced may begin.
- Discuss plans for maintenance; continue support of generalization.

Independent Performance
- Students able to use task and self-regulation strategies independently; teachers monitor and support as necessary.
- Fading of overt self-regulation may begin.
- Plans for maintenance and generalization continue to be discussed and implemented.

Each stage is discussed in detail and then followed by an example of SRSD in the classroom. The stages of instruction, however, represent merely the framework of instruction. Thus, this description is followed by a discussion of critical characteristics of SRSD instruction and guidelines for evaluation of this process.

STAGE 1: DEVELOP BACKGROUND KNOWLEDGE

During this stage, background knowledge and any preskills (e.g., vocabulary, concepts) students need for learning and using the writing or self-regulation strategies are developed. For example, if students are going to learn a story-writing strategy (such as the Who, When, and Where [WWW] strategy for story writing included in this book), they must understand the vocabulary related to story parts, including who, when, and where, or for older students, setting and characters. Preskills and background knowledge should be developed far enough to allow students to move into the next stages. Their development can continue into Stages 2 (Discuss It) and 3 (Model It); however, it is usually best if preskills are mastered by Stage 4 (Memorize It). Background knowledge and preskill development activities depend on the learner and the knowledge and skills that must be developed. These skills can be developed in regard to both the composition and self-regulation strategies that are to be mastered.

The concept and use of self-instructions are often introduced in Stage 1. The teacher and students might collaboratively create self-instructions relevant to composition. For example, a student who tends to act impulsively might say to himself, "Remember, I need to take my time and go slow." A student with a low tolerance for frustration might say, "I'm not going to get mad. Getting mad makes me do bad." Students can practice using such self-instructions in a variety of situations as a part of preskill development; these self-instructions can then be incorporated into the later stages of strategies instruction. This may be particularly helpful for students who have not previously learned to use self-instructions.

In addition, the teacher can discuss with students how the things they say to themselves can either help or hurt them. Students might discuss the self-speech they currently use when asked to write and whether it helps them or needs to be changed. Negative or ineffective self-statements such as "I'm no good at this" or "I hate writing" can be identified, and the ways these statements interfere with performance can be discussed.

STAGE 2: DISCUSS IT

During this stage, the teacher and students discuss the *significance* and *benefits* of the writing and self-regulation strategies to be learned. Each step in the writing strategy is discussed, as are any mnemonics to be used. The importance of student effort in strategy mastery is also emphasized. Throughout instruction, it is essential that students recognize and discuss the role of effort in learning and using strategies, and that they see their efforts paying off in better writing. This emphasis on knowing more about the strategy and how it works, along with student effort, helps set the stage for the development of positive attitudes about writing. The *goals* of strategies instruction are discussed and determined. This stage enables students to make a commitment to strategy mastery and participation as a partner/collaborator while helping to establish motivation.

Along with their teacher, students may also examine their current performance on the targeted composing skill. Compositions from students' portfolios or those written before strategies instruction began can be read and analyzed. For example, if the story grammar strategy has been discussed, students' selected stories can be analyzed to see how many common story elements are included. In addition, students may graph the number of elements present in their stories. Graphing of current performance can help set the stage for both goal setting and self-monitoring. If current performance is examined to help set the stage for strategies instruction, it should be done in a positive, collaborative manner with the teacher stressing that students were not expected to have all the common story parts when these stories were written because they hadn't yet learned the strategy.

The teacher and students also discuss how and when to use the strategy. This discussion should not be limited to the writing task at hand. At this time, students can begin to identify opportunities to use the strategy in new situations or for other appropriate tasks (e.g., the story grammar strategy might be useful in writing a book report). However, the teacher should be sure that the proposed benefits of the strategy are expressed reasonably so that students do not develop unreasonable expectations. In addition, the teacher and students should discuss writing tasks in which this strategy would *not* be useful (e.g., the story-writing strategy would not be useful for writing a science report).

STAGE 3: MODEL IT

During this stage, the teacher or a peer models the composing strategy and selected types of self-instructions, thinking aloud while writing an actual composition. Types of self-instructions that can be introduced include problem definition (*What is it? What do I have to do here?*), focusing attention and planning (*I need to concentrate. First I need to . . . then . . .*), strategy step statements (*I need to write down my strategy reminder*), self-evaluation and error correcting (*Have I used all of my parts? Oops! I missed one. I'd better add it*), coping and self-control (*I can handle this. I need to go slow and take my time*), and self-reinforcement (*I like this ending!*). All of these forms should not be introduced at once. Instead, teachers should select types of statements and model statements specific to the needs and characteristics of their students. It is also important that the model demonstrate coping with difficulty, such as having trouble thinking what to do next or forgetting a strategy step, and then model how one successfully deals with a particular difficulty. Students can help the teacher when difficulties are encountered.

It is important that modeling be natural and enthusiastic and that the self-instructions have appropriate phrasing and inflection. The self-instructions modeled should be matched to students' verbal style and language. Later on, the students will develop their own statements. The modeled statements are critical in helping them do this. Teachers often ask if they have to model without student input at this stage. This is up to the teacher. To keep students engaged, a teacher might involve students in using the strategy steps and thinking of good writing ideas. However, the teacher must stay in control of the process and be sure that use of the strategies for writing and self-regulation is clearly demonstrated.

If students initially use prompts (they are typically used, as will be seen in the lesson plans), such as a graphic or chart listing the strategy steps or detailing a mnemonic and a graphic organizer for writing, the model should use them as well. The teacher can also set a goal for her or his composition, such as including all seven story parts, and evaluate the composition to see if that goal was met. Students can also be involved in the writing process by helping the teacher or peer model during planning and writing.

After self-regulation of the writing strategy has been modeled, the teacher and students should discuss the importance of the self-statements used during modeling as well as the goal setting and self-assessment. At this point, students typically begin developing their preferred self-instructions, recording them on paper or on bulletin boards. These self-instructions will be used in later stages; modeling, reexplanation, and further development of self-instructions can occur in later stages as needed. Teachers and students can discuss the strategy steps and instructional components and then collaboratively decide if any changes are needed to make the strategy more effective and efficient. This can be discussed again in later stages. Generalization of the strategy to other tasks and settings can also be discussed further.

Teachers who have used SRSD have either creatively augmented live modeling or come up with alternatives. One teacher who was uncomfortable with modeling from memory or from notes when he first began strategy instruction came up with an innovative approach that worked well for him and his students. He worked out his modeling script, making sure he had all of the components, steps, and self-instructions he wished to model. He then put his self-talk on audiotape, reading from the script but speaking naturally and appropriately. He played this tape with his writing group, using the overhead projector to simultaneously plan for a composition. When modeling planning using the strategy prompt and graphic organizer was completed, the teacher and his students collaboratively wrote the actual composition, using the notes generated while modeling. In addition, teachers have successfully incorporated videotapes of peers who have already learned the strategies modeling their use of the writing and self-regulation strategies.

One of the aspects of modeling that makes it such a powerful procedure is the extent to which the model's performance can be individualized to meet the needs of a particular student or group of students. When teachers first prepare to model for their students, they often find it helpful to brainstorm together. As teachers become more practiced and adept at modeling, they find the preparation for this stage much easier. Modeling scripts developed by three groups of teachers during a workshop are presented in Table 2.2. Each group identified and discussed a particular student or group of students for whom the modeling was intended and then identified particular needs or goals relevant to this student or group. The same picture was used by each group as a story prompt to facilitate comparing and contrasting the different scripts. Each group then developed a script for modeling the story-writing strategy. As you will see, the scripts differ in ways that make them responsive to the needs of the target students, yet each script is based on the same strategy.

STAGE 4: MEMORIZE IT

During this stage, students are required to memorize the steps in the composing strategy and the meaning of any mnemonics used. Although the task of memorizing the strategy steps and mnemonics begins in earlier stages (as will be seen in the lesson plans), it is important that teachers be sure that their students have them memorized at this

Table 2.2. Teacher modeling scripts

The following three scripts were devised by three groups of teachers using the same picture as a story starter; each group identified students for whom the modeling was constructed. In Chapter 6, we provide an updated, slightly different set of lesson plans for teaching the story-writing strategy.

SCRIPT 1

Developed for a small group of fourth grade students; two students experienced a great deal of frustration with writing and often gave up before finishing their compositions.

1. What am I supposed to do? I am supposed to follow the five writing steps for a story. I need to look at the picture first.

2. Next I need to brainstorm for ideas. I need for my mind to be free. I need to think of all the ideas I can. If I try, I can do this. This looks like . . . three people sitting around boxes, eating lo mein.

3. Next I need to write down the story reminder: **WWW, What = 2, How = 2.** I'm really having a good time. I like to use my imagination.

4. Step 4 is to fill in my reminder. The first **W** is *who*. Who is the main character? The kid. Who are the other characters? The mother and father. No. That's not exciting. I'm going to make it an aunt and uncle. Let's see. Now, the next **W** is *when?* Boy, this sure is taking a long time. But when I finish it, I'll be really proud. When does the story take place? The story takes place at night. It's dark. They're eating dinner. The next **W** is *where.* Where does the story take place? Hmmm . . . Is this their old house or their new house? Are they going or coming? I think the aunt and uncle are moving into a new house right next door to the kid's house. Good, now this is getting easier.

    What = 2. What does that mean? The first ***what*** is: What does the main character want to do? The little boy is hoping his aunt and uncle let him stay the night to play in the boxes and sleep on the floor. The other ***what*** is: What happens when he tries to do it? He finishes his dinner, doesn't spill anything, is polite. They say okay. The little boy is going to stay the night, plays in the wooden crates, and gets stuck. Okay, I'm rolling now. The next step is **How = 2**. The first *how* is: How does the story end? The story ends when the aunt and uncle call the fire department. They come and cut the crate with an ax. I'm almost done now. I'm doing a good job. Last **H** is: How does the main character feel? The little boy was really scared, but now he is relieved and decides to go home for the night. Wow, that sure took me a long time, but I did it. I knew I could if I tried.

5. Now all I have to do is write the story.

    The Story. My aunt and uncle are moving into the house next door to me. I'm having Chinese dinner with them. I hope they will let me stay for the night. I'll be real polite.

    They are going to let me stay! I play in the empty wooden crates, but I get stuck. My aunt and uncle call the police who ax the crate open. I decide to go home to my house. My aunt's house is too exciting.

    Let's see. Does my story have all the parts? Yes, it will have all the Ws and W=2 and H=2. Does my story make sense? Yes, it does. It happened to my little brother so I know it makes sense. I did my best. I think I'll give a copy of this to my brother.

SCRIPT 2

Developed for a small group that included a male student with learning disabilities; this student has difficulty with reading and becomes anxious and frustrated with writing but loves math and science and telling stories. To help with this student's level of anxiety, modeling was done slowly and calmly.

(Review the five writing steps on the chart first and then model.) What is it I have to do? I have to write a story that will be fun for my friends to read. Relax, take my time. What is my first step? I need to look at the picture and decide what is happening. The family in the picture is eating Chinese food in their house. It looks like they just moved. They must be hungry. Good. I think I know what I'll write. Now I must really concentrate. This is going to be the best story ever. What are the story parts? *(See chart.)* **WWW, What = 2; How = 2.** First, who are the main characters? I'll name them Mr. and Mrs. Wiz and their son Gerald, whose nickname is Gee. When is the story happening? It is a Saturday in September. Where does the story take place? They have just moved to Florida right next to Disney World. Mr. Wiz works for Disney and Gee loves Space Mountain. Mrs. Wiz is a semi-pro golfer (like my mom). What is it I have to do next? **What = 2.** I don't need to rush or worry; stay calm and go slowly. What do they want to do? They want to eat, unpack, and get settled in their new house. What happens? They finish eating and go to unpack the china when a ghost jumps out of the box. Who's Gee Wiz going to call? Ghostbusters? Wow, this is great! The Ghostbusters' line is busy, so the Wizzes jump on their three-seater 1972 Harley Low Rider. I can add more to this later. What will the Wizzes do when they get to the Ghostbusters' office? First, when Mrs. Wiz rings the doorbell, green slime runs over her hand. She screams! Ooo! This is neat, but I've got to get back to the main idea. Egon, one of the Ghostbusters, answers the door. "Hello. Ghostbusters. What can I do to help you?" Egon asks. Gee Wiz grabs Egon's leg and screams. "There's a ghost in our house." Mr. Wiz calmly says, "We need your help, now." Egon quickly sets off the Ghostbuster alarm and all the Ghostbusters get ready for the assignment. The Wizzes lead the way to their new house. OK, I have good notes for this part. The next step is: How does the story end? They get the ghost out of their new house? How will they do it? The Ghostbusters chase the ghost in and out of every room. Egon whispers to the other Ghostbusters, "We've got to corner him in the basement; it's our only hope. We've got to make the ghost think he's chasing us." Everyone runs down the stairs to the basement, screaming and yelling as if they were afraid of the ghost. The ghost quickly glides after them, hooting and hollering. Just as the ghost is about to corner them, the Ghostbusters turn on their blasters, open the trap, and zap the ghost into the trap. Everyone could hear the ghost screaming, "I'll get you yet!" "Yea!" shouted the Wizzes.

(continued)

Table 2.2. (continued)

"Thank you," replied the Ghostbusters, and off they drove, leaving the relieved and happy Wizzes in their new house. How do the main characters feel? Gee Wiz is really disappointed because he could not have a pet ghost. Mr. and Mrs. Wiz, on the other hand, are pleased as punch that their house is ghost-free. The Wizzes happily continue to unpack. Let me check my steps. Did I complete each? Yes. My notes are good to start with. I could probably work on the ending a little more. Now I can start writing my story. *(Write story with student's help.)*

SCRIPT 3

Developed for a small group of students experiencing severe problems with composition; none of these students has written a complete story.

What is it I have to do? Write a story.

What is my first step? Look at the picture and let my mind be free.

What do I see? I'll make a list.

1. I see people: Mother, father, child.
2. What are they doing? Eating.
3. Where are they eating? At home.
4. Home doesn't look right, does it? No.
5. Maybe they just moved in. Sounds good.
6. I don't see anything else right now. Let's see if I can write a story. OK?

Now I need my story parts reminder. One step at a time.

W—*Who* is the main character? The little boy *(teacher makes notes)*. Who else is in the story? Mother, father.

W—*When* does the story take place? Hmmm . . . I think I'll look at the picture. I see a window. It's dark outside—must be at night. **W**—*Where*. Looking at the picture, it looks like they moved into a new house.

Now I need **What = 2**. *What* does the main character want to do? Hmmm . . . My main character is the little boy and he is trying to eat. *What* happens when he tries to do it?

Hmmm . . . Let's look at the picture. What do I see the boy doing? He is trying to get the food before his mother gives it to him. Mom doesn't look mad. Maybe they were both going for the last piece of food and the boy got it first. I like that. Let's look at the story parts reminder.

Now I need. **How = 2**—*How* does the story end? The boy says, "Boy that was a good dinner." I think that says it all. How does the main character feel? The boy feels full and sleepy.

Now I think I'm ready to write my story. The first thing I'll do is look at the five writing steps.

1. Look at the picture. Yes, I did that. It is about a family eating dinner.
2. Let my mind be free. I did a lot of brainstorming.
3. Write down the story parts reminder. I have it right here.
4. Write down story ideas for each part. Yes, I did it!
5. Now I'll write the story.

The Last Morsel

This story is about a boy and his mother and father. [That sounds good. Look at the story parts reminder and see what the next part is.] It's dark outside and they just moved into a new house [looks fine]. [What happens?] The boy is trying to eat and he and his mother are both going for the last piece of food. [OK. I know now what to write.] The boy tells his mother, "Ha! I beat you!" His mother starts to laugh. [I like that. OK. Now I can finish this story.] The boy finishes his dinner and says, "That was good. Now I'm ready for bed." [Now I need a title. What's another word for food—*morsel*. Yes, I like that. How about this—The Last Morsel.]

point. This stage is especially important for students who experience learning or writing difficulties because such students often experience memory problems as well. A strategy that cannot be recalled cannot be used. As one student stated, "You can't use it if you can't remember it!" Students who have already memorized the strategy will not need further practice in Stage 4. Once the strategy is memorized, students may paraphrase as long as the meaning remains intact. Students might also be asked to memorize one or more self-instructions from the personal lists they generated in Stage 3. Students can be prompted to use these statements in various appropriate contexts throughout the first four stages of strategy instruction; use of these self-statements will then come more easily in the next stage.

STAGE 5: SUPPORT IT

In the same way scaffolding provides support as a building is constructed, teachers at this stage support, or *scaffold*, students' strategy use. During this stage, students employ the strategy, self-instructions and other self-regulation procedures as they actually compose. The teacher provides as much support and assistance as needed and will write collaboratively for a time with students who need this level of support to be successful. Criterion levels should be gradually increased until final goals are met. Prompts, interaction, and guidance are faded at a pace appropriate to individual students until each student is effectively using the writing and self-regulation strategies without assistance. Throughout this stage, the teacher and students plan for and initiate generalization and maintenance of the strategies. This stage typically takes the longest of all the stages for those students who struggle with writing; students must be given adequate time and support to master the strategies.

Research and teachers' experiences clearly show that this stage is critical for students who find writing difficult (Graham & Harris, 2003; Harris & Graham, 1992; Harris, Graham, & Mason, 2003). In fact, without this stage, it has been determined that struggling writers show little or no improvement even after all four previous stages have been sufficiently completed. Only with support and collaborative writing, fading support until the student is writing independently, do these students make the strategy their own. More capable students may need little or no time in this stage. This is so important that we often remind teachers: Please Don't P.E.E. in the Classroom—*P*ost, *E*xplain (even model), and *E*xpect. Success with SRSD depends on using all the stages for students who have difficulty with writing.

STAGE 6: INDEPENDENT PERFORMANCE

If students have not already made the transition to use of covert ("in the head") self-instructions, doing so is encouraged at this stage as students use the strategies independently. Self-regulation procedures are continued, but they can be gradually faded as determined by the teacher and individual students. Plans for maintenance and generalization (e.g., booster sessions) continue to be implemented, and the teacher and students collaboratively evaluate strategy effectiveness and performance.

METASCRIPT

As we noted earlier, the six stages of instruction should not be followed like a cookbook. Good cooks take a recipe and personalize it. The acquisition stages in our SRSD model represent a *metascript*, providing a general format and guidelines. It is important for teachers to personalize and individualize strategy instruction to meet both the needs of their students and their own preferences and requirements. There are many ways in which the stages can be reordered, combined, and made recursive. For example, for some students, Stage 1 (Develop Background Knowledge) may not be necessary. Stage 4 (Memorize It) might be combined with Stage 2 (Discuss It). This may be particularly appropriate in situations where students have had previous strategies instruction, the composition strategy is complicated, and the teacher wants to be sure of some degree of strategy mastery before modeling to enhance the effects of modeling. In some instances, teachers have chosen to introduce self-instructions or some subset of self-instructions in Stage 2 (Discuss It) rather than waiting until Stage 3 (Model It).

One teacher came up with an innovative approach: She combined Stage 3 (Model It) and Stage 5 (Support It). Her middle-school students had been learning writing strategies for some time, and the strategy on which they were working was a developmental extension of one they had previously mastered. She believed that combining these two stages would be beneficial and more efficient. After discussion of the new strategy, she used it to plan and create aloud her own persuasive essay while students followed the same strategy steps to plan and write their own essays. Our observations of her lessons and her students' essays indicated that this worked well.

It should be noted that the stages presented in this book do not necessarily correspond to individual lessons. In fact, stages in lessons are typically combined, as can be seen in the lesson plans. Furthermore, teachers and students take as many class periods as necessary to complete any given lesson plan; for example, lesson plan 1 may take only one class period, while lesson plans 2 through 6 may each take several class periods to complete.

Finally, there are many other ways that teachers can effectively modify the lesson plans in this book. For example, in the story-writing lesson plans, pictures are used as story starters. Teachers are not required to use these pictures or any pictures at all. Students can select their own story ideas, story starters can be used (e.g., "Corey was a huge, friendly black dog. One day, Corey . . ."), or other options can be determined. Because most SRSD work has been done as part of research projects in teachers' classes, aspects of instruction have been standardized. Teachers, however, do not have this limitation. In the story-writing lesson plans, very short stories are provided to read with students so they may find the story parts. Teachers may find it preferable to use the literature they are reading in their classrooms during this part of SRSD, which we encourage.

CHARACTERISTICS OF EFFECTIVE STRATEGY INSTRUCTION

As previously noted, SRSD has multiple components. Our work with teachers and students, however, has shown us that the *characteristics* of strategies instruction must also be carefully considered. Discussion of the six major characteristics of SRSD critical to the success of this approach follows.

Collaboration

Throughout this book, emphasis is placed on the importance of interactive instruction and each student's role as an active collaborator in the learning process. Although the teacher initially provides whatever degree of scaffolding or support is needed, responsibility for recruiting, executing, monitoring, and modifying strategies is gradually transferred to the student. For example, students can act as collaborators in determining the goals of instruction; completing tasks; implementing, evaluating, and modifying the writing and self-regulation strategies; and planning for maintenance and generalization. Students also collaborate with and provide support for one another. The areas and ways in which students can collaborate are up to the imagination and willingness of teachers and students.

Individualization

SRSD can be used effectively when working with individuals or groups (including entire classes where appropriate). Whether instruction occurs individually or in groups, the preskills, skills, strategies, and self-regulation procedures to be developed should be responsive to the teacher's understanding of the learners and the tasks and tailored to students' capabilities. When it is appropriate to teach the self-regulation and composing strategies to a group of students, aspects of the instruction can still be individualized. It is important, for example, that students develop their self-instructions in their own words. This can be done in a group situation by modeling and discussing types and purposes of self-instructions and then having each student develop her or his own self-statements. Alternatively, students might pair up or work as a group to help one another determine self-statements.

It is important that students progress through the stages of strategies acquisition at their own pace. A large group may break down into smaller groups when necessary, or the teacher may need to work with some students on an individual basis. Students who master the strategies more quickly than their peers may act as peer tutors or provide support and assistance to others. Finally, while a group of students may be working on mastering a particular set of composing and self-regulation strategies, goals can be individualized. More capable writers can have more challenging goals, such as including dialogue in their stories, using varied sentence structures, or creating plot twists.

Cognitive and affective goals can be tailored to individual student needs. One student may be using self-statements aimed at coping with frustration, while another student's self-statements may focus on developing a stronger sense of self-efficacy ("I can do this if I try hard and use my strategy"). The teacher can also provide individually tailored feedback and reinforcement to facilitate such goals, as well as help students recognize improvements in performance and the usefulness of strategy instruction. Ongoing self-evaluation using techniques such as self-monitoring or portfolio assessment can also foster individualization.

Mastery-Based Instruction

Strategy instruction focuses on targeted affective, cognitive, and writing goals. Instruction to meet these goals should be mastery-based, meaning that students should proceed through instruction at their own pace rather than on a preset schedule or timeline. This need not imply mastery at each stage of strategy instruction. Rather, the stages are frequently recursive, and thus teachers may return to any stage at any time with criteria for progression becoming higher as the student recycles through the stages. For example, developing background knowledge and preskills is an early stage in our instructional model; however, students need not fully master preskills before advancing to the next stages. Preskill development can continue throughout the first three or four stages; however, students should achieve a high level of preskill mastery before the later stages of strategy instruction (e.g., memorizing strategy steps, engaging in collaborative practice). If mastery of a particular stage or skill is taking an inordinate amount of time, the teacher should reconsider what strategy is being taught and the methods being used for teaching it.

Anticipatory Instruction

The multiple aspects of strategy instruction should be carefully considered and well planned for in advance. In addition, we recommend that teachers attempt to anticipate glitches. Teachers should brainstorm things that could go wrong or prove difficult, particularly in light of their understanding of their students and the writing task. This sort of thinking ahead helps teachers prepare for and possibly avoid difficulties, even those that had not been anticipated. Once students become involved in the planning and implementation of strategies instruction, they should also be involved in the planning process of anticipating glitches.

Booster sessions are particularly important as a form of *relapse prevention* and should be collaboratively planned for in advance. At the end of formal strategy instruction, the teacher and students should discuss a plan for keeping the strategy alive. As part of this plan, booster sessions can be anticipated or even scheduled. A booster session can consist of elements such as

- Reviewing or renewing self-regulation procedures, such as goal setting or self-monitoring
- Reviewing the strategies mastered
- Practicing the mastered strategies in a collaborative manner
- Discussing any changes in a strategy or use of a strategy on the students' part (the teacher should be alert to changes that both subvert or weaken the strategy and those that improve it)
- Engaging in collaborative problem solving regarding any problems students have experienced with a strategy or adaptations of a strategy across the curriculum
- Discussing successful experiences with strategy use or generalization
- Continually planning for anticipated glitches

Enthusiastic Teachers Working within a Support Network

Enthusiastic, responsive teaching is an integral part of SRSD. The teacher plays an important role in helping students understand the meaning and efficacy of strategies, as well as the importance of their own efforts. In addition to establishing the credibility of strategies, teachers must also serve as models of self-regulated, strategic performance and establish a collaborative, supportive environment for strategy mastery and autonomous, reflective learning.

Given the complexity of strategy instruction, we have found that understanding and implementing strategy instruction is much easier for teachers when they work with other teachers to learn the processes involved and have opportunities to share both successes and failures. Moreover, the impact of instruction on students is much greater and maintenance and generalization of strategic performance across the curriculum and grades is more likely when strategies instruction is embraced across a school or district. Finally, principals, learning specialists, and other school administrators play critical roles in providing leadership and support for the nurturing and use of writing and self-regulation strategies. Organizational support is an important factor in successful strategies instruction.

Developmental Enhancement

To teach a strategy well, teachers must help students see the meaning and significance of the strategy, along with its strengths and weaknesses. This requires an understanding of where the strategies to be taught fit in with the larger scheme of things in terms of students' development as writers. A skillful, effective writer employs strategies and conventions of the craft the way a jazz musician uses a melody. The mature writer is able to profit from the variations, the riffs, the twists, and, ultimately, the meaning of the strategies and conventions of writing. As writers mature, they continually refine, combine, and enhance the strategies they have mastered or created, using them in more sophisticated ways. Teachers can facilitate this process by collaboratively planning for and supporting their students in the increasingly sophisticated use of the strategies they have learned.

THE STORY-WRITING STRATEGY: AN ILLUSTRATION

Coauthor Barbara Friedlander successfully used SRSD to help her students master a story-writing strategy. Barbara was conducting Writers' Workshop one class period a day with typically achieving fifth-grade students and several students with learning disabilities. Most of the students had been in Writers' Workshop for the past 3 years. These students were used to choosing their own topics and genres, determining the content and purpose of their writing, selecting pieces for completion and publication, using peers and teachers as a resource, and peer editing.

Barbara carefully considered both the learners in this group and story writing as a composition task. Her reading of stories the students had written indicated that although some students used all seven common story parts, most neglected two or more. Furthermore, all students, including those who used all of the parts, had the potential to improve their story writing by including greater detail, elaboration, goals, and actions. Barbara also considered the affective and cognitive characteristics of the individual students in this group; she had been working with these students for the past 2 years and had the advantage of knowing them well. Most of the students enjoyed writing and were comfortable doing it. However, a few of the students (including two who were identified as having learning disabilities and two who were not) still evidenced anxiety about composing and difficulties with writing. These students needed a stronger sense of motivation, enhanced self-efficacy, and more internal attributions (what Barbara termed an "I can do this if I try" attitude). Finally, Barbara knew that these students would be going to middle school the following year, where they would face increased demands for writing projects (e.g., book reports and biographies) that could be informed by knowledge and the use of a story-writing strategy. She also felt that such knowledge could benefit many of the students in terms of reading comprehension.

Barbara decided to offer these students instruction on a story-writing strategy within the process approach used in her Writers' Workshop. She wanted to make it possible for her students to master the story-writing strategy and to grow as writers, yet continue to maintain control over the content and purpose of their stories and use the strategy within the writers' community already established (i.e., using peers as a resource, peer editing, publication).

Barbara decided to follow the stages typically used in SRSD with a few modifications. She reversed the order of Stages 1 and 2 and used these stages recursively. She planned and conducted her instruction in the manner described as follows.

Stage 1: Discuss It

Barbara decided to begin with a conference to offer SRSD instruction in story writing to her students and then work with those who chose to learn the strategy at this time. During this conference, she and the students discussed the common parts of a story, the goal of instruction (i.e., to write better stories that are more fun for students to write as well as for others to read), and how inclusion and expansion of story elements can improve a story. Barbara also briefly outlined the instructional procedures that would be followed to help students master the strategy, stressing the students' role as collaborators during strategy mastery, implementation, and evaluation. She noted the possibility of acting as peer tutors for other students who wished to learn this strategy in the future. The importance of student effort in strategy mastery was also emphasized. Perhaps due to her enthusiasm or the way she explained the strategy instruction, all of Barbara's students opted to participate.

Stage 2: Develop Background Knowledge

Barbara knew that her students were comfortable with the vocabulary involved in the story-writing strategy and mnemonic. She therefore decided to focus on the story mnemonic itself during this stage. This was done in several ways. Each student was given a small chart that provided the mnemonic. After discussing the meaning of each element, students identified elements in literature they were currently reading for fun or for other classes. Because Barbara wanted students to generalize their understanding of story elements to reading comprehension, she spent a significant amount of time discussing how students can use story elements to help them grasp the meaning in other people's writing. Also highlighted were the different ways in which various authors developed or used story parts. Students then generated ideas for story parts as a group, using a story idea offered by a student, a picture, or another story origin. Barbara explained that they needed to memorize the mnemonic. She provided practice in several ways (e.g., with and without a chart present, through rehearsal, using partner testing). Finally, Barbara had each student select one or two of their previously written stories and then determine which of the story elements were present in each one.

She explained and demonstrated graphing of the number of story elements in each story and also discussed how students would continue to use the graph for self-monitoring and self-evaluation throughout instruction. With students whose graphs indicated that they typically used all or nearly all of the story parts, Barbara discussed how they could improve their parts with more detail, elaboration, and action.

Stage 1 Repeats: Discuss It Further

Barbara further discussed the story-writing strategy with her group of students using the overhead projector. Each student had his or her own small chart with the steps on it as well. Barbara and her students discussed the steps in the strategy; she asked the students to tell her what they thought the reasons were for each step. The group then discussed how and when to use the strategy. Although the discussion began with story writing, Barbara also asked the students to consider other times they might employ the strategy. Linkages to writing book reports and biographies as well as to reading were discussed. Barbara further established the point that strategies cannot work without first being mastered, and she emphasized the role of student effort in strategy mastery and management.

Finally, Barbara decided to introduce one form of self-instructions—creativity self-statements. She modeled for the students the way she often used statements to herself to free up her mind and think of good story ideas and parts. Among the self-statements she modeled were

- *Let my mind be free.*
- *Think of fun ideas.*
- *Think of something no one else might think of.*
- *Take my time, good ideas will come to me.*

Some students offered examples of their own self-statements. After discussing how these self-statements were helpful, the students generated their own preferred creativity self-statements, recorded them on paper, and practiced using them to generate story parts.

Stage 3: Model It

Barbara asked her students to get out their strategy steps charts and their lists of creativity self-statements. She then shared a story idea with them that she had been thinking about using and began modeling use of the story-writing strategy by planning and writing a story while "thinking out loud." She encouraged the students to help her as she planned and made notes for each story part. As she wrote the first draft of her story (changes or additions to her plans were made as she wrote), she modeled five additional types of self-instructions:

1. Problem definition (*What do I have to do? I need to . . .*)
2. Planning (including use of each of the strategy steps)
3. Self-evaluation (*How am I doing? Am I using each step? Can I think of more details?*)
4. Self-reinforcement (*I really like this idea.*)
5. Coping (*I can do this if I try. Don't worry, worry doesn't help. Take my time.*)

Barbara made sure to model coping with difficulty and frustration while she wrote. She also had her students help her by reminding her which step came next in the strategy or suggesting what she might try saying to herself.

After completing the story, the group again discussed the importance of what they said to themselves while they worked and identified the types of self-statements the teacher had used. Although Barbara did not expect all of the students to use all of these types of self-instructions, she made each type available to the group. The students provided examples of personal positive self-statements, and then generated and recorded their own examples of the types of self-instructions. Finally, Barbara asked the students to consider the strategy steps and mnemonic and to suggest any changes they thought were needed to make the strategy more effective or efficient. The students did not suggest any changes. Barbara asked them to continue considering this as they worked with the strategy.

Stage 4: Memorize It

Barbara asked her students to practice the strategy alone or with a partner in any way they liked, and noted the importance of memorizing the strategy (paraphrasing was allowed as long as meaning remained intact). She also asked the students to select and memorize statements from their personal lists. Some of the students memorized the steps, mnemonic, and self-statements easily, while others had more difficulty doing so. At this point, instruction continued on a small-group or individual basis. Barbara moved into the next stage of instruction with each group or student when they were ready to do so. Perfect recall of the strategy steps, mnemonic, and self-statements was not always necessary for beginning Stage 5 (Support It), as Barbara explained that memorization of these things could continue as they kept working with the strategy. Barbara prompted individual students to use their self-statements both during writing time and at other appropriate times; this continued both during and after instruction.

Stage 5: Support It

Barbara initiated goal setting, self-monitoring (continuing the graphs the students had started in Stage 2), and self-reinforcement with her students as they began collaborative practice. The goal for each student was to include all seven story parts stated in the story-writing strategy. Barbara believed this to be a reachable goal for all of the students—and she was correct. All of the students were able to meet this goal. Each time a student completed a story, Barbara and the student independently counted the number of story parts included, compared counts, graphed the number on the student's graph, and compared this number to the previously set goal. Self-reinforcement was encouraged when students met or came close to their goals. Barbara also provided social reinforcement; concrete, external reinforcement was not used.

Story writing during this stage began with Barbara collaboratively planning a story with each student; each student then wrote her or his story independently. Barbara made sure that the student was using the strategy steps and mnemonic. She modified her input and support to meet the individual needs of each student. Some students required a great deal of prompting, guidance, and support, while others needed very little. Prompts (the charts and self-statement lists), guidance, and support were faded at a pace appropriate to individual students, and Barbara began encouraging students to use covert self-speech. Barbara found that this took less time than she had anticipated, and most students were ready for independent performance after two or three collaborative experiences.

Also during this stage, Barbara had a conference with all of the students together to discuss and plan for strategy maintenance and generalization. The students decided upon review and booster sessions as necessary to help them maintain strategic performance, and also discussed opportunities they might have for generalization. (One student reported using the strategy in English class when reading stories, while another reported using the strategy to help write outlines; several students mentioned writing stories at home.) Finally, throughout this stage, the students were available to one another as resources or for peer editing, as typically is done during Writers' Workshop.

Stage 6: Independent Performance

Students independently planned and composed stories using the story grammar strategy and self-instructional statements. The students typically used fewer self-instructions at this point than they had in earlier stages; this was appropriate, as strategy use was becoming more fluent. Barbara provided positive and constructive feedback as appropriate to each student and continued to encourage the use of covert self-instructions. The students were asked to use the charts only if necessary and to try to write without them; continued use of planning on paper was encouraged. Most of the students did not use the charts, but instead used sheets of paper to record the story grammar mnemonic and their initial ideas. Some students, however, no longer wrote out ideas for every story part. These students told Barbara that they didn't need to because they had the parts in their heads and were ready to write. She told them this was fine, but reminded them to check their drafts to be sure they had included all of the parts, as well as detail and elaboration.

The students continued the goal-setting and self-monitoring procedures independently for two more stories and were then told that use of these procedures for future stories was up to them. As the students reached independent performance, they became available to help with collaborative practice with other students. The stories students wrote were revised and edited following the Writers' Workshop procedures used in Barbara's classroom.

Once again, a group conference was held to evaluate the story grammar strategy and instruction. The students were pleased with the strategy and their use of it. Barbara initiated a discussion of the strategy's weaknesses at this point and explained to the students that other story structures did exist (e.g., that used by African tribal storytellers), and that the students might want to compare and contrast these story grammars or learn new story strategies in the future. The students indicated an interest in doing so.

The plans for maintenance were reviewed, and Barbara indicated that she would periodically check with the students to see if they remembered the strategy and if they were using it. Booster sessions would be scheduled if needed. Generalization of the strategy and the self-instructions was also discussed again. Several students mentioned using the mnemonic in reading or for other writing assignments. One student reported using the mnemonic to write a "tall tale" in another teacher's class, while other students mentioned using it for journal writing and when writing for the school newspaper. These reports were confirmed by other teachers who reported to Barbara that some students were using both the mnemonic and some of their self-statements in their classes. One teacher noted that several students were using the mnemonic for both writing and revising. Barbara planned to continue to prompt generalization in writing as well as other areas of the curriculum.

IMPLEMENTATION AND EVALUATION

Implementation and evaluation of the strategy acquisition and management stages occur concurrently and reciprocally. Evaluation focuses not only on composition skills and processes but also on cognitive and affective changes and development. Because evaluation is ongoing and formative, as well as summative, changes can be made in the strategy or the instructional procedures as needed throughout instruction.

In the illustration involving Barbara's class, evaluation occurred throughout instruction and at the end. The students were involved in evaluation through the use of their graphs and in discussions about the strategy and instructional procedures. Barbara had previously taught this strategy, and several changes had been made in both the strategy and the instructional procedures in earlier years; no new changes were made by this group. Barbara also engaged in a form of portfolio assessment, looking through the students' earlier writings and comparing them with stories written during and after strategy instruction. Both she and her students found that strategy use significantly improved their story writing. Barbara informally assessed the students' attributions, their attitudes toward writing and the use of strategies, and their views of themselves as writers through individual and group discussions. She felt that positive changes were occurring in these areas for nearly all the students, particularly those who had been anxious about writing or critical of their abilities. Stories written by Barbara's students follow.

STORIES FROM BARBARA'S CLASS

These two stories were written by Jill, a typically achieving student. The first was written before strategy instruction and the second was written after the instruction had been completed.

Untitled • One day a boy went to a pond near his house. When he got to the pond he watched a frog jump around. Then the frog jumped over to the boy, they stared at each other. Suddenly the frog jumped away and the boy never saw him again.

Dreams! Dreams! Dreams! • Once there was a penguin named Rubin. There was nothing special about Rubin. He was just a black and white penguin. Rubin lived in the San Diego Zoo. He loved the zoo. Then one day he saw a boy that came to visit the zoo wearing shorts with sailboats on them. Rubin loved the shorts. Rubin also wanted them. That night Rubin had a dream. It was about Rubin getting the shorts. Once he got the shorts he had gotten a Walkman. Rubin dreamed that after he got the Walkman, he turned it on and started to dance. Rubin danced all night in his dream. When Rubin got up he was sad because he had only dreamed it. • *The End*

The following two stories were written by Christie, a student with learning disabilities. The first was written before strategy instruction and the second was written after the instruction had been completed.

Untitled • A monkey named Joe was bored when he got up from his nap. His friend Fred was on the telephone with his boss. He was moping around the house for a half hour. Then he got hungry so he went in the kitchen to get something to eat. He saw Fred's wallet on the table. He picked it up and looked inside and saw money. He saw credit cards and lots of money. First he picked up the 100 dollar bill but it was old and written on the right so he put it down. Then he picked up a one dollar bill and it was brand new. Then his friend got off of the telephone and saw Joe with his dollar and said what are you doing? Joe just made a face.

Baseball and Tommy • One hot, humid day in April (April 22, 1990) there was Tommy, who lived in Maryland–Virginia. Tommy is a short boy, he is 9 years old with brown hair. And he loved to wear his red hat, blue jeans, and his gray sweatshirt. One afternoon Tommy saw his friends (Jim, Fred, Scott, Tod) were playing ball. But when he went home he tried to play but he was not good. He practiced and practiced, finally he was getting good. So when he told his friends they said, "Let's see how good you are." So they went to Tod's house and played in his backyard. It was a hot, humid day so they had to stop. They went in and got drinks. Then Scott said, "Hey, you're pretty good." "Thank you," Tommy said. When Tommy tried out for the team (neighborhood) he made it. When he got home he was so proud of himself. He told his father and his father said if you're so good then try out for the school team. The next day he watched the team and tried to learn the plays. When he went home he played with his friends, like the team. The next day he went in to talk with the coach and ask if he could try out. The coach said sure. We're looking for another player. So Tommy went for it and made the team. When he got home he told his father. His father was so proud he took him out for ice cream. Tommy's father said, "I am sorry for acting so rude before and being so forceful." Tommy said, "It's ok." • *The End*

The following story was written by a student named Vanessa after strategy instruction. Although she was one of the more developed writers in the class, Vanessa typically did not use all of the story parts in her pre-SRSD compositions; her goals during instruction also included using more elaboration, detail, and actions in her stories.

The St. Patrick's Day Leprechaun • One day in Doggy Land, Valerie (a poodle) was walking through the forest. It was March 31, 1990. Valerie was a white poodle with a green bow in her hair. Since it was St. Patrick's Day, Valerie was going to find a leprechaun.

She was skipping along when all of a sudden she heard a moan. Then she heard a whimper. Now, Valerie was a very curious dog. She started to walk east. That was where the sound was coming from. In surprise she found out that it was a dog too. He was tan and white with big, brown, sad eyes. He also had on a green top hat and a bow-tie with clovers on it. It was a leprechaun! Valerie said, "Why are you crying Mr. Leprechaun?"

"Because I have scratched my paw on a thorn bush! Could you please help me'" begged the leprechaun. Well, Valerie wanted a little something out of this too. So she said, "Only if you give me three wishes!"

"Oh, all right!" said Mr. Leprechaun. Valerie got a band-aid out of her purse and put it on the leprechaun. He felt much better. "Now what do you wish for?"

"I want a bike, a new dress, and a pot of gold!" said Valerie. Out of mid-air came a bike, and a new dress. "But where's my pot of gold?" asked Valerie.

"Well for that we'll have to go over the rainbow. Hop on!" shouted Mr. Leprechaun. Together they rode up onto the rainbow on the magic carpet. When they got on top they slid down. They landed on a cloud. Under a rock was the pot of gold.

After that Valerie went home. She laid her things down on the table. She was thirsty from the long ride. She went into the kitchen. When she came back her bike, dress, and pot of gold were gone. "Oh no!" thought Valerie. She ran back to the woods. But he wasn't there. She looked up at the sky. The rainbow was gone! For it was only her imagination. • *The End*

Analyses of stories written in Barbara's classroom before and after SRSD indicated that the students improved greatly in the number of story parts included in their stories. The few students who were already using all of the parts showed improvement in detail and action in their stories. The students showed improvement in the quality of their writing as well; word choice improved and the inclusion of details increased, as did other characteristics for individual students.

In addition to these writing measures, an interview was held with each student and with another teacher who was working with Barbara at the time. All of the students indicated that they believed the story grammar strategy had improved their writing. Those students who had already been using all of the parts noted that they now used greater detail and more action. The mnemonic was the aspect of instruction most frequently nominated as most enjoyable. One student commented, "The WWW, What = 2, How = 2 builds up your resources." None of the students indicated any problems with incorporating strategy instruction into the process approach (Writers' Workshop) being used in their school. The other teacher working with Barbara during Writers' Workshop that year said that as she worked with the students, she could see "light bulbs going on." She mentioned that one student had commented, "Now this story writing makes sense." Although most of the students were already familiar with the parts of a story, mastery of the strategy helped them to better understand what they already knew. The students were also able to generalize the strategy across teachers. Some students were observed by other teachers using the strategy instruction in other subjects during that school year and the next year as well.

In conclusion, when the students ask, "What should I write about?" or "How do I get started?" or simply say, "I'm just no good at writing," SRSD will help them deal with these concerns and put them on the path to becoming effective writers. This book includes Lesson Plans that provide a metascript that can be followed or adapted to meet the needs of individual students, allowing all students to learn the "tricks" of writing.

REFERENCES

Graham, S., & Harris, K.R. (2003). Students with learning disabilities and the process of writing: A meta-analysis of SRSD studies. In H.L. Swanson, K.R. Harris, & S. Graham (Eds.), *Handbook of learning disabilities* (pp. 323–344). New York: Guilford Press.

Harris, K.R., & Graham, S. (1992). Self-regulated strategy development: A part of the writing process. In M. Pressley, K.R. Harris, & J.T. Guthrie (Eds.), *Promoting academic competence and literacy in school* (pp. 277–309). San Diego: Academic Press.

Harris, K.R., Graham, S., & Mason, L. (2003). Self-regulated strategy development in the classroom: Part of a balanced approach to writing instruction for students with disabilities. *Focus on Exceptional Children, 35*(7), 1–16.

Chapter 2 Self-Test

1. Students engaged in SRSD should
   a. Complete a stage of instruction and not return to it
   b. Allow the teacher to complete assessments of their initial writing and their improvements over time
   c. Collaborate with teachers to improve their self-regulation of critical writing strategies

2. True or False
   The Develop Background Knowledge must always precede the Discuss It stage.

3. True or False
   If done in a supportive manner, showing students how to graph their current performance can help set the stage for both goal setting and self-monitoring.

4. The Support It stage involves
   a. Collaboratively writing with students while gradually fading prompts and supports until students are using writing and self-regulation strategies independently
   b. Individual or small-group instruction as needed
   c. Both A and B

5. "Please don't P.E.E. in the classroom" means you should not
   a. *P*ost, *E*xplain (even model), and *E*xpect strategic performance.
   b. *P*re-test, *E*xtensively teach, and *E*xpect difficulties.
   c. *P*romote strategies, *E*ncourage, and *E*valuate.

6. True or False
   When Develop Background Knowledge, Discuss It, Model It, and Memorize It are done well, few struggling writers need the Support It stage.

7. True or False
   Teachers should follow the Lesson Plans in this book exactly as they are written.

8. True or False
   Each SRSD stage of instruction represents one lesson.

9. True or False
   Throughout SRSD, students should act as collaborators in ways such as determining goals, evaluating instruction and progress made, and planning for maintenance and generalization.

10. We recommend that
    a. Teachers model self-instructions that students will copy exactly.
    b. Teachers work with other teachers to maximize the effectiveness of SRSD and make learning to do SRSD easier.
    c. All preskills are mastered before moving to Stage 3 of instruction.

Answers: 1. c 2. False 3. True 4. c 5. a 6. False 7. False 8. False 9. True 10. b

Chapter 3

Self-Regulation
and the Writing Process

The struggling writer asks his teacher, "How does Josh decide what to write about?" "How does Anna think of a topic?" "How does Emma know how to revise her report?" The teacher answers, "Johnny, Anna, and Emma all self-regulate, and I am going to teach you how to do it too. Are you ready?" The struggling writer answers with an enthusiastic smile, "I'm ready."

Along with powerful writing strategies, SRSD includes explicit development of critical self-regulation strategies, including goal setting, self-instructions, self-monitoring, and self-reinforcement. Experienced writers use these powerful self-regulation strategies throughout the writing process, and young students can learn to use them too. Many struggling writers have difficulty with self-regulation, and they will therefore need explicit instruction and support in their development from their teachers. SRSD helps teachers nurture and support these critical skills as students learn to write. Each of the following forms of self-regulation can be seen in the SRSD Lesson Plans in this book.

GOAL SETTING

The act of goal setting serves several key functions. First, it enhances attention, motivation, and effort. Second, it provides information as to what is desired or required for the writing task at hand. Goal setting also facilitates planning and strategic behavior while prompting self-evaluation and self-determined consequences.

The process for goal setting includes the following five steps:

- Ask the students to set their goals, breaking them into sub-steps as needed.

- Have the students devise their own plans for meeting their goals and assessing their progress.

- Set the plans into operation.

- Require the students to monitor their progress.

- Reset or revise goals as necessary.

Properties of Goals

The properties that are critical to the successful use of goal setting in writing and other academic areas are *specificity*, *difficulty*, and *proximity*.

Specificity

The student's goal should provide a clear indication of what is required for the task. It must be explicitly stated in order for the student to gauge his or her progress.

Difficulty

Goal difficulty refers to how hard or challenging a goal is for a particular student. Goals that are challenging yet doable lead to better performance than goals that are easy. More difficult goals, however, lead to better performance only when the student possesses the capability needed and has made a commitment to pursue and achieve the stated goal. Thus, when students want to set goals that are too difficult, the teacher must work with them to set initial challenging yet doable goals.

Proximity

Goals that are proximal are close at hand and can be completed in a minimal amount of time (e.g., *Write three pages in my journal today*). Goals that will take a longer time to reach (e.g., *Write 30 pages in my journal over the next two weeks*) are called *distal*. Proximal goals lead to higher levels of performance than distal goals because they yield more opportunities for determining how things are going (e.g., daily journal entries, assessment of task behavior, work completion) and provide more occasions for inducing an individual to take action.

Practical Considerations

Goal Acceptance and Commitment

Teachers should ensure that students establish appropriate goals for their writing, but ultimately, each student must make the commitment. There are several ways that teachers can foster students' goal acceptance and commitment.

- Be supportive. Providing encouragement is vital to the process.

- Listen to students' opinions about their goals, encourage them to ask questions, and then ask them what they plan to do to in order to meet their objectives.

- Demonstrate the benefit of the goals being set. Students are more likely to accept goals if they see them as valuable. One way that teachers can make a writing goal more attractive is to link its accomplishment to a visible improvement in performance.

- Nothing succeeds like success. Goals are more likely to be accepted by students if they have a high expectation for achieving them. When students have a history of success in meeting their goals, they are more likely to be confident and try to achieve even higher goals.

Feedback

Timely and frequent feedback encourages evaluation and control of one's own behavior on an ongoing basis. Feedback, or knowledge of how one is doing, is necessary if an individual is to track his or her progress and attain a desired goal. For school-age children, feedback on their work toward attaining goals can be obtained from the teacher and peers or through self-assessment.

SELF-INSTRUCTIONS

Expert writers commonly "talk to themselves" as they write. They engage in a running dialogue with themselves, making comments about where they are in the process, what needs to be done next, why some ideas do or do not work at any given point, how they will phrase certain ideas, whether readers will understand what they are saying, what a great job they are doing, and so forth. Although this dialogue is occasionally spoken aloud (overt), it is neither intended nor adapted for communication with others. Most of this private, self-speech serves the general cognitive functions of orienting, organizing, and structuring the author's behavior. In effect, writers tell themselves what to do while they write, setting and staying with a plan and helping themselves over rough spots.

Self-instructions are a form of self-speech, which is self-regulatory. In people's everyday lives, self-speech can be overt or covert, voluntary or involuntary. Most children naturally use self-speech to help orient, organize, structure, and plan behavior; to help consciously understand or focus on a problem or situation; to overcome difficulties; to help deal with anxiety, frustration, or other forms of arousal; and to provide self-reinforcement.

Deliberate self-instructions can greatly help students through the writing process. They direct students' attention to relevant events, stimuli, or aspects of a problem. This helps students interrupt or control an automatic or impulsive response (i.e., to stop and think). Self-instructions assist students in generating and selecting alternative courses of action. They focus thinking, increase memory for steps and procedures, and help children perform a sequence of actions or steps.

Self-instructions state criteria for success and enhance positive attitudes about and attention to the task. They also reinforce and help maintain task-relevant behaviors and provide ways of coping with failure and self-reinforcing success.

Six Types of Self-Instructions

There are six basic types of self-instructions that can be used throughout the writing process: problem definition, focusing of attention and planning, strategy implementation, self-evaluation, coping and self-control, and self-reinforcement. These labels are not typically used with students; however, they are presented here for the benefit of teachers.

Problem Definition

When beginning to write, students must define the problem/situation. They must size up the nature and demands of the task and ask themselves, "What do I have to do here?" and "What is my first step?" They then define the task (e.g., "I want to write a convincing essay").

Focusing of Attention and Planning

Students use these statements to focus their attention and begin to develop their plans. They may think, "I need to concentrate, be careful, and think of the steps. To do this right, I need to make a plan. First, I need to . . . and then . . . ."

Strategy Implementation

Self-instructions assist students in self-regulating strategy use. They tell themselves, "First, I will write down my essay writing reminder. The first step in writing an essay is . . . . My goals for this essay are . . . and I will self-record on . . . ."

Self-Evaluation

While they write, students can use self-instructions to evaluate performance, thus catching and correcting errors. They think, "Have I used all of my story parts? Oops, I missed one. That's okay. I can revise." They will also identify when they have done a step correctly or met a goal, naturally leading to self-reinforcement.

Coping and Self-Control

Self-instructions can also help students cope and exercise self-control. They may say to themselves, "Don't worry. I can handle this. I know the steps," or "It's okay to feel a little anxious—a little anxiety can help."

Self-Reinforcement

Self-instructions include positive, reinforcing statements such as, "I'm getting better at this!" or "I like this ending. Wait until my teacher reads this!" Self-reinforcement requires self-evaluation compared with a specific criterion. Students must be able to accurately know when self-reinforcement is warranted.

Practical Considerations

When students are first learning to use self-instructions, it may be best to start with only one type or one specific self-instruction that fits a particular need for the individual student. Otherwise, students might be overwhelmed with too many statements to remember and use. It is very important that individual students develop self-instructions in their own words. Self-instructions are most effective when they are matched to students' verbal style and language level. In addition, some students (particularly older students) may be resistant to thinking aloud and should not be forced to do so. These students can be asked to use their self-instructions in their heads or keep a list of them nearby to consult as needed.

Correspondence between saying and doing is also important when self-instructions are used. Merely saying the right things or doing the action or task and then saying the self-instruction is usually ineffective. Students may need some assistance in developing a close correspondence between self-instructions and the writing behaviors or cognitions they are meant to control. Most students who have been in SRSD classes, including those with severe learning and writing problems, have caught onto the use of self-instructions quickly. This has helped them become ready to expand their repertoires.

SELF-MONITORING

Self-monitoring occurs when an individual self-assesses whether a behavior has occurred and then self-records the results (Nelson & Hayes, 1981). Self-monitoring in writing can occur in three areas: attention, performance, and strategy use. In the SRSD Lesson Plans in this book, students learn to self-monitor their writing performance and their use of writing strategies. Self-monitoring strategies are most effective with students who possess the required skill but do not apply it.

Self-monitoring contains two elements: self-assessment and self-recording. Although self-assessment can be done without self-recording, most students benefit more when they use the two together. Self-monitoring can occur before students begin to write, while they write, or after they have a completed draft. For self-monitoring to be effective, both the self-assessment and self-recording procedures must be easy for students to use independently. Many students have stated that self-recording is their favorite self-regulation procedure.

Self-Assessment

Self-assessment involves determining whether or not, how often, or for how long an event or behavior has occurred. For example, students might ask themselves whether all of the parts of a good story were used, or they might determine how many words were written in the story or how much time they spent writing.

Self-Recording

Self-recording involves having students record whether or not, how often, or for how long a selected behavior or event occurs. Self-recording could consist of circling "yes" or "no" on a questionnaire or entering data on a graph or chart. Individual graphs or charts are frequently used for self-recording, as they present a picture of a student's performance over time and allow the student to see improvement. This visual record of improvements has proven to be highly motivating to the majority of writers with whom we have worked. Each Lesson Plan in this book includes a form of charting, or self-recording, performance throughout the lesson, such as recording the number of story parts included in a student's story on a Story Rockets graph.

Practical Considerations

At least initially, it is preferable for students and their teacher to decide collaboratively what will be self-assessed. Self-assessment prompts students to compare their own performance with standards for acceptable performance, therefore the teacher and students should also collectively determine the criteria that a performance requires to be considered acceptable. Because the goal is for students to eventually self-assess independently, the self-assessment procedures must be within each student's capabilities, otherwise means to support independent self-assessments must be found. Self-assessment is integrated into the Lesson Plans in this book, but teachers can determine additional performance criteria for self-assessment beyond what is in these lessons, and self-assessment can also be used in other ways throughout the school day.

One teacher recently taught her students to self-monitor the number of times they wrote their spelling words in a 15-minute practice period each day; students then entered their counts on their individual graphs. Happily, these students found the self-monitoring procedures to be quite motivating, and, as a result, they increased their daily number of spelling practices from approximately 20 to approximately 75; on some days, a few students' practice counts exceeded 120.

The steps used to teach self-monitoring are meant to be applied in a flexible way and can be modified to meet teacher and student needs. The steps used to help students self-monitor are incorporated into the Lesson Plans in this book; however, teachers can use these steps outside of SRSD across the curriculum.

Step 1. Determine and define explicitly what students will self-monitor

Step 2. Gather information on the students' current performance on the behavior or event to be self-assessed. For writing, one or two recent compositions finished before SRSD begins typically make for a sufficient sample. This baseline data helps to demonstrate progress throughout instruction.

Step 3. Briefly describe the purpose of self-monitoring and the benefits students will derive. This is typically begun by saying something like, "I would like to teach you something that will help you to help yourself write good stories." Then discuss the benefits of independently self-monitoring in future tasks.

Step 4. When the purpose of self-monitoring is clear and the students have indicated a willingness to self-monitor, instruct the students in the procedures involved. Students and teachers should discuss

- What will be self-assessed
- What criteria are desirable
- How to count and record the targeted aspect of writing
- When self-monitoring is to occur

After outlining these steps for the students, the teacher models them, verbalizing what is being done at each step. The teacher then asks the students to talk the teacher through each step, and finally, the students model the procedures and verbalize the steps independently. These steps are important to ensure that each student clearly understands the self-monitoring procedures, as well as the behavior or event to be self-monitored, and can easily carry out the self-monitoring procedures independently.

SELF-REINFORCEMENT

Josh begins to plan his writing task and says, "That was a good idea. Keep up the good work." Anna makes a list of topics and says, "I did a good job thinking of ideas. I am proud of myself." Emma rereads her work and says, "My character is described really well for the reader." Self-reinforcement occurs when students choose and administer reinforcers for themselves when a criterion for performance has been met or surpassed. In SRSD, self-reinforcement occurs through the use of positive, rewarding self-statements.

Practical Considerations

Although we have not used other reinforcers (e.g., tokens, points) in most of our SRSD work with students, teachers can determine if such reinforcers are needed. Teachers are encouraged, however, to try SRSD without them first and to use them only if necessary. The exception is current studies concerning students with emotional and behavioral disorders (Lane, Graham, Harris, & Weisenbach, in press; Lane, Harris, Graham, Weisenbach, Brindle, & Morphy, in press), where SRSD is used within a schoolwide positive behavioral support program.

Self-regulation is a powerful tool for students who are struggling academically. Once struggling writers take ownership of and know how to use self-instructions, goal setting, self-monitoring, and self-reinforcement, they will know how Josh thinks of creative ideas, how Anna chooses her writing topic, and how Emma goes about revising her work. The students will know the "trick" and be ready to write.

REFERENCES

Lane, K., Graham, S., Harris, K.R., & Weisenbach, J.L. (in press). Teaching writing strategies to young students struggling with writing and at-risk for behavioral disorders: Self-regulated strategy development. *Teaching Exceptional Children.*

Lane, K., Harris, K.R., Graham, S., Weisenbach, J., Brindle, M., & Morphy, P. (in press). The effects of self-regulated strategy development on the writing performance of second grade students with behavioral and writing difficulties. *Journal of Special Education.*

Nelson, R.O., & Hayes, S.C. (1981). Theoretical explanations for reactivity in self-monitoring. *Behavior Modification, 5,* 3–14.

Chapter 3 Self-Test

1. Self-instructions should be
   a. Required to be used aloud for all students
   b. Targeted to particular needs or characteristics of students
   c. Recited exactly the way the teacher uses them

2. The self-statement "What do I have to do here?" is an example of
   a. Problem definition
   b. Focusing of attention and planning
   c. Strategy implementation

3. The self-statement "First, I will write down my essay writing reminder" is an example of
   a. Self-reinforcement
   b. Focusing of attention and planning
   c. Strategy implementation

4. The self-statement "Have I supported my opinion with reasons?" is an example of
   a. Self-reinforcement
   b. Self-evaluation
   c. Coping and self-control

5. The self-statement "Don't worry. I can do this if I try." is an example of
   a. Self-reinforcement
   b. Self-evaluation
   c. Coping and self-control

6. True or False
   The teacher should teach all six types of self-statements to all students.

7. True or False
   Goal setting enhances student attention, motivation, and effort.

8. The teacher can foster student goal setting by
   a. Listening to the students' opinions about their goals
   b. Analyzing the students' writing samples and determining writing goals
   c. Using the curriculum standards to set individual student's writing goals

9. True or False
   When using these Lesson Plans, teachers should use self-monitoring only for those aspects of writing already targeted in the lessons.

10. True or False
    Students should set their own goals, regardless of how challenging or proximal they may be.

Answers: 1. b 2. a 3. b 4. b 5. c 6. False 7. True 8. a 9. False 10. False

Chapter 4

SRSD

Making It Work

"Okay, students, begin writing."

The students look at the clean, white, lined paper and their newly sharpened pencils and begin to think. Some students start writing and others continue to sit quietly and look around the room. One student says to himself, "I can do this if I try. I know the trick. I'll use my strategies." Another student says, "What do I need to do? I need to write a good story that has all the parts." As the teacher conferences with a student, she looks up to see all her students writing. She is now ready for the next step in SRSD. She wonders how she can refine her lessons, how she can be sure the students will use the strategies she taught them in other academic settings, and how she can continually assess her students' writing skills.

In this chapter, we will present the guidelines for evaluating SRSD and further discuss ways to achieve generalization and maintenance of writing and self-regulation strategies.

PRINCIPLES OF EVALUATION

Include Students as Co-Evaluators

Students should be included as partners in the strategy evaluation process. Not only does co-evaluation increase their sense of ownership and reinforce the progress they are making, but it also provides teachers with greater insight into the effectiveness of the strategies and SRSD instruction. Students can participate in many ways, such as learning to evaluate their writing based on their goals (self-assessment), or discussing with the teacher the components of instruction that are most helpful to them or where they would recommend changes. Co-evaluation has advantages for teachers as well. It provides a practical means for reducing the teacher's load. Students share this load by completing part of the evaluation process.

What things can students be expected to evaluate? The most obvious thing is their written products. In the lesson plans in this book, students learn to evaluate their writing based on their goals. If a strategy is designed to help students produce more support for their arguments, use certain types of words, include specific parts, or make revisions, students can learn to make and record their performance in these areas. Teachers must monitor the accuracy of students' assessments (more so at first), but with practice, students will become more precise in their evaluations.

Students can participate in other ways. They can discuss with the teacher the components of instruction that are most helpful to them, alert the teacher if something is not working for them, and make suggestions as to where they would recommend changes. By asking students to share their reflections, teachers gain valuable insight into their progress and readiness for moving on. Collaborative peer evaluation, such as peer-revising strategies (Graham, Harris, & Mason, 2005; Harris, Graham, & Mason, 2006), is also a valuable component of the assessment process.

Students can also assist in the decision-making process during instruction. Helping students ask appropriate self-questions is another effective way to help them evaluate their own progress. Appropriate self-questions include

- Am I ready to move to the next step?

- Have I used all of my story parts?

- Think back. Have I had any problems with this?

- Do I need to do anything different?

- Do I need to ask the teacher or a friend for help?

Once students are effectively using a writing strategy, teachers are encouraged to solicit recommendations and feedback concerning what students liked and did not like about the strategy and instructional procedures. The students are unlikely to use, adapt, or maintain writing strategies that they do not view as being efficient, effective, useful, or reasonable. Sample questions to ask students include

- What did you like about the strategy that you learned?

- What did you not like about this strategy?

- What would you change or do differently if you were teaching these strategies?

- Did the strategy help you write better? Why or why not?

- Will you continue to use the strategy? Why or why not?

- What did you like about the activities used to learn the strategy?

ASSESS CHANGES IN STUDENT WRITING BEHAVIOR, ATTITUDES, AND COGNITION

The effects of strategy instruction are not limited to what students write. The writing strategies lessons provided in this book are also designed to change how students go through the process of composing, such as increasing the time spent in advanced planning. In addition, it can be expected that students' confidence in their writing will increase, their attitude toward composing will become more positive, and their writing anxiety will decrease as they become more proficient at using writing strategies to meet their goals as writers. Thus, an evaluation that concentrates only on changes in students' written products will not provide an entire picture of the results of SRSD.

Writing Measures

Determining the appropriate writing measure depends on the particular strategy being taught, the components used to teach the strategy, and the amount of time available to the teacher and students. The lesson plans in this book include assessments by teachers and students, such as determining the number of story parts in a newly written story or the number of reasons given in a persuasive essay. Teachers, however, can add to or change these targets for assessment depending on the topic on which they are focusing or the students' needs. Measures of writing performance can be differentiated for students depending on their goals and current abilities.

Attitudes

Assessing students' attitudes toward and beliefs about writing is typically done through conversations with students as well as by observation. Indications of students' attitudes and beliefs about writing can be gained by discussing the amount of writing they do away from school and assessing spontaneous statements they make about writing assignments. If the desired changes in attitude are not taking place, the components of instruction can be modified or strengthened (i.e., developing new self-statements to cope with worry or anxiety) as needed. Developing a sense of self-efficacy (e.g., the "I can do this if I try" attitude) is an important part of SRSD. Students should be able to indicate the importance of both effort on their part and the strategies they have learned in writing.

Cognition

During and after SRSD, it is important to determine if students are using the cognitive processes targeted by assessing if learning the strategy changed their approach to writing. The most direct way of doing this is to observe what students do while they write. For example, the teacher should determine whether students write down the mnemonics and then make and organize their notes before writing. Some students may reach a point where they no longer need to do so, but the teacher must be sure they are still using all of the elements of writing they have learned. If they are not, they may need a booster session or encouragement to go back to the mnemonics and make notes. Teachers can also watch for indicators such as students spending more time planning after instruction, students quietly instructing themselves as they write.

Some changes in cognition, however, may be difficult to observe. Discussion can help the teacher gauge changes in students' knowledge about writing, the genre in which they are working, and the writing process. Some questions that may be appropriate to ask students before and after strategy instruction include

- What is good writing?

- What kinds of things do good writers say to themselves while they write?

- What things do you most like to say to yourself while you write? Why?

- If you were having trouble with a writing assignment, what kinds of things would you do?

- What kinds of things did you do that helped you plan this paper?

Remember that some changes take more time to become evident. Changes in attitude, for instance, may not occur immediately after a strategy is taught. Rather, some changes may occur only after students see more tangible payoffs, such as satisfaction with gradual improvements in their writing or better grades on their assignments.

ASSESS WHILE INSTRUCTION IS IN PROGRESS

It is important to evaluate students' progress during instruction, as opposed to only when instruction is "done." Thus, the aspects of writing performance, attitudes, and cognition should be assessed throughout instruction as appropriate. This will give teachers a better understanding of what individual students need to achieve success. Furthermore, if a strategy is too difficult or too easy for a particular student, the teacher will be able to modify the strategy or develop a more appropriate one.

It is also important to ensure that each stage and component of SRSD instruction is carried out as intended. Many teachers find it helpful to keep a file in which they jot down their informal observations on how things are going. This could include such things as what went well during instruction, what was problematic, who was progressing, who was having trouble, and ideas for the next day. Each student should keep a "writing folder" containing instructional materials such as charts, papers, notes, and plans on which they are working. This allows the teacher to survey student papers to note areas in which progress is evident and areas still in need of work.

ASSESS STUDENTS' USE OF THE STRATEGY OVER TIME AND IN NEW SITUATIONS

A key challenge in teaching writing strategies is flexible and continued use of the strategies over time. Students may not continue to use a target strategy once instructional supports are no longer in place. Furthermore, students might not be able to successfully adapt the strategy to new but appropriate situations. Therefore, it is beneficial to actively enhance maintenance and generalization of strategy usage from the very beginning of SRSD instruction, as well as to help students continue to develop and adapt the strategies over time.

Examples of procedures for enhancing maintenance and generalization include

- Periodically inviting students to explain the purpose of the strategy and to reiterate the basic steps

- Asking students to keep records of each time they use a strategy

- Asking students to keep records of how they modify the strategy for new tasks

- Observing students to see if they are using the strategy when they are completing relevant assignments

- Asking students if they are using the strategy in relevant assignments

Ultimately, the goal is to determine if students need additional support to consistently apply the strategy in appropriate situations.

INVOLVE OTHER TEACHERS IN THE EVALUATION PROCESS

When students are being taught a writing strategy that can be applied in a number of different content areas or classrooms, teachers are encouraged to involve other teachers in the evaluation process. The aim is to determine if the strategy is being applied successfully in these other settings. Other teachers should also be asked if the strategy is effective and appropriate for students' needs in their classes, and if not, how it could best be modified.

One of the major advantages in involving other teachers in the evaluation process is that they are often willing to help promote maintenance and generalization. They can provide reminders for students to use the strategy, help students with a particular step if they are having trouble, or suggest modifications to make the strategy more effective for whatever task is at hand. This involvement encourages collaboration with other teachers and can help promote generalization.

USE PORTFOLIO ASSESSMENT PROCEDURES

Portfolio assessment provides a way for the teacher and students to evaluate their successes and challenges. Although the lesson plans in this book do not call for portfolios, teachers are encouraged to include students' writing before and after SRSD in portfolios. There are at least three basic types of portfolios.

1. Students can keep a biography of their work, collecting pieces that portray the stages and development of a piece.

2. Students can collect a diverse range of works, such as stories, essays, journal entries, poems, and letters.

3. Students can analyze and self-critique their own work over a period of time. They can be encouraged to look for changes in their written papers and the way they go about the process of writing. Students can note what satisfies them and what does not work and identify areas that require further development.

Having students keep portfolios is beneficial to both teachers and students. Students learn to engage in reflective self-evaluation, an important part of becoming self-directed learners. Portfolios can help students more clearly see writing as a process, as their collections reveal the changes in their writing and their use of the composing processes. Teachers, in turn, can use these portfolios both for assessment and to share and communicate improvements in students' writing to parents and others.

A FEW FINAL TIPS FOR SRSD

Take It Slow

Many teachers often want to start SRSD with a challenging writing area or with a particular student who has very severe problems with writing. We recommend that teachers just starting out with strategy instruction proceed slowly. They should begin with relatively simple strategies in areas where they are comfortable and anticipate success, and they should work with students who are willing to learn the strategies. As teachers and students become more comfortable with SRSD, they can move on to greater challenges.

Take Advantage of Strategies and Lessons Already Developed

It is often easier to begin strategy instruction with an existing, proven strategy, such as any of those presented in this book. Once the teacher and students are familiar with SRSD, they can work together to create and evaluate new strategies. Teachers may need to create new strategies to address their unique needs and situations; researchers have yet to validate strategies for all genres or writing tasks.

Collaborate with Others

When possible, it is recommended that teachers collaborate with other teachers, other professionals, or paraprofessionals as they become strategies instructors. Supportive feedback and the opportunity to brainstorm when difficulties are encountered are very helpful when first trying SRSD. Other professionals may also be able to support elements of SRSD. For example, one teacher involved the speech-language therapist in her school for those students who were receiving services from her. The speech-language therapist helped these students become more fluent with the vocabulary involved in their writing, as well as with the use of self-instructions.

SRSD provides teachers with many ways to differentiate instruction depending on students' needs and strengths. Effective assessments will help teachers recognize the full potential of this approach.

INTRODUCTION TO THE LESSON PLANS

Lesson plans are presented next. A careful reading of the first four chapters in this book will be helpful in using these lesson plans appropriately. As was explained in Chapter 2, these lesson plans represent metascripts—a general plan and guidelines for teaching the strategies. Following the discussion in Chapters 2 and 3, teachers will need to modify these lesson plans to fit students' needs and classroom objectives. As noted in Chapter 1, a prescribed sequence is not recommended for teaching the writing strategies in this book. The strategies are not arranged from most to least critical, nor are specific grade levels stated for strategies. Teachers and administrators must decide which strategies to use at which time and with which students within the larger context of the curriculum and the students' needs. More than one strategy for the same genre may be used with different students in the same classroom.

These lesson plans are not "scripted." At some points in the lessons, specific wording is suggested for the purpose of being as clear as possible for those who are unfamiliar with self-regulated strategy development (SRSD) instruction. Lesson plans are accompanied by support materials for teachers. These may include strategy graphics that can be copied for students and used to make overheads, strategy prompt mnemonic charts, self-statement sheets, goal-setting materials, and progress graphing sheets. All of these materials can be reproduced as needed for educational purposes.

STRATEGY FOR ENHANCING WORD CHOICE

Chapter 5: Vocabulary Enrichment

Vocabulary Enrichment focuses on brainstorming and using action words, action helpers, and describing words in the context of story writing. Good word choice is difficult for many struggling writers, yet it is critical to the evaluation of writing quality. Although story writing is the context here, this strategy can also be adapted for other writing tasks. Lesson plans are provided for using action words only. These lesson plans can be modified easily to teach use of action helpers and describing words.

STRATEGIES FOR STORY WRITING

Chapter 6: POW + WWW

POW + WWW is a story-writing strategy that focuses on the basic steps of writing and the common parts of a good story. This set of lesson plans, and all of the following, use the full SRSD procedures.

Chapter 7: POW + C-SPACE

POW + C-SPACE is a more sophisticated strategy for story writing and is appropriate for students who understand the common parts of a good story and can do more advanced writing.

STRATEGIES FOR NARRATIVE, EXPOSITORY, AND PERSUASIVE WRITING

Chapter 8: POW + TREE

The POW + TREE strategy assists students in learning how to write an opinion essay. Lessons and materials are presented for both younger and older students.

Chapter 9: STOP and DARE

STOP and DARE is a more sophisticated strategy for writing a persuasive essay that addresses both sides of an issue.

Chapter 10: Report Writing

Report Writing assists students in determining what they know about a topic and in gathering additional information, planning, and writing a report.

Chapter 11: PLANS

PLANS is a goal-setting strategy applied to writing an essay. The same strategy can also be adapted to other writing tasks.

STRATEGIES FOR REVISING

Chapter 12: SCAN

SCAN is a strategy for revising a persuasive or opinion essay.

Chapter 13: Compare, Diagnose, and Operate

The strategy in this chapter provides a framework for the revising process, helping students learn to *Compare*, *Diagnose*, and *Operate* (CDO). The criteria for revision in this strategy focus on substance rather than form.

Chapter 14: REVISE

REVISE is a strategy used to revise an essay.

Chapter 15: Peer Revising

The strategy discussed in this chapter is for peer revising. Peers learn how to communicate effectively as well as how to help one another improve their writing.

STRATEGY FOR A WRITING COMPETENCY TEST

Chapter 16: PLAN & WRITE

PLAN & WRITE is designed to help students prepare for a state competency test. PLAN & WRITE can be revised to meet the demands of different state writing tests.

STRATEGY FOR READING AND WRITING INFORMATIONAL TEXT

Chapter 17: TWA + PLANS

TWA + PLANS is a strategy designed for reading expository text and writing informative essays. It can be used for information text as found in science and social studies content classes.

Remember to personalize the plans to meet the needs of your students and classroom objectives. We hope that this book's lessons will help your students not only improve their writing skills but also learn to enjoy the process of writing.

REFERENCES

Graham, S., Harris, K.R., & Mason, L. (2005). Improving the writing performance, knowledge, and motivation of struggling young writers: The effects of self-regulated strategy development. *Contemporary Educational Psychology, 30*, 207–241.

Harris, K.R., Graham, S., & Mason, L. (2006). Improving the writing, knowledge, and motivation of struggling young writers: Effects of self-regulated strategy development with and without peer support. *American Educational Research Journal, 43*(2), 295–340.

Chapter 4 Self-Test

1. One advantage to co-evaluation is that
   a. It increases the student's sense of ownership.
   b. The student is the more active participant.
   c. It provides more accurate grading.

2. True or False
   Students are usually accurate the first time they self-evaluate.

3. True or False
   When students are more confident about their writing, writing anxiety decreases.

4. Assessing students' attitudes and beliefs about writing can be determined by
   a. Examining their portfolios
   b. Their documented mastery of strategy instruction
   c. Conversations and observations of the student

5. True or False
   Changes in attitude may not occur immediately after a strategy is taught.

6. True or False
   Teachers who have carefully read this book and study the Lesson Plans are encouraged to start SRSD with their students who are having the most severe writing problems.

7. True or False
   Once students are doing well and formal SRSD instruction is over, it is not necessary to re-assess the student's skills.

8. True or False
   To help students continue developing and adapting the strategy over time, the teacher could ask the students to keep records of the times they use specific strategies.

Answers: 1. a   2. False   3. True   4. c   5. True   6. False   7. False   8. True

Part 2

Section I

Strategy for Enhancing Word Choice

Chapter 5

Vocabulary Enrichment

MATERIALS
Vocabulary Strategy Chart: Action Words
Vocabulary Strategy Chart: Action Helpers
Vocabulary Strategy Chart: Describing Words
Use Action Words!
Use Action Helpers!
Use Describing Words!
My Self-Statements
Vocabulary Graph
Story Questionnaire
Vocabulary Enrichment Certificate

NOTE: These lessons are for action words only. The lessons can be easily modified to teach use of action helpers and describing words. Materials for action helpers and describing words are included. Teachers can also decide to teach more than one word type at a time.

LESSON 1

LESSON OVERVIEW

The teacher will describe, discuss, and model the best way to write a story using the five-step Vocabulary Enrichment Strategy for action words. The teacher will then support the students' practice using the five strategy steps for action words in writing their stories. Lesson 1 typically takes more than one class period to complete. If appropriate, the teacher can use the term *verbs* for action words.

STUDENT OBJECTIVES

The students will evaluate their prior use of action words to write a story. They will begin using the five-step strategy to include more action words in their story writing. Once they have written a story, the students will complete a story questionnaire.

MATERIALS

One copy for each student:
- Use Action Words!
- Vocabulary strategy charts
- Vocabulary Graph
- Vocabulary Self-Statements

- Picture prompts for story writing (provided by teacher)
- Two stories previously written by each student
- Story Questionnaire
- Paper and pencils

SET THE CONTEXT FOR STUDENT LEARNING

Tell your students that they will be learning a new writing trick that will help them write better stories. This trick will help make their writing more interesting for others to read.

DEVELOP THE STRATEGY AND SELF-REGULATION

Step 1: Introduce Action Words

Say, *"Good stories use many action words."*

- Ask, *"What is an action word?"* Solicit responses, and then

    1. Go over the Use Action Words! chart, including definitions and examples.

    2. Ask the students to suggest three more action words, and then ask for different words for the same things (e.g., What is another word for *shouted*?).

    3. Using a picture prompt, ask the students to identify three or four action words that can be seen or suggested in the picture; write them down as they are given (the picture prompt needs to include a great deal of action).

    4. Ask the students to use these action words in sentences. They must be good meaningful sentences. Demonstrate how you can have more than one action word in a sentence; have the students try making sentences with two or more action words.

Step 2: Review Current Writing Performance for Action Words

Say, *"Remember the stories you wrote for me the other day?"* Ask the students to read and review their two stories, instruct the students to count the number of action words in each story, and help each student as needed.

- Introduce the graphing chart. Explain and model how to count different action words from a story. (You can use a simple story you write or select one or two written by the students.) Be sure to stress that the words must be different. The same action word only counts once!

- Explain the goal, which is to write better stories. Say, *"Good stories use many action words. This makes the story more fun to read. Our goal is to have a better story and more action words the next time."*

Step 3: Describe the Learning Strategy

Say, *"I will teach you how to think of more good action words."* Using the same picture as before, tell the students that to think of good action words, they must be creative and let their minds be free.

- Tell the students to look at the picture to think of more action words. Explain that sometimes you say things to yourself when you want to think of more action words (e.g., "I have to let my mind be free." "If I take my time, good words will come to me." "Think of new words for old ideas." "What *doing* words are in this picture?"). Tell the students that these things are not always said aloud but are often said inside your head.

- Say, *"The things you say to yourself will help you to work. What things do you want to say to yourself to help you think of action words?"* Try to get two or three self-statements from each student.

- Ask the students to record their self-statements on their self-statements chart as appropriate.

- Say, *"Look at this picture again. Tell yourself how to think of good action words. Tell me four or five more good action words."* Help the students as necessary. Don't go on until you get three or four additional action words. The students should keep their list of self-statements in front of them.

Say, *"I am going to teach you five steps for writing good stories with more action words."*

- Give each student the appropriate vocabulary strategy chart. Describe and discuss the five steps.

- Ask the students to read the five steps aloud together.

Step 4: Model the Strategy

Keep the vocabulary strategy chart, Use Action Words!, and self-statements charts out where the students can refer to them.

- Using the same picture, model the entire process by writing an actual short story. Be sure to use problem definition, planning, the five strategy steps, and self-evaluation and self-reinforcement self-statements as you model as seen next. You can have the students assist you as you write.

Say, *"What do I have to do? I have to write a good story. A good story uses many action words. I need to remember my steps. Step 1 says, 'Look at the picture and write down good action words.' I need to say to myself, 'Let my mind be free.'"* Pause. *"Think of new words for my ideas."* Think of some words aloud and write them at the top of the paper. *"If I take my time, good words will come to me."* Pause and then list words as before. *"Good! I like these words. I can think of more good words while I write. Step 2 says, 'Think of a good story idea for my words.'"* Pause and think. *"I've got an idea! I'll write about _____. Step 3 says, 'Write my story—make sense and use good action words.'"* Write the story, talking briefly. Use self-statements as you write (e.g., "How shall I start?"). Pause and think of a first sentence. Don't hurry, but don't slow it down unnaturally. *"Take my time."* At least once or twice ask, *"Am I using good words?"* When the story is written, say, *"Good, now I'm ready for Step 4, which says, 'Read my story and ask—did I write a good story? Did I use good action words?'"* Read the story to yourself, and then answer your question. *"I like my words. Step 5 says, 'Fix my story—can I use more good action words?'"* Look back through the story and add one or two more words. Be sure to talk aloud as you do this. *"Good work! I'm done! It'll be fun to show my story to others."* Ask the students to help you count the action words in your story and graph the number of words on the graphing chart.

- Self-Statements

   1. Say, *"Remember the things I said to myself to help me write my story."* Ask the students if they can remember 1) things you said to yourself to get started, 2) things you said while you worked (try to get some creative self-statements as well as remembering steps), and 3) things you said to yourself when you finished. Prompt, and if they can't remember what you said to yourself, remind them of the phrases you used.

   2. Allow the students to add to their individual self-statements chart. Each student should have at least one thing to say to get started. For example, "What do I have to do?" or "I have to write a good story with many action words."

   3. Each student should have at least one thing to say while you work. For example, "I have to remember the five steps."

   4. Each student should have at least one thing to say when you're finished. For example, "I did a great job with action words" or "Good action words!"

   5. Note that we don't always have to say these things aloud; once we learn them, we can think them in our heads or whisper them to ourselves.

Step 5: Rehearse the Five Strategy Steps

- The students must be able to recite all five steps from memory. Wording doesn't have to be exact. The students can paraphrase, but the meaning cannot be changed.

   1. Orally review the five steps. Read them from the vocabulary strategy chart. Tell the students that they will need to memorize the five strategy steps.

   2. Give the students time to practice. Practice the steps in any way you think is helpful. Read with the chart up. Put the chart down, write, cover, say, and so forth.

   3. Give each student the opportunity to paraphrase all five steps from memory.

GO TO STEP 6 ONLY IF YOU HAVE TIME. IF NOT, GO TO WRAP-UP.

Step 6: Students Practice Strategies and Self-Instructions

- Give the students the opportunity to practice the strategy steps. Review student goals by having all the students look at their graphing charts and goals to have more words than their earlier written stories. Help the students set reasonable goals for the number of action words in their next story. You can prompt and provide positive and corrective feedback. Be supportive and offer plenty of encouragement. You can use the same picture or a new picture. Review the students' self-statements and the vocabulary strategy chart before they begin. The students can refer to either as necessary.

- Have the students count the number of action words in their stories. Count and compare counts to verify that the students have done this correctly. Let the students record the number of action words on the graphing chart.

- Have each student complete the Story Questionnaire.

WRAP-UP

Encourage the students to think about what they have learned because next time you'll give them a quiz (non-graded) on the five steps!

LESSON 2

LESSON OBJECTIVES
The teacher will model use of the five-step strategy for action words without looking at the vocabulary strategy chart.

STUDENT OBJECTIVES
The students will state the five-step strategy from memory. The students will develop goals for action words and write a story using the five-step strategy. The students will complete a Story Questionnaire following writing a story. This lesson should be repeated as necessary until students are ready for Lesson 3.

MATERIALS

One copy for each student:
- Use Action Words!
- Vocabulary strategy charts
- Vocabulary Graph
- Vocabulary Self-Statements

- Picture prompts for story writing (provided by teacher)
- Two stories previously written by each student
- Story Questionnaire
- Paper and pencils

SET THE CONTEXT FOR STUDENT LEARNING

- Ask the students if they have been thinking about what they have learned about story writing and action words.

- Review the meaning of action words. Look at the Use Action Words! and the vocabulary strategy chart. Ask the students if they noticed any action words in their reading.

- Ask the students if they can state the five strategy steps without looking at the vocabulary strategy chart. They can paraphrase, but it is important that the whole concept is remembered. Provide prompts, encouragement, and reinforcement for their efforts.

- Practice the five strategy steps if necessary or have the students practice together.

DEVELOP THE STRATEGY AND SELF-REGULATION

Step 1: Review Self-Statements

Give each student his or her self-statements chart; review all of their self-statements and the purposes for the statements. Remind the students that the things they say to themselves will help them work while writing a story.

Step 2: Model without the Vocabulary Strategy Chart

- Ask the students to put all charts and materials in their folders or desks.

- Model the entire strategy process by writing a short story without referring to any support materials. Be sure to continue using problem definition, planning, strategy step usage, self-evaluation, and self-reinforcement self-statements. You can have the students assist you as you write.

Say, *"What do I have to do? I have to write a good story. A good story uses many action words. I need to remember the five strategy steps. Step 1 says I need to look at the picture and write down good action words. Let my mind be free."* Pause. *"I need to think of new words for my ideas."* Think of some words aloud and write them down at the top of the paper. *"I need to take my time so that more good words will come to me."* Pause, and then list words as before. *"Good! I like these words. I can think of more action words while I write. Step 2 says I need to think of a good story idea for my words."* Pause and think. *"I've got an idea. I'll write about . . . . Step 3 says that I need to write my story and remember to use good action words."* Talk yourself briefly through writing the story. Think aloud things like *"How shall I start?"* Pause and develop a first sentence. Say, *"Don't hurry, but don't slow it down unnaturally."* At least once or twice ask, *"Am I using good action words?"* When the story is written, say, *"Good, now I'm ready for Step 4, which says I should read my story and ask if I used good action words."* Read the story to yourself. *"Step 5 says that I need to fix my story. Can I use more good words?"* Look back through the story and add one or two more words, verbalizing as you do. *"Good work! I'm done! It'll be fun to show my story to others."*

- Count and graph the number of action words used.

Step 3: Student Practice of Strategies and Self-Statements

- Tell the students that they will now write a story using the five-step vocabulary strategy. Ask them to look at their graphing chart and set a goal to write more action words than the previous time. Provide prompts, give positive and corrective feedback, be supportive, and offer plenty of encouragement. Encourage the students to use the five steps for writing a story without referring to the vocabulary strategy chart.

- Have the students count the number of action words in their stories. Count and compare counts. Let the students record the number of action words on the graphing chart.

- Have each student complete a Story Questionnaire.

WRAP-UP

Remind the students to think about what they have learned and to use the five-step strategy whenever they are writing a story.

LESSON OBJECTIVES

The teacher will guide the students to independent strategy use when writing a story.

STUDENT OBJECTIVES

The students will independently write a story with action words. When finished, they will complete a Story Questionnaire.

MATERIALS

One copy for each student:

- Use Action Words!
- Vocabulary strategy charts
- Vocabulary Graph
- Vocabulary Self-Statements
- Picture prompts for story writing (provided by teacher)

- Two stories previously written by each student
- Story Questionnaire
- Vocabulary Enrichment Certificate
- Paper and pencils

SET THE CONTEXT FOR STUDENT LEARNING

- Ask the students if they have been thinking about what they have learned about story writing and action words.

- Review the meaning of action words. Look at the Use Action Words! chart.

- Ask the students if they can state the five strategy steps without looking at the vocabulary strategy chart. They can paraphrase, but it is important that the whole concept is remembered. Provide prompts, encouragement, and reinforcement for their efforts.

- Practice the five strategy steps if necessary or have the students practice together.

DEVELOP THE STRATEGY AND SELF-REGULATION

Step 1: Move from Guided to Independent Practice

- The students will use self-statements while using the five-step strategy to write a story, but this time they will work without the teacher modeling first. Check the students' strategy use with as little prompting as possible, but prompt the students if they omit a step.

- Have the students count the number of words in their stories. Count and compare counts.

- Let the students record their number of action words on their graphing chart.

- Have each student complete a Story Questionnaire.

- Have the students share their stories with a peer or with the group.

WRAP-UP

Remind the students to think about what they have learned and to use the five-step vocabulary strategy whenever they write stories.

- Repeat this lesson as needed until the students can independently use the five-step vocabulary strategy for writing stories with action words.

- Lessons 1, 2, and 3 can be repeated for teaching the students to increase their use of *action helpers* and *describing* words in their story writing. As you focus on using action helpers, remind the students to keep using good action words as well. As you focus on describing words, remind the students to continue to use both action words and action helpers as well.

- Give each student who has successfully learned to use the vocabulary enrichment strategy a Certificate of Achievement.

Vocabulary Strategy: Action Words

Strategy Steps:

1. Look at the picture and write down good action words.
2. Think of a good story idea for my words.
3. Write my story. Make sense and use good action words.
4. Read my story and ask myself, "Did I write a good story? Did I use good action words?"
5. Fix my story. Can I use more good action words?

Vocabulary Strategy: Action Helpers

Strategy Steps:

1. Look at the picture and write down good helper words.
2. Think of a good story idea for my words.
3. Write my story. Make sense and use good helper words.
4. Read my story and ask myself, "Did I write a good story? Did I use good helper words?"
5. Fix my story. Can I use more good helper words?

Vocabulary Strategy: Describing Words

Strategy Steps:

1. Look at the picture and write down good describing words.
2. Think of a good story idea for my words.
3. Write my story. Make sense and use good describing words.
4. Read my story and ask myself, "Did I write a good story? Did I use good describing words?"
5. Fix my story. Can I use more good describing words?

USE ACTION WORDS!

Action words tell what people, things, or animals do. They are *doing* words.

- He **JUMPED** and **SHOUTED** at the game.
- The man **WORRIED** and **THOUGHT** about her.
- The book **FELL** to the floor.
- The horse **GALLOPED** down the road.

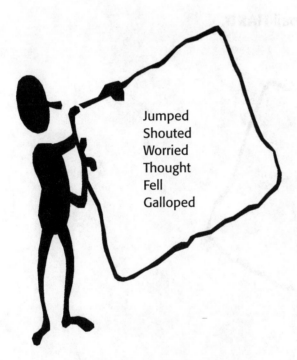

Jumped
Shouted
Worried
Thought
Fell
Galloped

USE ACTION HELPERS!

Action Helpers are words that go along with action words. They help tell more about the action by telling how the action is done.

- The dog ran **QUICKLY.**
- The book fell **QUIETLY.**
- The boy ran **FAST.**
- The taxi drove **SLOWLY.**
- The man laughed **LOUDLY.**
- The woman pounded the nail **HARD.**

Quickly
Quietly
Fast
Slowly
Loudly
Hard

Although many action helpers end in **LY**, thre are also many that do not!

USE DESCRIBING WORDS!

Describing words tell more about people, animals, places, or things. They help to paint a picture. Describing words may tell about color, shape, number, size, feeling, smell, sound, taste, and so forth.

- The **SICK** girl went home.
- There were **FIVE** boxes.
- The **PRETTY** leaf was **RED.**
- The **ROUGH** wood hurt her **SORE** feet.
- The city was **DIRTY.**
- The **BIG, ROUND** box is mine.

Sick   Sore
Five   Dirty
Pretty   Big
Red   Round
Rough

My Self-Statements

Things to say when I'm getting started:

_____

_____

_____

_____

_____

_____

Things to say while I work:

_____

_____

_____

_____

_____

_____

Things to say when I'm finished:

_____

_____

_____

_____

_____

_____

Vocabulary Graph

	12	11	10	9	8	7	6	5	4	3	2	1

| | 12 | 11 | 10 | 9 | 8 | 7 | 6 | 5 | 4 | 3 | 2 | 1 |

Color in your chart up to the number of good vocabulary words you used.

Story Questionnaire

Please answer each question below. Circle your answer.

When you wrote your story:

1.	Did you look at the picture and write down good action words?	YES	NO
2.	Did you let your mind think free?	YES	NO
3.	Did you like the words you thought of?	YES	NO
4.	Did you remember your goal—to use more good action words than last time?	YES	NO
5.	Did you think of a good story idea?	YES	NO
6.	Did your story make sense and use good action words?	YES	NO
7.	Did you read your story and then fix it?	YES	NO
8.	Did you take your time?	YES	NO
9.	Did you remember to use everything you know about writing stories to help you while you wrote?	YES	NO
10.	Did you tell yourself that you did a good job?	YES	NO

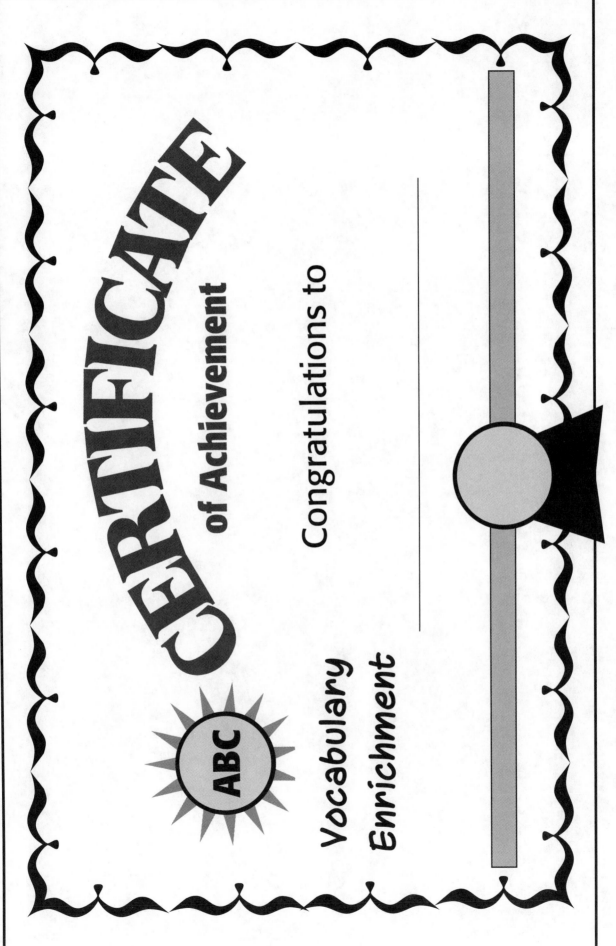

CERTIFICATE
of Achievement

ABC

Congratulations to

Vocabulary
Enrichment

Section II

Strategies for Story Writing

Chapter 6

POW + WWW

P = Pick my idea.

O = Organize my notes.

W = Write and say more.

W = Who is the main character?

W = When does the story take place?

W = Where does the story take place?

W = What does the main character do or want to do; what do other characters do?

W = What happens then? What happens with other characters?

H = How does the story end?

H = How does the main character feel; how do other characters feel?

MATERIALS

POW + WWW Mnemonic Chart
Cue Cards with Pictures
Cue Cards without Pictures
Graphic Organizer with Pictures
Graphic Organizer without Pictures
Story Rockets Graph
My Self-Statements
Transfer Sheet
POW + WWW Certificate
Bulletin Board:
  • Self-Statements "Explosions"
  • POW + WWW Writing Sheet

LESSON 1

LESSON OVERVIEW

The POW + WWW, What = 2, How = 2 strategies will be introduced in this lesson. The teacher and the students will collaboratively locate the story parts Who, When, Where, What = 2, How = 2 in two stories. The students will begin to learn the two strategies. They will establish writing partners and concept of transfer.

STUDENT OBJECTIVES

The students will identify the seven parts of WWW, What = 2, How = 2 in two stories.

MATERIALS

One copy for each student:
- POW + WWW mnemonic chart
- Graphic organizers

- Transfer sheet
- *Freddie the Fish* and *The Sly Fox* stories
- Paper, pencils, and scratch paper

SET THE CONTEXT FOR STUDENT LEARNING

 Introduce yourself as a writing teacher. Say, *"I'm going to teach you some of the tricks for writing. First, we will learn a strategy, or a trick, that good writers use when they write. Then we will learn the trick, or the strategy, for writing good stories."*

DEVELOP THE STRATEGY AND SELF-REGULATION

Step 1: Introduce POW

- Put out the POW + WWW mnemonic chart so that only POW shows.

- Emphasize that POW is a trick good writers often use for many things as they write.

  P = *P*ick my Idea

  O = *O*rganize my Notes

  W = *W*rite and Say More

- Emphasize that POW can be remembered because it gives the students POWER when they write.

- Practice POW; turn the mnemonic chart over. Ask each student to explain what POW stands for and provide help as needed. Continue to provide assistance until you feel sure that each student understands the meaning behind POW. Some students may not understand what it means to make notes. Discuss and demonstrate as needed.

- Briefly discuss good stories. Ask the students to describe things that make stories good. Be sure the following components are discussed:

  1. Good stories are fun to write and fun for others to read.

  2. Good stories make sense and have several parts.

 Say, *"We will learn a trick to help us remember and use the parts of a good story."*

Step 2: **Introduce WWW, What = 2, How = 2**

- Introduce WWW. Uncover the POW + WWW chart to display WWW. Say, *"Let's identify the parts of a good story."* Have the students look at the chart. Briefly discuss each W. You can use the word *character* for *Who.* For *When,* ask the students to tell you how a person explains *When* in a story (i.e., *When* did the story happen?) Give examples (e.g., "Once upon a time," "A long time ago," "Yesterday," "Wednesday afternoon at 4:00"). Ask the students for examples of what might be *Where* in a story (i.e., *Where* did the story take place?).

- Uncover What = 2. Explain and briefly discuss each *What.* Brainstorm examples of how a writer might tell each. Use stories the students know or are currently reading for examples.

- Uncover How = 2. Explain and briefly discuss each *How.* Brainstorm examples of how a writer might tell each. Use stories the students know or are currently reading for examples.

Step 3, Part 1: **Find Parts in a Story**

 Say, *"We will read a story to find out if the writer used all of the parts that make a good story."* (Leave the mnemonic chart out where the students can see it.)

- Lay out a graphic organizer or write it on the board. Point out the mnemonic chart (WWW, What = 2, How = 2) at the top and review the ideas for which it stands.

> **Modification:**
> Use the Graphic Organizer with Pictures for young students or those students who have difficulty with the language concepts.

- Give each student a copy of the story (*Freddie the Fish*); ask them to read along silently while you read the story aloud. Read the story aloud a second time and tell the students to raise their hands when they hear *Who, When,* or *Where* in the story. Call on students as they raise their hands and ensure that all students have a turn. As they identify *Who, When,* and *Where,* write each response in the appropriate space on the graphic organizer. DO NOT USE FULL SENTENCES. DO THIS IN NOTE FORM.

> **Modification:**
> Use additional stories for young students or those students who have difficulty with the language concepts.

- Tell the students that they are now looking for the two *Whats* and the two *Hows.* Briefly review what each means. Remind the students to raise their hands when they hear one in the story. Read the story from the beginning. Stop as hands are raised; write each *What* and each *How* in the appropriate space on the graphic organizer. DO NOT USE FULL SENTENCES. DO THIS IN NOTE FORM. If you get to the end of the story and the students have not identified all of the parts, go back over the story and help as needed. Be encouraging and positive throughout.

> **Modification:**
> If the students are unfamiliar with writing notes, include a mini-lesson on note writing here.

- After finding all of the parts, ask the students to find words in *Freddie the Fish* that they could change into "million-dollar words." These are good vocabulary words; each good word is worth a million dollars. For example, you could change *big* to *huge* (or *gigantic*) and so on.

> **Modification:**
> The students who have difficulty remembering the mnemonic and the parts will be given extra practice called "rapid-fire practice" in the next lessons.

Step 3, Part 2: **Practice the POW + WWW Mnemonic**

- Practice the POW + WWW mnemonic. Turn the mnemonic chart and the students' papers over. Ask the students to tell you what the mnemonic is. (They should respond, "WWW, What = 2, How = 2.") Ask the students to write the reminder on scratch paper. If the stu-

dents have trouble, turn the chart back over and allow them to look. Keep doing this until all students can tell you the reminder and write it on paper from memory.

- Practice the story parts. Ask the students to explain the parts. (Keep the chart turned over, but allow the students to look at the WWW, What = 2, How = 2 they wrote on their scratch paper.) Help as needed. Practice until you feel confident that the students can identify and understand all the parts.

Step 4: Find Parts in a Second Story

Do a second story (*The Sly Fox*). Leave out the mnemonic chart. As before, remind the students to raise their hand when they hear a story part. Be sure that each part is identified. Do not write the parts out this time. Point to—or ask the students to point to—where each part goes on the chart. Find words that can be changed to million-dollar words—for example, you can change *looked* to *hunted*—or look for where you could add million-dollar words.

TRANSFER LESSON: ESTABLISH PARTNERS AND TRANSFER

1. Tell the students that you want them to use POW + WWW in their other classes whenever they can, and that they will act as partners to help each other do that. Create partners or small groups to remind each other.

2. Describe and discuss Goal 1 for next time, which is to use all or parts of POW and/or WWW in other classes or for other writing tasks. Brainstorm together some classes or other writing tasks where POW + WWW could be used, being sure to note that POW should be used whenever WWW is used. Other ideas could include book reports, letters to friends, reports on special topics, articles for a school newsletter, stories about something that happened to them or a special event, and so forth. [Briefly note that for some tasks, like writing a report, all parts of the WWW trick might not be appropriate to use, and they must change WWW to fit the kind of report they need to write, or not use all of WWW, What = 2, How = 2 in situations where it doesn't make sense.]

3. Tell the students to report back to you about using all or any parts of POW + WWW next time (e.g., the students might report making notes for a writing task before they wrote). Show the students their transfer sheets, and explain that they will write down each time they use all or any part of POW + WWW outside of this class. They will also get to draw a star on the graph for each entry. Briefly discuss the word *transfer*, which means to move from one place to another (e.g., "I transferred schools" means "I moved from one school to another"). Emphasize that you want them to transfer what they learn about POW + WWW from this class to other classes and other writing tasks.

4. Describe and discuss Goal 2 for next time, which is to help their partners by reminding each other when they might transfer POW + WWW; report back on times they helped one another transfer by reminding their partners. Explain that they will write down and put a star next to each time they tell you about the ways they helped their partners transfer all or any part of POW + WWW. Ask them to tell you what *transfer* means and make sure they understand it!

WRAP-UP

Announce a test (no grade) for the next session. For this test, the students will write out POW and the WWW mnemonic and tell what the letters stand for from memory. Have the students take their scratch paper with POW + WWW, What = 2, How = 2.

TRANSFER LESSON

Remind the students that they will fill in the transfer sheet the next time.

Freddie the Fish

Last summer, Freddie, a big fish with black and white stripes, lived in a big pond just outside of town. One day, Freddie was happily swimming around the pond when he saw a big, juicy worm floating in the water. Freddie was hungry and decided that the worm would be a nice snack. He swam silently over to the worm and bit into it. Suddenly, he felt himself being pulled through the water and into a boat! Oh, no! He had been caught by a fisherman! Freddie felt sad and wished he had been more careful.

(Adapted from a folktale)

The Sly Fox

Once upon a time, a sly fox lived in a den in the forest. Every day the fox looked for food. He often wished for something different to eat. He thought of the rats and bugs he usually ate. Somewhere in the forest there had to be something more interesting to eat.

Suddenly, the fox saw a robin up in a tree eating just what he wanted—a piece of cheese. The fox began to climb the tree. Just as he was getting close, the bird flew to another tree. The fox's mouth was watering as he stared up at the cheese. He did not want to eat a rat when he could have cheese. "That bird will fly away again if I try climbing the tree!" he thought, "But I have to have that cheese."

Then the fox decided to try to trick the robin into giving up the cheese. "Mrs. Robin," says the fox, "I have heard that your voice is the best in the forest. I would love to hear one of your songs for myself." The proud robin lifted her head to sing, but when she opened her mouth the piece of cheese fell to the ground. The fox laughed as he looked up at the bird. He was glad that it had been so easy to fool the robin.

So the fox ate the cheese, while the robin went hungry. Then the fox went on his way looking for dessert. He was proud of himself for being smarter than the robin.

(Adapted from a folktale)

LESSON 2

LESSON OVERVIEW

The POW + WWW, What = 2, How = 2 strategies will be reviewed. The students will examine a story that they had previously written and look for the number of story parts. This current progress for each student will be graphed and a goal set to get all seven story parts next time. The students will record their transfer efforts.

STUDENT OBJECTIVES

The students will identify parts in a story, establish current practice, and set a goal for writing stories with seven parts.

TRANSFER LESSON

The students will orally state where they transferred either POW or WWW and tell how they helped their partner.

MATERIALS

One copy for each student:
- Mnemonic chart
- *The Tiger's Whiskers* story
- One previously written story by each student
- Graphic organizers
- Story Rockets graph
- Paper, pencils, and scratch paper

- Transfer sheet
- Cue Cards with or without pictures for practice. As with the graphic organizer, card picture cues can be used to help younger students or those with language difficulties.

Modification:
Use the Graphic Organizer with Picture Cues for young students or those students who have difficulty with the language concepts.

SET THE CONTEXT FOR STUDENT LEARNING

Test to see if the students remember POW + WWW, What = 2, How = 2.

- Provide the students with scratch paper. Ask them to write down POW and then ask them what it stands for. If the students have trouble remembering POW, continue to practice it until they can recall it without difficulty.

- Ask the students to write WWW, What = 2, How = 2 on the scratch paper. If a student has trouble, be supportive and prompt as needed.

- Ask the students to explain the meaning of WWW, What = 2, How = 2. Ensure that every student has an opportunity to answer.

- It is essential that each student memorize the reminder. If some students have trouble with this, spend a few minutes practicing it. Tell the students that you will test them each day to make sure they can recall it. Remind the students that they can practice memorizing the parts.

Modification:
See how fast the students can tell you what each letter stands for, using cue cards.

TRANSFER LESSON

Review and record transfer.

1. Review the meaning of transfer briefly.

2. Ask the students to report back when they use all or parts of POW and/or WWW in other classes or for other writing tasks. If necessary, brainstorm together some classes or other writing tasks where they could use both POW and WWW. Be sure the students understand that they should use POW with WWW whenever they use WWW. Other writing tasks could include book reports, letters to friends, reports on special topics, articles for a school newsletter, stories about something that happened to them, or a special event. Briefly remind the students that for some tasks, such as writing a report, all parts of the WWW trick might not be appropriate to use, and they should change WWW to fit the kind of report they need to write. Fill in the transfer sheet. Star each recorded item.

DEVELOP THE STRATEGY AND SELF-REGULATION

Step 1: **Identify Story Parts**

If necessary, go through one more story sample (*The Tiger's Whiskers*) and have the students verbally identify the story parts.

Step 2: **Establish Current Level of Performance**

 Say, *"Remember the story you wrote for me the other day?"* Pass out the students' previously written stories.

- Tell the students to read their stories and see which parts they have. (You will need to work out ahead of time which parts they had and which ones they were missing.)

- Briefly note with the students which parts they have and which they don't. As a group, briefly note common parts that are missing.

- Note also that even though a student has a part, he or she might be able to make that part better next time. This will make his or her story more fun to write and to read. Discuss examples of how students could do each using either their stories, *Freddie the Fish*, or *The Tiger's Whiskers:*

  - It can have more than one character.

  - It can tell more about when and where.

  - It can have more things happen (action).

  - It can tell more about characters' feelings.

  - It can have an interesting ending.

  - It can use good word choice (e.g., color words) or "million-dollar" words.

  - It can use an interesting first sentence.

- Introduce the Story Rockets graph. Give the students graphs and have them fill in the number of parts they had in their pretest story. Be very positive; tell them that they are just now learning the trick of writing good stories and it is okay if they do not have all of the parts.

- Explain the goal, which is to write better stories. Remind the students that good stories are fun for them to write and for others to read. They have all the parts, each part is well done, and the story makes sense.

 Say, *"Our goal is to have all of the parts and better parts the next time we write a story."*

WRAP-UP

- Remind the students of the POW + WWW, What = 2, How = 2 test again next time.

- If the students are still having trouble finding the seven parts in the stories you have read, plan to read another story aloud at the beginning of the next lesson.

TRANSFER LESSON

Remind the students that they will fill in the transfer sheet again next time.

The Tiger's Whiskers

A long time ago, there was a woman who lived with her son in the forest. One day, her son got very sick. The woman was very sad and wanted her son to get well. She tried everything she could think of, but nothing worked. At last she remembered that medicine made from a tiger's whisker would help him get well. So the woman set out to get a tiger's whisker. She went to a tiger's cave and put food in front of the cave and sang soft music. The tiger came out, ate the food, and thanked the woman for the music and the food. The woman quickly cut off one of his whiskers and ran home. The woman's son got well and the woman was very happy.

(Adapted from a folktale)

LESSON 3

LESSON OVERVIEW

The teacher will model using the POW + WWW strategies for writing a story. Self-statements as a self-regulation procedure will be established.

STUDENT OBJECTIVES

The students will write the POW + WWW mnemonic from memory. The students will listen to a teacher-modeled lesson. The students will record things they can say to themselves when writing.

MATERIALS

One copy for each student:
- Mnemonic chart
- Story samples (*The Farmer's Story, Charlie the Cat*)
- Turtle picture prompt
- Graphic organizers
- Story Rockets graph
- Self-Statements sheet

- Paper, pencils, and scratch paper
- Transfer sheet
- Cue cards with or without pictures for practice. As with the graphic organizer, card picture cues can be used to help younger students or those with language difficulties.

Modification:
Use the Graphic Organizer with Picture Cues for young students or those students who have difficulty with the language concepts as needed during this lesson. If your students have demonstrated an understanding of all the story parts, you may begin to use the Graphic Organizers without Pictures.

SET THE CONTEXT FOR STUDENT LEARNING

Test to see if the students remember POW + WWW, What = 2, How = 2. Do it aloud to save time. It is essential that each student memorize these parts of the strategy. If the students have trouble with this, spend a few minutes practicing it (use cue cards). Tell them that you will test them on it each day to make sure they understand it.

TRANSFER LESSON

Record and review transfer. See Lesson 2 for detailed steps.

Modification:
Continue use of cue cards with students who are having difficulty remembering either the mnemonic or parts. Students can query each other in pairs, using the Cue Cards.

DEVELOP THE STRATEGY AND SELF-REGULATION

Step 1: Find Story Parts

If the students are still having trouble finding the seven parts, read another story (*The Farmer's Story* or *Charlie the Cat*) aloud.

- Discuss using million-dollar words (included at the end of this lesson).

Step 2: Model POW

Lay out a copy of the POW + WWW, What = 2, How = 2 Graphic Organizer.

Say, *"Remember that the first letter in POW is P, which stands for Pick my idea. We will now practice how to think of a good story idea and good story parts. To do this, we must be creative. We have to think free."*

- Say, *"Look at the turtle picture."* Tell the students the things you say to yourself when you want to think of good story ideas or parts. Be sure to say, *"I have to let my mind be free,"* *"If I take my time, a good idea will come to me,"* *"Think of new, fun ideas,"* and *"What ideas for parts do I see in this picture?"* Explain that the things students say to themselves will help them work. Note that it's not always necessary to think out loud and that the students can think these things in their heads.

- Ask the students, *"What things do each of you want to say to yourself to help you think of good story ideas and good parts?"* Try to get two or three self-statements from each student. If the students give you negative statements (e.g., "I'm not good at ideas"), discuss briefly that there are some things we wouldn't want to say to ourselves because they may get in the way of doing a good job. Help your students think of things to say that will help them work. Record the students' self-statements on their self-statements chart. Leave the sheets out where they can be seen.

Step 3: Model WWW, What = 2, How = 2

 Say, *"The second letter in POW is O, which stands for Organize my notes. I am going to write a story today with your help. I will use my mnemonic to help me. I will use this page to make my notes and to organize them; you will do this, too, the next time you write a story."* Briefly review while pointing at the seven parts of a good story on the graphic organizer. Say, *"What should my goal be? I want to write a good story. A good story has all seven parts, makes sense, and is fun for me to write and for others to read."*

Step 4: Model Writing a Story

- Keep the POW + WWW, What = 2, How = 2 mnemonic chart and the students' self-statements sheets out where they can be seen or use the blackboard.

- Model the entire process, writing an actual story as you go (using the turtle picture prompt). Use problem definition, planning, self-evaluation, and self-reinforcement self-statements as you work. Use "million-dollar words" (good vocabulary words—each is worth a million dollars!). Follow the steps, filling in ad lib statements where indicated. Ask the students to help you with ideas but be sure that you remain in charge of the process.

 Say, *"What do I have to do? I have to write a good story. A good story makes sense and has all seven parts. Remember P in POW—Pick my idea. Let my mind be free."* Pause. Say, *"Take my time. A good story idea and good parts will come to me."* Pause.

- Say, *"Now I can do O in POW—Organize my notes. I can write down story part ideas for each part. I can write ideas down in different parts of this organizer as I think of them."* Be sure to model moving in and out of order during your planning. Students can help you think of ideas. *"What ideas do I see in this picture?"* Talk out and fill in notes for who, when, and where. *"For who I see . . . For when I can write . . . Let's see, for where it's . . . Good! I like these parts! Now I better figure out two whats and two hows. Let my mind be free! Think of new, fun ideas."* Talk out and briefly write notes for the two *whats* and the two *hows*. Do not use full sentences. Use coping statements at least twice. *"Let's see, for the story question, 'What does the main character want to do,' I think . . . for the next what question, 'What happens when she tries to do it,' I think . . . I can add more action by writing about . . . . For the ending, I can*

say . . . For the feeling, story part, I can write about . . . ." After generating notes for all the story parts, say, *"Now I can look back at my notes and see if I can add more notes for my story parts."* Actually show the students how to add more notes. Model that and be sure to use coping statements, *"I can also look for places where I can use million-dollar words."* Model this.

- Say, *"Now I can do W in POW—Write and say more. I can write my story and think of more good ideas or million-dollar words as I write."* Talk yourself through writing the story; the students can help. Use a clean piece of paper and print. Start by saying, *"How shall I start? I need to tell who, when, and where."* Pause to think and then write out sentences. Be sure to add one or two more ideas and million-dollar words, and note these on your plan as you write. Don't hurry, but don't slow your writing down unnaturally. Ask yourself at least twice, "Am I using good parts?" and "Am I using all of my parts so far?" Again, use coping statements. Ask yourself, "Does my story make sense?" When your story is finished, say, *"Good work. I'm finished. It'll be fun to share my story with others."*

Step 5: Student Self-Statements

Add to the students' self-statements sheets. Ask the students if they can remember 1) the things you said to yourself to get started; 2) the things you said while you worked (try to get some creative statements, coping statements, statements about remembering the parts, and self-evaluation statements); and 3) the things you said to yourself when you finished. Tell the students what you said if they can't remember and discuss each statement. Make sure that each student adds these items to his or her list.

- What to say to get started: This should be along the same lines as, "What do I have to do? I have to write a good story with good parts and with all seven parts," but it should be in the students' own words.

- Things to say while you work: These should be appropriate to the needs of individual students and in the students' own words; any of the types of self-statements may be used.

- Things to say when finished: These should be be self-reinforcing-type sentences in the students' own words.

- Note that these things do not have to be spoken aloud; once the students learn them, they can think in their heads or whisper to themselves.

Step 6: Model Graphing Success

Graph the story parts written during the modeled lesson on a blank Story Rockets graph. Ask the students, *"Does this story have all seven parts?"* Using positive self-statements, model self-reinforcing. Tell yourself and the class that you did a good job—you like your story.

WRAP-UP

Remind the students of the POW + WWW, What = 2, How = 2 test again next time.

TRANSFER LESSON

Remind the students that they will fill in the transfer sheet again next time.

The Farmer's Story

Many years ago there was an old farmer who lived near the woods. He owned a donkey. The farmer wanted to put his donkey in the barn. First he pushed him, but the donkey would not move. Next, the farmer tried to frighten the donkey into the barn. He asked his dog to bark at the donkey, but the lazy dog refused. Then the farmer thought that his cat could get the dog to bark. So he asked the cat to scratch the dog. The dog began to bark. The barking frightened the donkey and he jumped into the barn. The farmer was very proud of himself.

(Adapted from a folktale)

Charlie the Cat

Once upon a time, a large tomcat named Charlie lived in a big, old house. Charlie was a tough cat, and all the other cats (and some dogs!) were afraid of him. One day, Charlie's owners brought home two new young cats, Paddy and Lucy, which made Charlie furious. He didn't want any other pets in *his* house! Charlie ran right out of the house and climbed up on his favorite fence. Suddenly, a big thunderstorm started. The lightning startled Charlie, and he fell off the fence and into a wire pen below. Charlie cut his foot when he fell, and he couldn't get out of the pen. Yowl! Yowl! cried Charlie. All of a sudden, he saw Paddy and Lucy coming to help him. The two young cats went right to work, digging hard until they had dug a big hole under the pen. Charlie escaped right through the hole! He was so relieved to be free again. Now Charlie was happy to have Paddy and Lucy live in *their* house together.

LESSON 4

LESSON OVERVIEW

The students and teacher will collaboratively write a story using POW + WWW, What = 2, How = 2. The teacher must provide the support needed to ensure that all students are successful in writing a story that contains all seven parts. The teacher should reinforce the students' use of self-instructions and good word choice. The story should make sense and include million-dollar words.

STUDENT OBJECTIVES

The students will write POW + WWW, What = 2, How = 2 from memory and be able to state the meaning of each part. The students will collaboratively write a story that has seven story parts.

MATERIALS

One copy for each student:
- Mnemonic chart
- Boy on alligator picture prompt
- Graphic organizers
- Story Rockets graph
- Self-Statements sheet
- Paper, pencils, and scratch paper
- Transfer sheet
- Cue cards with or without

pictures for practice. As with the graphic organizer, picture cues can be used to help younger students or those with language difficulties. Students should have memorized the strategy by this lesson; however, some students may still need practice to maintain memorization.

Modification: Use the graphic organizer with picture cues for young students or those students who have difficulty with the language concepts as needed during this lesson. If your students have demonstrated an understanding of all the story parts, you may begin to use the graphic organizers without pictures.

SET THE CONTEXT FOR STUDENT LEARNING

Test to see if the students remember POW + WWW, What = 2, How = 2. Do it aloud to save time. It is essential that each student memorize these parts. If the students have trouble with this, spend a few minutes practicing it. Tell the students you will test them on it each day to make sure they understand it.

TRANSFER LESSON

Record and review transfer. See Lesson 2 for detailed steps.

DEVELOP THE STRATEGY AND SELF-REGULATION

Step 1: Collaborative Writing

- Support It. Give the students a blank graphic organizer and ask them to take out their self-statements list. Place the boy on the alligator picture where the students can see it. This time let the students lead as much as possible in planning and writing, but be sure to prompt and help as much as needed. The students can share and use the same ideas, but each student should write his or her own story using his or her own notes. Go through each of the following processes.

Say, *"The first letter in POW is P for Pick my idea."* Refer the students to their self-statements for creativity or thinking free. Help each student get an idea.

- Say, *"The second letter in POW is O for Organize my notes. I will use my mnemonic to help me. I will use this organizer to make my notes and organize my notes."*

- Review the steps. Say, *"What should my goal be? I want to write a good story that has all seven parts, makes sense, and is fun for me to write and for others to read."* After the students have generated notes for all the story parts (help the students as necessary or allow them to help each other), say, *"I must remember to look back at my notes and see if I can add more notes for my story parts."* Help each student actually do this. Remind the students to look for more ideas for good word choice or million-dollar words. Finally, say, *"The last letter in POW is W for Write and say more."* Encourage and remind the students to start writing by saying, *"What do I have to do here? I have to write a good story that has all seven parts and makes sense. I can write my story and think of more good ideas or million-dollar words as I write."* Help the students as much as necessary for them to complete the writing process, but try to let them do as much as they can alone. Encourage them to use other self-statements of their choice while they write. If the students do not finish writing in this lesson, they can continue at the next lesson.

Step 2: Graph Story Parts

Have each student graph his or her story. Ask each student to determine if his or her story has all seven parts. The students can then fill in the story rocket. Reinforce the students for reaching all seven parts (the teacher should prompt and support during planning and writing so that all students have all seven parts).

WRAP-UP

- Remind the students of the POW + WWW test again next time.

- Remind the students that they will fill in the transfer sheet again next time.

This lesson can be repeated, using picture prompts of your choice, if the students need additional support and practice before Lesson 5.

LESSON 5

LESSON OVERVIEW

The students will continue to review POW + WWW, What = 2, How = 2 in this lesson. It is critical that the teacher provide each student with the assistance necessary to be successful. In other words, Support It! The students will be weaned off the graphic organizer and will make their own notes. This lesson should be repeated, using picture prompts of your choices until the students can independently write the mnemonic and a story with all seven parts. Additional lessons to enhance transfer, Lessons 6 and 7, follow.

If you feel that the students are not ready to move on to writing notes with scratch paper instead of the graphic organizer, repeat Lesson 4 with other practice picture prompts of your choice and go on to this lesson when they are ready. You can repeat Lesson 4 more than once.

STUDENT OBJECTIVES

The students will write the mnemonic and state orally what each part represents. The students will write notes for the POW + WWW, What = 2, How = 2 strategies on a blank sheet of paper. The students will write a story that includes all seven story parts.

MATERIALS

One copy for each student:
- Mnemonic chart
- Squirrel at table and girl at door picture prompts

- Story Rockets graph
- Self-Statements sheet
- Paper, pencils, and scratch paper
- Transfer sheet

SET THE CONTEXT FOR STUDENT LEARNING

Test to see if the students remember POW + WWW, What = 2, How = 2. Do it aloud to save time. It is essential that each student memorize these parts. If the students have trouble with this, spend a few minutes practicing it. Tell the students you will test them on it each day to make sure they understand it.

TRANSFER LESSON

Record and review transfer.

DEVELOP THE STRATEGY AND SELF-REGULATION

Step 1: Wean Off Graphic Organizer

Explain to the students that they won't usually have a graphic organizer with them when they have to write stories, so they can make their own notes on blank paper. Show them how to write down the mnemonic at the top of the page.

- POW

- WWW, What = 2, How = 2

Then have them make a space on the paper for notes for each part.

Step 2: Collaborative Writing

Support It. Ask the students to get out their self-statements list. Put out the squirrel at the table and the girl at the door picture prompts. Each student can select one about which to write. Let the students lead as much as possible, but prompt and help as much as needed. The students should make notes on the same paper on which they wrote their mnemonic. The students can share ideas, but each student should write his or her own story using his or her own notes. Go through each of the following processes.

 First, say, *"Remember that the first letter in POW is P for Pick my idea."* Refer students to their self-statements for creativity or thinking free. Help each student get an idea.

- Next, say, *"The second letter in POW is O for Organize my notes. I will use my mnemonic to help me. I will use this piece of paper for writing and organizing my notes."*

- Review the process. Say, *"What should my goal be? I want to write a good story that has all seven parts, makes sense, and is fun for me to write and for others to read."* After the students have generated notes for all seven story parts, say, *"Remember to look back at my notes and see if I can add more notes for my story parts."* Help each student actually do this. Remind them also to look for more ideas for good word choices or million-dollar words.

- Finally, say, *"The last letter in POW is W for Write and say more."* Encourage and remind the students to start by saying, *"What do I have to do here? I have to write a good story that has all seven parts and makes sense. I can write my story and think of more good ideas or million-dollar words as I write."* Help the students as much as they need to do this, but try to let them do as much as they can alone. If parts can be improved, or better word choices can be used, you can make suggestions. Encourage the students to use other self-statements of their choice while they write.

Step 3: Graph Progress

Ask the students to determine if their stories have all seven parts and then fill in their graphs. Reinforce the students for reaching seven story parts. The students can revise their stories if they leave out parts and their graph. The teacher can have the students share their stories in appropriate ways.

WRAP-UP

Remind the students of the POW + WWW, What = 2, How = 2 test again next time.

TRANSFER LESSON

Remind the students that they will fill in the transfer sheet again next time.

Powerful Writing Strategies for All Students by K. Harris, S. Graham, L. Mason, & B. Friedlander.

LESSON 6

LESSON OVERVIEW

This is a repeat of Lesson 5 with a story starter prompt instead of a picture prompt. The students will be given the opportunity to practice transferring the strategy.

STUDENT OBJECTIVES

The students will write the mnemonic and state orally what each mnemonic part represents. The students will write notes for the POW + WWW, What = 2 and How = 2 strategies on a blank sheet of paper. The students will transfer the strategy to a written story prompt.

MATERIALS

One copy for each student:
- Mnemonic chart
- *Rock* and *Cassie the Dog* prompts
- Story Rockets graph

- Self-Statements sheet
- Paper, pencils, and scratch paper
- Transfer sheet

SET THE CONTEXT FOR STUDENT LEARNING

Test to see if the students remember POW + WWW. Do it aloud to save time. It is essential that each student has memorized the strategy. Tell the students that they will learn to use their strategy a new way.

TRANSFER LESSON

Record and review transfer.

DEVELOP THE STRATEGY AND SELF-REGULATION

Step 1: Review Making Notes Using Mnemonic

Remind the students that they won't usually have a graphic organizer with them when they have to write stories, so they can make their own notes on blank paper. If needed, help them write down the reminder at the top of the page.

Step 2: Collaborative Writing/Support It

- Ask the students to get out their self-statements list. Put out the story prompts *Rock* and *Cassie the Dog* or write them on the board. Discuss how this is different. Ask, *"What can we transfer? Yes, POW + WWW still works!"*

- This time, the students should do as much as possible independently. Each student should pick one story prompt. Help only if needed. The students should make notes on the paper. They should repeat each of the processes as were completed in Lesson 5. The students should write their own stories using their own notes.

Say, *"Remember that the first letter in POW is P for Pick my idea."* Refer the students to their self-statements for creativity or thinking free.

- Say, *"The second letter in POW is O for Organize my notes. I will use my mnemonic to help me."*

- Finally, say, *"The last letter in POW is W for Write and say more."* Encourage and remind them to start by saying, *"What do I have to do here? I have to write a good story that has all seven parts and makes sense."*

Step 3: Graph Performance

Have each student read aloud and then graph his or her story. Ask the students to determine if their stories have all seven parts and then fill in the graph. Reinforce them for reaching seven, or have the students revise if necessary.

WRAP-UP

Remind the students of the POW + WWW test again next time.

TRANSFER LESSON

Remind the students that they will fill in the transfer sheet again next time.

Repeat this lesson if the students are unable to transfer the strategy independently.

Write a story about a
rock with this message
written on it:

"Rub me and see what happens!"

Cassie is a big, happy dog. Her fur is mostly black, but she has white paws and a big white spot on her back.

Write a story about Cassie the dog.

LESSON 7

LESSON OVERVIEW

This is a repeat of Lesson 6, but this lesson takes place in a setting different from where the prior lessons have occurred. The students will be given the opportunity to practice transferring the strategy.

The teacher should arrange to have the students write a story in a new class or other setting, or write one at home.

STUDENT OBJECTIVES

The students will write the mnemonic and state orally what each mnemonic part represents. The students will write notes for the POW + WWW, What = 2 and How = 2 strategies on a blank sheet of paper. The students will transfer the strategy to a different setting.

MATERIALS

One copy for each student:
- Mnemonic chart
- Story picture prompts
- Story Rockets graph

- Self-Statements sheet
- Paper, pencils, scratch paper, and certificate
- Transfer sheet

SET THE CONTEXT FOR STUDENT LEARNING

Test POW + WWW for review. Do this out loud to save time. Tell the students that they will use their strategy in a new place.

TRANSFER LESSON

Record and review transfer.

DEVELOP THE STRATEGY AND SELF-REGULATION

Step 1: Review Making Notes

Remind the students that they won't usually have a graphic organizer with them when they have to write stories, so they can make their own notes on blank paper. If needed, help them write down the reminder at the top of the page.

Step 2: Collaborative Writing/Support It

- Ask the students to get out their self-statements sheet. Put out the story picture prompts. Discuss how this is different. Ask, *"Can we transfer POW + WWW to another classroom? Yes, it still works!"* Can we transfer this strategy to use at home?

- This time, the students should do their stories independently. Help only if needed. The students should make notes on the paper. They should use all of the steps in the POW + WWW strategy. Have the students use the remaining story prompt or select another story idea.

Step 3: Graph Performance

Have the students bring their stories to class and then graph their stories. Ask them to determine if their stories have all seven parts and then fill in the graph. Reinforce the students for reaching seven, or have them revise if necessary.

WRAP-UP

Repeat this lesson if the students are not able to transfer the strategy independently. If the transfer was sucessful, give the students the POW + WWW Certificate.

POW + WWW Lesson Checklists

LESSON 1

_____ Set the context for student learning.

Step 1. Discuss and Describe the Strategy: POW

_____ Explain *Pick my idea*

_____ Explain *Organize ideas*

_____ Explain *Write and say more*

_____ Practice **POW**

_____ Discuss good stories

Step 2. Discuss and Describe the Strategy: WWW

_____ Explain *Who*

_____ Explain *When*

_____ Explain *Where*

_____ Explain *What=2*

_____ Explain *How=2*

Step 3. Find Parts in Story

_____ Introduce graphic organizer

_____ Read *Freddie the Fish*

_____ Find **WWW**

_____ Find *What=2*

_____ Find *How=2*

Step 4. Practice WWW, What=2, How=2

_____ Practice reminder and parts

Step 5. Find Parts in Story—*The Sly Fox*

_____ Find *WWW*

_____ Find *What=2*

_____ Find *How=2*

Step 6. Establish Partners and Transfer

_____ Tell students that they will act as partners

_____ Discuss Goal #1

_____ Introduce chart

_____ Discuss Goal #2

Wrap-Up

_____ Give students folders

_____ Announce a test for next class

_____ Remind students to transfer

LESSON 2

_____ Set the context for student learning. Test and practice **POW** and **WWW.**

_____ Review meaning of transfer

_____ Complete transfer charts

Step 1. Find Parts in Story

_____ Read *The Tiger's Whiskers*

_____ Find *WWW*

_____ Find *What=2*

_____ Find *How=2*

Step 2. Establish Current Level of Performance

_____ Pass out students' previously written stories

_____ Students read stories and find parts

_____ Note common missing parts

_____ Discuss making stories better

_____ Introduce story rockets

_____ Explain goal

_____ Establish goal

Wrap-Up

_____ Have students put their work in their folders

_____ Announce a test for the next class

_____ Remind students to transfer

LESSON 3

_____ Set the context for student learning. Test and practice **POW** and **WWW.**

_____ Record and review transfer.

Step 1. Find Parts in Story (If Needed)

_____ Read *The Farmer's Story* or *Charlie the Cat*

_____ Find **WWW**

_____ Find *What=2*

_____ Find *How=2*

Step 2. Model **Pick My Idea** and Establish Self-Instructions

_____ Get materials ready

_____ Model *Pick my idea*

_____ Model self-instructions

_____ Record self-statements

Step 3. Model **Organize My Notes**

_____ Get materials ready

_____ Model *Organize my notes*

Step 4. Model Writing a Story

_____ Get materials ready

_____ Model self-statements throughout process

_____ Model *Pick my idea*

_____ Model *Organize my notes*

_____ Model *Write and say more*

Step 5. Student Self-Instructions

Add to students' lists:

_____ Things to say when you get started

_____ Things to say while you work

_____ Things to say when you are finished

Step 6. Model Graphing Success

_____ Graph this story

Wrap-Up

_____ Have students put their work in their folders

_____ Announce a test for next class

_____ Remind students to transfer

LESSON 4

_____ Set the context for student learning. Test **POW** and **WWW.**

_____ Record and review transfer

Step 1. Collaborative Writing

_____ Get materials

_____ Help students develop an idea

_____ Help students *organize notes*

_____ Encourage students to *write and say more*

Step 2. Review Story and Graph

_____ Review story

_____ Complete graph

_____ Reinforce for reaching seven parts

Wrap-Up

_____ Have students put their work in their folders

_____ Announce a test for next class

_____ Remind students to transfer

LESSON 5

_____ Set the context for student learning. Test **POW** and **WWW**.

_____ Record and review transfer

Step 1. Wean Off Graphic Organizer

_____ Model making notes

Step 2. Collaborative Writing

_____ Get materials

_____ Help students develop an idea

_____ Help students _organize notes_

_____ Encourage students to _write and say more_

Step 3. Review Story and Graph

_____ Review story

_____ Complete graph

_____ Reinforce for reaching seven parts

Wrap-Up

_____ Have students put their work in their folders

_____ Announce a test for the next class

_____ Remind students to transfer

LESSON 6

_____ Set the context for student learning. Test **POW** and **WWW.**

_____ Record and review transfer

Step 1. Review Making Notes

_____ Help students make notes if necessary

Step 2. Collaborative Writing

_____ Discuss transferring strategy to different prompt

_____ Help students develop an idea

_____ Help students *organize notes*

_____ Encourage students to *write and say more*

Step 3. Review Story and Graph

_____ Review story

_____ Complete graph

_____ Reinforce for reaching seven parts

Wrap-Up

_____ Have students put their work in their folders

_____ Announce a test for next class

_____ Remind students to transfer

LESSON 7

_____ Set the context for student learning. Test **POW** and **WWW.**

_____ Record and review transfer

Step 1. Review Making Notes

_____ Help students make notes if necessary

Step 2. Collaborative Writing

_____ Discuss transferring strategy to different setting

_____ Help students develop an idea

_____ Help students _organize notes_

_____ Encourage students to _write and say more_

Step 3. Review Story and Graph

_____ Review story

_____ Complete graph

_____ Reinforce for reaching seven parts

Wrap-Up

_____ Have students put their work in their folders

_____ Announce a test for next class

_____ Remind students to transfer

POW

Pick my idea.

Organize my notes.

Write and say more.

WWW What = 2 How = 2

Who is the main character?

When does the story take place?

Where does the story take place?

What does the main character do or want to do; what do other characters do?

What happens then? What happens with other characters?

How does the story end?

How does the main character feel; how do other characters feel?

Cue Cards with Pictures

Where does the story happen?

When does the story happen?

Who is the main character?

How does the main character feel?

How does the story end?

What happens then?

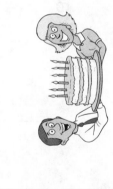

What does the main character do?

Cue Cards without Pictures

Where does the story happen?

When does the story happen?

Who is the main character?

How does the main character feel?

How does the story end?

What happens then?

What does the main character do?

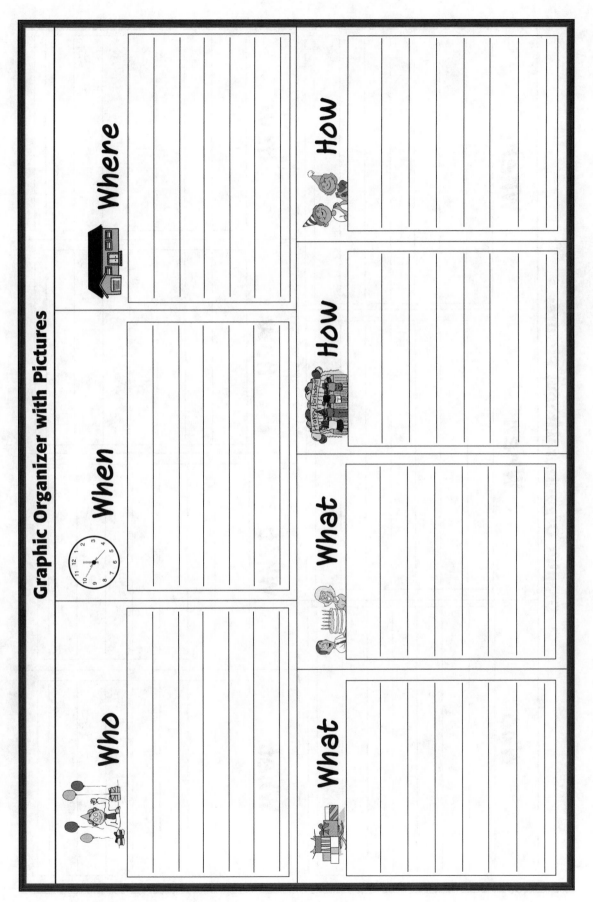

Graphic Organizer with Pictures

Who

When

Where

What

What

How

How

119

Graphic Organizer without Pictures

Who	When	Where

What	What	How	How

Story Rockets

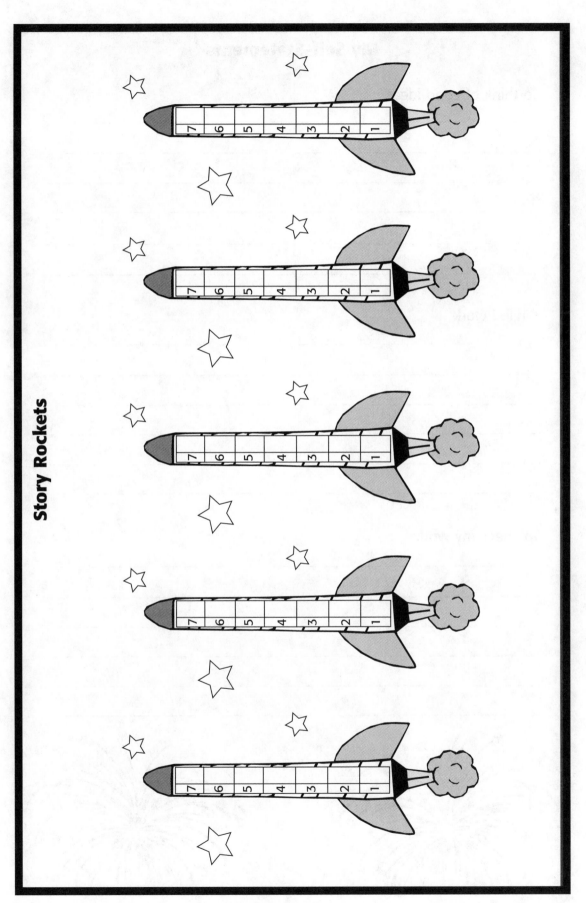

My Self-Statements

To think of good ideas:

_____
_____
_____
_____
_____
_____

While I work:

_____
_____
_____
_____
_____
_____

To check my work:

_____
_____
_____
_____
_____
_____

I Transferred My Strategy	I Helped My Partner

Self-Statements Explosions

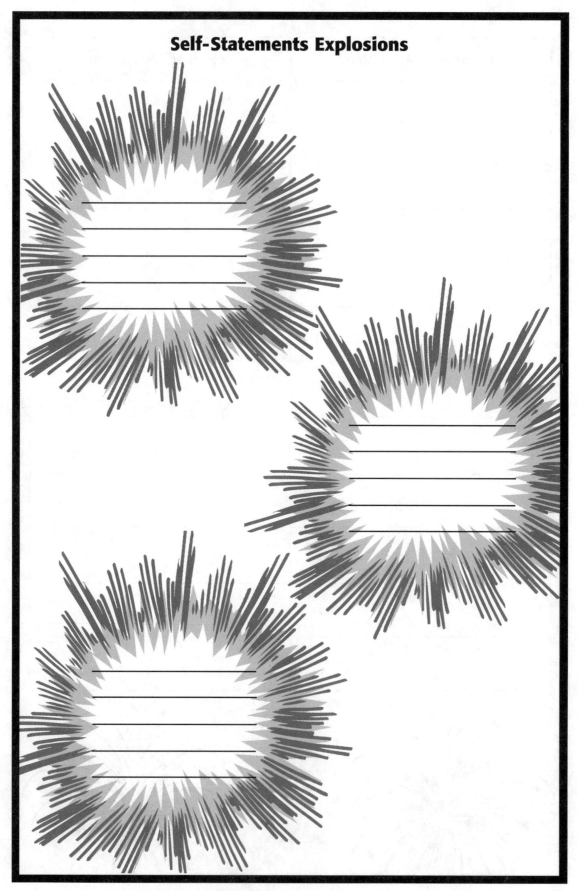

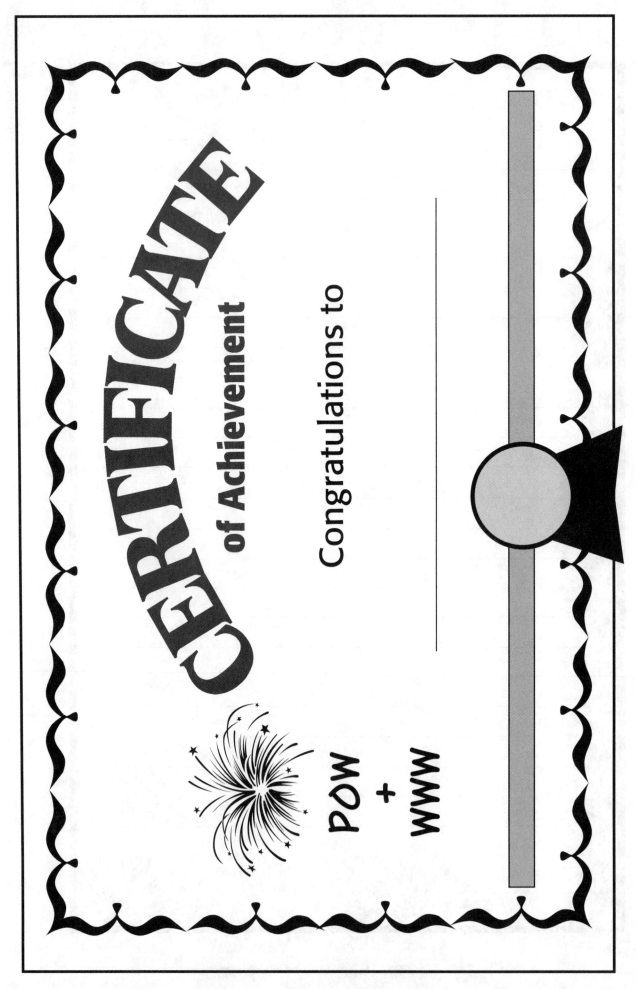

CERTIFICATE

of Achievement

Congratulations to

_____

POW
+
WWW

Chapter 7

POW + C-SPACE

P = Pick my idea.	
O = Organize my notes.	
W = Write and say more.	

C =	Characters
S =	Setting
P =	Purpose
A =	Action
C =	Conclusion
E =	Emotions

MATERIALS
POW + C-SPACE Mnemonic Chart
Graphic Organizer
Story Rockets Graph
Cue Cards with Pictures
Cue Cards without Pictures
Revising Your Plan
POW + C-SPACE Certificate
Bulletin Board:
- Writing Paper

LESSON 1

LESSON OVERVIEW

The purpose of learning the POW + C-SPACE strategies will be established in this lesson. The students will begin learning the parts of a story and memorizing the mnemonic POW + C-SPACE.

STUDENT OBJECTIVES

The students will review the parts of a story and practice orally rehearsing the parts of a story and the mnemonic POW + C-SPACE.

MATERIALS

One copy for each student:
- POW + C-SPACE mnemonic chart
- POW + C-SPACE Graphic Organizer

- Story examples (select your own story or see POW + WWW lessons for samples)
- Student folders
- Paper and pencils

SET THE CONTEXT FOR STUDENT LEARNING

Explain to the students that they are going to learn a method for writing better stories. After they have learned this method, they will publish their best stories in a class magazine.

DEVELOP THE STRATEGY AND SELF-REGULATION

Step 1: Explain POW + C-SPACE

 Ask, *"What makes a story good?"* Discuss what makes stories fun to read. Use stories that the students have recently read to help identify what makes a good story.

- Explain that good stories have several parts. Introduce the POW + C-SPACE mnemonic chart and briefly explain the parts, relating this to previous discussion.

- Explain what the letters POW stand for and then discuss what the parts are like in good stories that students have read. Talk about character and setting first. Note that *setting* includes time and place. Explain that good stories have interesting characters and good descriptions of setting.

- In explaining a story's *problem,* note that the main character in a story has a problem or something that he or she wants. What is the character's main problem? What does he or she want? The story is all about what the character does to solve the problem or to get what he or she wants (*action*). The conclusion is the end; at the end, the character may or may not solve the problem. A good story also lets the reader know how the main character feels (*emotion*).

Step 2: Read Story and Identify Parts

- Explain to the students that they are going to listen to some stories and identify the story parts. Give each student a copy of the mnemonic chart and graphic organizer, as well as a copy of the story that they will read along silently with you. Teachers should select a short story ahead of time to use here, or they can use a story from Chapter 6. Tell them to raise their hands when they identify the *character* and *setting.* Read the story aloud.

- Call on the students for answers and have them identify the appropriate parts on their organizers. If time allows, the teacher or students can make notes for each story part on a blank organizer or on the blackboard.

- Continue reading and ask the students to listen for the *problem, action, conclusion,* and *emotion.* If the students do not find all the parts, go back through the story and help them as necessary.

Step 3: Begin Memorizing POW + C-SPACE

Turn over the chart and the students' papers. Ask the students to tell you the mnemonic. They should respond, "POW + C-SPACE." Call on the students in turn to explain what the letters stand for and what they mean. Make sure that each letter is repeated a few times and that all the students have a chance to participate. Ask the students to write out the reminder and which part is represented by each letter. Students can also practice what each part is done or with a partner using cue cards. Tell them that next time you will ask them to write out the mnemonic and explain what it means. This will be like a test, but it will not be graded.

Step 4: Read Another Story

Read a second story and have the students identify the parts as before. Be sure that all students are comfortable with all of the story parts.

WRAP-UP

Have the students put all of their work from the day in their folders. Remind them that they will be asked to remember POW + C-SPACE at the next class.

LESSON 2

LESSON OVERVIEW

The students will review the parts and mnemonic for the POW + C-SPACE strategy. The students will then review their current level of performance by finding the story parts in a previously written story. The teacher will model the use of POW + C-SPACE for planning and writing stories.

STUDENT OBJECTIVES

The students will practice orally rehearsing the parts of a story and the mnemonic POW + C-SPACE. The teacher will model using the POW + C-SPACE strategies. The students will listen to a modeled lesson.

MATERIALS

One copy for each student:

- Mnemonic chart
- Graphic organizer
- Story Rockets graph
- Story examples and picture prompts (select your own or see POW + WWW for samples)

- One previously written story by each student
- Large chart paper
- Student folders
- Paper, pencils, and cue cards (if needed)

SET THE CONTEXT FOR STUDENT LEARNING

Ask the students if they remember the parts of a story. Have them write the mnemonic using only the letters. Then ask them to explain what each letter represents.

> **Modification:**
> If the students are having difficulty memorizing the parts, practice with the cue cards. Peers can quiz each other or see how fast they can say each part.

DEVELOP THE STRATEGY AND SELF-REGULATION

Step 1: Review Stories and Graph Performance

- Give each student a story he or she wrote previously. Ask them to read their stories to themselves and see which parts their stories contain and which parts are missing. (You will need to work out the answers ahead of time.) Confer briefly with each student, making note of what they have and what is missing. Maintain a positive tone.

- As a group, share stories (whole stories or parts). Comment on the good parts. Briefly note which parts are missing from many stories. Note that even if the parts are present, it may be possible to make them better (e.g., the characters and setting could be described more, there could be more action, the ending could be interesting, feelings could be emphasized).

- Give each student a Story Rockets graph. Have them graph the number of parts their story had on the rocket. Be very positive. Remind the students that they are just now learning this trick for story writing and it is okay if they do not have all of the parts.

Step 2: Describe the Strategy

- Tell the students that you are going to teach them a strategy for writing stories that contain all the parts and are interesting to read. Explain that good writers take some time to plan their stories before writing so they have some good ideas to start with. Tell them that you will be using pictures to help plan their stories.

- Briefly describe the steps in the POW strategy. (Strategy usage will be modeled later in this lesson.)

 Say, *"Pick your ideas and think. Think who is going to read your story. Once you know who your readers are, you can make the story interesting to them. Think about what kind of story you want to write. What do you want to do with this story? Do you want to make it funny, exciting, scary, or sad? Do you want to work on including all the parts, making it longer, or achieving some other personal goal?"*

- *Organize* your *notes* and the *parts.* Explain to the students that they should look at the picture and get ideas for the parts. If they relax and let their minds be free, ideas will come to them. They can start with any of the parts. They might start with *character,* but they could also start with some *action* or with the *setting.* They can change the parts as they plan.

- *Write* and say more. As they write their stories, the students should follow their plans and add more ideas and details to make it interesting.

Step 3: Model the Strategy

- Lay out a picture prompt and the graphic organizer.

- Keep the mnemonic chart out and refer to it for each step.

- Model the entire strategy, including planning and writing the story. Work on large chart paper or the blackboard and print so that the students can read it. You must work out the story you are going to plan in advance and practice what you will say. The following are some general guidelines:

  1. Verbalize each step.

  2. Include some general problem definition ("Let's see. What do I have to do next?"), creativity ("Let my mind be free and ideas will come to me"), and self-evaluation statements ("That's pretty good").

  3. Work slowly enough so that the students can follow what you are doing, but quickly enough so that you don't lose their interest.

  4. Get started by yourself, but to keep the group involved, have the students assist you.

 Say, *"What am I going to do? I'm going to write a good story. A good story has all the parts and is interesting to read. What's the first step? Think who and what? Who am I writing this for? What kind of story do I want to write? I want to write a story that is exciting and that has plenty of good action in it."* As you go, write, Who? (students) What? (exciting action).

- Say, *"What is the next step? I have to plan the parts of the story, so I will write down the mnemonic on my organizer."* Model this. *"Now I will look at the picture and think of ideas for the parts. I just relax and let my imagination work. What does the picture make me think of? I see . . . I wonder . . . Maybe . . . Or maybe . . . That could be the*

problem . . . I like that idea. I'll note . . . on the organizer. Good, I have a problem. I need a good character. Who is . . .?" Talk out your ideas and make brief notes on the organizer. Finish by reviewing the parts to yourself and saying that you have ideas for all the parts and they make sense, which is good. You can ask the students to contribute ideas.

- Say, *"Now I have to write the story. I can add more ideas and details while I write."* Talk yourself through writing the story on the chart paper. Keep thinking aloud, referring to your plan and adding ideas. Allow the students to assist you.

Step 4: Graph Performance

- Have the students assist you in counting the number of story parts you have in your story.

- Show the students how you would graph your number of story parts.

WRAP-UP

Have the students put all of their work from the day in their folders. Remind them that they will be asked to remember the mnemonic and parts for the next class.

LESSON 3

LESSON OVERVIEW

The students and teacher will collaboratively write a story using POW + C-SPACE.

STUDENT OBJECTIVES

The students will orally rehearse the parts of a story and the mnemonic POW + C-SPACE. Collaboratively with the teacher, the students will write a story that has all the parts of C-SPACE.

MATERIALS

One copy for each student:
- Mnemonic chart
- Graphic organizer
- Picture prompt (select your own or use POW + WWW for examples)

- Student folders
- Paper and pencils

SET THE CONTEXT FOR STUDENT LEARNING

Ask the students if they remember the strategy and story parts. Have them write the mnemonic the story parts and review as in Lesson 2. Practice with cue cards if necessary.

DEVELOP THE STRATEGY AND SELF-REGULATION

Step 1: Practice Strategy with Group

- Explain that you all will plan and write one story together as a group. The students should use the mnemonic chart. Together, you will complete a graphic organizer and write the story on the chart paper.

- Show the students a picture prompt. Follow these general guidelines as you work together:

  1. Prompt the students to verbalize each step of the strategy and part of POW + C-SPACE.

  2. Give feedback to their responses. If an inappropriate response is given, work with the student to develop a better response.

  3. Provide help as needed.

  4. Prompt the students to "let their minds be free" as they think of ideas and check whether their plan makes sense.

Say, *"What is the first step in the strategy?"* The students should answer, *"Pick an idea and think who, what?"* Ask, *"What does that mean?"* The students should answer, *"Think about who we are writing for and what kind of story we are writing."* Ask, *"Who are we writing for? What kind of story are we writing?"* Briefly note the students' responses.

- Say, *"What is the next step? I must Organize my notes using C-SPACE. What should I do?"* Lead the discussion, making notes for each part and giving feedback.

- Say, *"What is the next step? I need to Write and say more. What should we remember while we write? We must follow the plan and add details or ideas to make it more interesting."* Take turns with the students, adding to the story as you write it on the chart paper. Comment on following the plan and adding ideas and details.

Step 2: Graph Performance

- Have the students count the number of parts in the story you wrote together.

- Have the students graph the number of parts on their Story Rockets graph.

WRAP-UP

Have the students put all of their work from the day in their folders. Remind them that they will be asked to remember the mnemonic and parts for the next class.

LESSON 4

LESSON OVERVIEW

With assistance from the teacher, the students will begin to write stories that include all of the necessary story parts.

STUDENT OBJECTIVES

The students will write the parts of a story and the mnemonic POW + C-SPACE. The students will plan and write stories with the six parts of C-SPACE.

MATERIALS

One copy for each student:
- Mnemonic chart
- Graphic organizer

- Picture prompt (select your own or see POW + WWW for examples)
- Student folders
- Paper and pencils

SET THE CONTEXT FOR STUDENT LEARNING

Ask the students if they remember the strategy and story parts. Have them write the mnemonic for the story parts and review as in Lesson 2. Practice with cue cards if necessary.

DEVELOP THE STRATEGY AND SELF-REGULATION

Step 1: Group/Individual Practice

- Explain to the students that they will plan a story together, and then each student will write his or her own version. Each student as well as the teacher will complete an organizer.

- Show the students a picture.

- Lead the students through the strategy. Follow the same general guidelines as before (e.g., prompt to verbalize steps).

- The students need not write all the same things on their own organizer, but they must write something appropriate for each part.

- Tell each student to write a story using the graphic organizer. As they write, monitor to ensure that they are using all the story parts. Provide help when necessary.

Step 2: Read Stories and Graph Performance

- Have the students share stories by reading them out loud. Allow the students to revise if they are missing a story part.

- Have the students graph the number of parts for their own story on their Story Rockets graph.

WRAP-UP

Have the students put all of their work from the day in their folders. Remind them that they will be asked to remember the mnemonic and parts for the next class.

LESSON 5

LESSON OVERVIEW

The students will memorize the mnemonic and parts of POW + C-SPACE. With the teacher's assistance, the students will plan and write their own stories.

STUDENT OBJECTIVES

The students will write the parts of a story and the mnemonic POW + C-SPACE. The students will write a story that has all the parts of C-SPACE.

MATERIALS

One copy for each student:
- Mnemonic chart
- Graphic organizer

- Picture prompt (select your own or see POW + WWW for examples)
- Student folders
- Paper and pencils

SET THE CONTEXT FOR STUDENT LEARNING

Ask the students if they remember the strategy and story parts. Have them write the mnemonic for the story parts and review as in Lesson 2. Practice with cue cards if necessary.

DEVELOP THE STRATEGY AND SELF-REGULATION

Step 1: Individual Practice

- Tell the students that they will plan and write their own story. Display a picture (or several if you want to give the students a choice). Remind them to use all steps of the strategy. Tell them that they can use their charts if necessary, and that you will check with them to see if they need any help using the strategy.

- Monitor the students' use of the strategy and confer with them as before. You can provide help as needed, but encourage them to do it on their own. Make sure that each student plans for and has all six parts in his or her story.

Step 2: Read Stories and Graph Performance

- Have the students share stories by reading them out loud. Allow revising if necessary.

- Have the students graph the number of parts in their own story on their Story Rockets graph.

WRAP-UP

- Have the students put all of their work from the day in their folders. Remind them that they will be asked to remember the mnemonic and parts for the next class.

- Repeat this lesson until the students demonstrate that they can plan by using the graphic organizer and mnemonic chart to write a story with the six parts of C-SPACE. Some students may need more time, practice, and assistance than others to complete this lesson.

LESSON 6

LESSON OVERVIEW
The students will memorize the mnemonic and parts of POW + C-SPACE. With the teacher's assistance, the students will plan stories, create their own notes, and write their own stories.

STUDENT OBJECTIVES
The students will write a story that has all the parts of C-SPACE. They will make their notes on a blank piece of paper.

MATERIALS

One copy for each student:
- Mnemonic chart
- Picture prompt

- Student folders
- Paper and pencils

SET THE CONTEXT FOR STUDENT LEARNING

Ask the students if they remember the strategy and story parts. Review as in Lesson 2.

DEVELOP THE STRATEGY AND SELF-REGULATION

Step 1: Individual Practice

- Tell the students that they will plan and write their own story. Remind them that they will not always have the graphic organizer, but they can make notes on a blank piece of paper. Demonstrate how this is done. Display some pictures. Remind the students to use all the steps of the strategy. Tell them that they can use their mnemonic chart if necessary, and that you will check with them to see if they need any help using the strategy.

- Monitor the students' use of the strategy and confer with them as before. You can provide help as needed, but encourage them to do it on their own.

Step 2: Read Stories and Graph Performance

- Have the students share stories by reading them aloud. Allow revising if necessary.

- Have the students graph the number of parts in their own story on their Story Rockets graph.

WRAP-UP

- Have the students put all of their work from the day in their folders. Remind them that they will be asked to remember the mnemonic and parts for the next class.

- Repeat this lesson until the students demonstrate that they can plan *without* using the organizer, but using blank paper for planning, to write a story with the six parts of C-SPACE.

LESSON 7

LESSON OVERVIEW

The students will learn how to work with a partner while planning a story. NOTE: Lesson 7 is optional. Furthermore, this lesson could be used before or after Lesson 5 to assist students who are having difficulty.

STUDENT OBJECTIVES

The students will listen to a modeled lesson about working with a partner to plan a story.

MATERIALS

One copy for each student:
- Mnemonic chart
- Revising Your Plan sheet
- Picture prompt (select your own)

- Student folders
- Paper and pencils
- Graphic organizer or blank sheet of paper (teacher decides which to use)

SET THE CONTEXT FOR STUDENT LEARNING

Review the purpose of cooperation and the overall purpose of the strategy. The students will add a step to the POW + C-SPACE strategy to help them learn to write more interesting stories. They will also be helping one another. Ask about ways they work together on their writing in class, such as sharing ideas or working in pairs. This will depend on the amount of peer revising that has been previously implemented. Here, students will help each other with their stories *before* they write them.

DEVELOP THE STRATEGY AND SELF-REGULATION

Step 1: Describe the Strategy

- Explain that the students will plan their stories alone, and then they will share their plan with a partner. Partners will discuss how to make their stories better, and then each student will write his or her story alone. Have the students write "Share Then Revise" next to the O in their POW + C-SPACE mnemonic chart.

- Explain that they will learn a strategy for helping one another improve their story plans. Show them the revised sheet.

 Say, *"The first step is to tell your story using your notes. You will be a storyteller, so try to make the story interesting as you tell it. You will follow the plan and say more."*

- Say, *"In the next step, the partner will tell what he or she likes best. Why is it important to tell about something that you like first? (You should start with a positive. It is easier to listen to suggestions if they know you like the story.")*

- Say, *"In the next step, the author and partner will discuss ways to make the story better. To do this, they will use C-SPACE. They will then think about each part of the story and come up with ways to make some parts better."* Make changes on your plan sheet.

- Say, *"The last step is for the author to make notes on the graphic organizer about changes and new ideas to include in the story. It is important to write down these ideas so you will not forget to use them when you write your story."*

- Say, *"Now you switch and the other student is the author, and you follow the same steps."*

Step 2: Explain Questions

Say, *"Let's talk about the questions to ask about each of the parts. The questions will help you think about how to make the story better. What makes characters and settings interesting?"* The students should cite such things as descriptions, good details, expressions of their personalities, and so forth.

- Say, *"What is the next part of a story after the character and setting? Right, it is the problem. What is the problem?"* The students should say that the main character has a problem or must pursue something he or she wants. *"The problem is very important; it is like the main idea of a story. The story is all about what the character does to solve a problem, so the writer should be sure that everyone can recognize the problem when reading the story. The question we want to ask about the problem is 'What is the problem? Can you tell what it is? Does it make sense?'"*

- Ask, *"What is the next part of a story? The next part is the action."* Discuss what makes for interesting action. Point out that the action should fit the problem.

- Ask, *"What is next? We have to reach the conclusion. What is the conclusion? It's what happens at the end of the story."* The students should understand that the problem is solved or that the characters sometimes fail to solve the problem and there is an unhappy ending. The question to ask about the conclusion is, "Is the problem solved?"

- Ask, *"What about emotions? What is important about emotions in stories?"* Discuss this with the students. Say, *"We will ask whether we can tell how the characters feel about the problem and the conclusion."*

Step 3: Model the Strategy (Teacher as Writer, Students as Partners)

Start with a picture and complete a graphic organizer or make notes on a blank piece of paper on which you write the mnemonic. Work out your story ahead of time. It should be a nearly complete story, but it should have plenty of room for improvement (e.g., lacks emotion, has poor descriptions of characters and setting). Tell the story to the group and prompt them to ask questions and make suggestions; follow all of the steps for working with a partner. Make notes and think aloud about how you would change and add to the story when you write it. Write it later and share it on another day, pointing out how much better it is; or have the students help you rewrite it.

The general guidelines for this modeling and guided practice are as before:

1. Prompt the students to verbalize the steps and questions.

2. Provide clear feedback and whatever help is necessary for the students to use the strategy appropriately.

3. Take suggestions from all the students.

Step 4: Pair Practice

Have partners plan and then write a story using these procedures. Have the students graph the number of story parts on their Story Rockets.

WRAP-UP

Make sure the students have copies of the new charts for their folders. Have the students put all of their work from the day in their folders. Repeat this lesson as needed.

POW + C-SPACE Lesson Checklists

LESSON 1

_____ Set the context for student learning.

Step 1. Discuss and Describe the Strategy: POW + C-SPACE

_____ Discuss good stories

Step 2. Find Parts in Story

_____ Introduce graphic organizer

_____ Read story

_____ Find parts of **C-SPACE**

Step 3. Practice POW + C-SPACE

_____ Practice mnemonic and parts

Step 4. Find Parts in Second Story

_____ Find parts in **C-SPACE**

Wrap-Up

_____ Give folders to students

_____ Announce test for next class

LESSON 2

_____ Set the context for student learning. Test and practice **POW + C-SPACE.**

Step 1. Establish Current Level of Performance

_____ Pass out students' previously written stories

_____ Students read stories and find parts

_____ Note common missing parts

_____ Discuss making stories better

_____ Introduce story rockets

_____ Explain goal

Step 2. Describe the Strategy

_____ Describe planning

_____ Describe steps in the strategy

_____ Describe "P"

_____ Describe "O"

_____ Describe "W"

Step 3. Model the Strategy

_____ Lay out materials

_____ Model planning

_____ Model writing a story

Step 4. Read Stories and Graph

_____ Read stories

_____ Graph stories

Wrap-Up

_____ Have students put work in folders

_____ Announce test for next class

LESSON 3

_____ Set the context for student learning. Test **POW + C-SPACE.**

Step 1. Collaborative Writing

_____ Get materials

_____ Develop an idea

_____ Organize notes

_____ Write and say more

Step 2. Review Story and Graph

_____ Review story

_____ Complete graph

_____ Reinforce for reaching seven parts

Wrap-Up

_____ Have students put work in folders

_____ Announce test for next class

LESSON 4

_____ Set the context for student learning. Test **POW + C-SPACE.**

Step 1. Collaborative Writing

_____ Get materials

_____ Develop an idea as a group

_____ Organize notes as a group

_____ Each student writes and says more independently

Step 2. Review Story and Graph

_____ Review story

_____ Complete graph

_____ Reinforce for reaching seven parts

Wrap-Up

_____ Have students put work in folders

_____ Announce test for next class

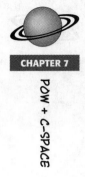

LESSON 5

_____ Set the context for student learning. Test **POW + C-SPACE.**

Step 1. Individual Practice

_____ Get materials

_____ Each student develops an idea

_____ Each student organizes notes

_____ Each student writes and says more

Step 2. Review Story and Graph

_____ Review story

_____ Complete graph

_____ Reinforce for reaching seven parts

Wrap-Up

_____ Have students put work in folders

_____ Announce test for next class

LESSON 6

_____ Set the context for student learning. Test **POW + C-SPACE.**

Step 1. Wean Off Graphic Organizer

_____ Get materials

_____ Help students develop an idea

_____ Help students organize notes on a blank piece of paper

_____ Encourage students to write and say more

Step 2. Review Story and Graph

_____ Review story

_____ Complete graph

_____ Reinforce for reaching seven parts

Wrap-Up

_____ Have students put work in folders

_____ Announce test for next class

LESSON 7

_____ Set the context for student learning. Test **POW + C-SPACE**.

Step 1. Describe the New Strategy

_____ Explain the new steps

_____ Model the steps

Step 2. Explain Questions

_____ Explain questions

_____ Model questions

Step 3. Model the Strategy (Teacher as Writer, Students as Partners)

_____ Plan

_____ Share

_____ Ask questions

_____ Revise plan

Step 4. Memorize Additional Steps

_____ Practice new steps

Wrap-Up

_____ Have students put work in folders

_____ Announce test for next class

POW

Pick my idea.

Organize my notes.

Write and say more.

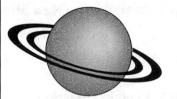

C-SPACE

Characters

Setting   Time and place

Purpose   What the main character tries
                to do

Action   What is done to achieve the goal

Conclusion   Results of the action

Emotions   The main character's reactions
                and feelings

Graphic Organizer

Purpose
What the Main Character Tries to Do

Setting
Time and Place

Characters

Emotions
The Main Character's Reactions and Feelings

Conclusion
Results of the Action

Action
What Is Done to Achieve the Goal

149

Story Rockets

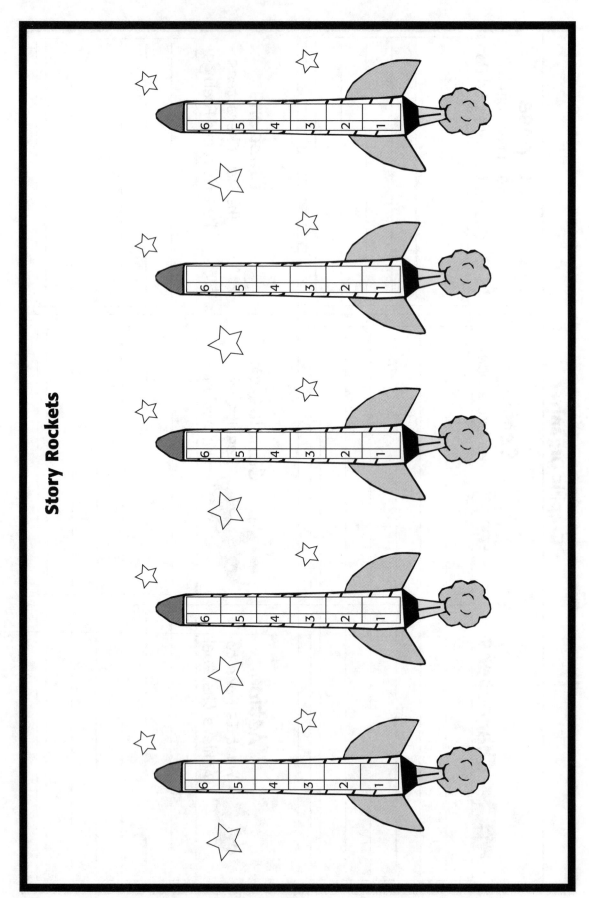

Cue Cards with Pictures

Purpose
What the Main
Character Tries to Do

Setting
Time and Place

Characters

Emotions
The Main Character's
Reactions and Feelings

Conclusion
Results of the Action

Action
What Is Done to
Achieve the Goal

Cue Cards without Pictures

Characters

Setting
Time and Place

Purpose
What the Main
Character Tries to Do

Action
What Is Done to
Achieve the Goal

Conclusion
Results of the Action

Emotions
The Main Character's
Reactions and Feelings

152

Revising Your Plan

TELL your story to a PARTNER and REVISE your plan.

Author: TELL story using notes.

Partner: TELL what you liked best.

Both: DISCUSS ideas using C-SPACE.

           C – Characters

           S – Setting

           P – Problem

           A – Action

           C – Conclusion

           E – Emotion

Author: Make NOTES on your plan sheet.

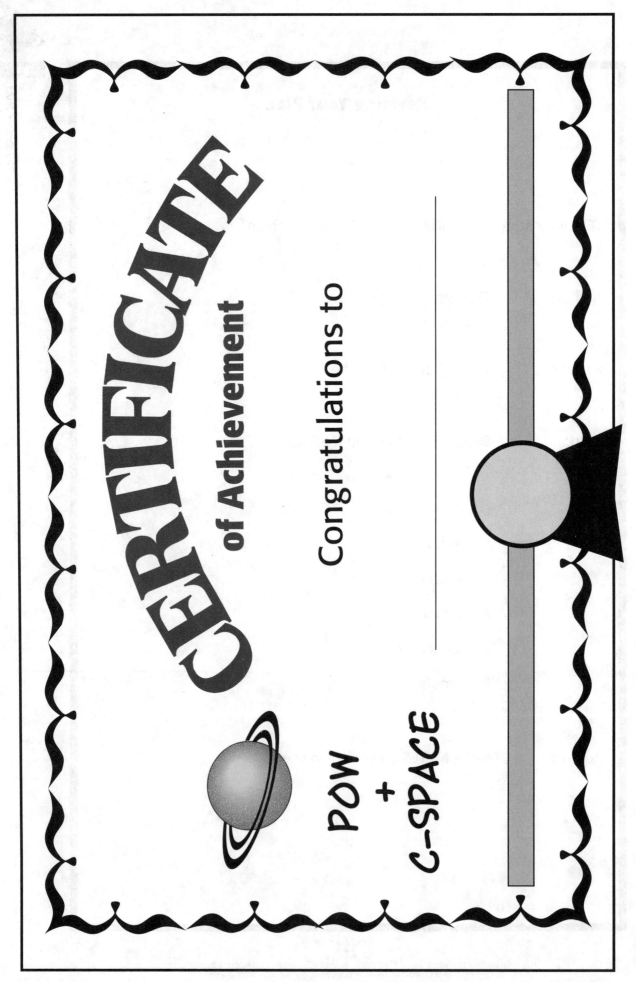

CERTIFICATE

of Achievement

Congratulations to

_____

POW
+
C-SPACE

Section III

Strategies for Narrative, Expository, and Persuasive Writing

Chapter 8

POW + TREE

P = Pick my idea.

O = Organize my notes.

W = Write and say more.

T = Topic Sentence

R = Reasons

E = Ending/Explain Reasons

E = Examine/Ending

MATERIALS
POW + TREE Mnemonic Chart for Younger Students
POW + TREE Mnemonic Chart for Older Students
POW + TREE Graphic Organizer for Younger Students
POW + TREE Graphic Organizer for Older Students
Transfer Sheet
Essay Rockets Graph for Younger Students
Essay Rockets Graph for Older Students
Essay Samples for Younger Students (6)
Essay Samples for Older Students (2)
Transition Words
Cue Cards for Younger Students
Cue Cards for Older Students
Essay Prompts
My Self-Statements
POW + TREE Certificate
Bulletin Board:
  • Writing Paper
  • Writing Self-Statements

LESSONS FOR YOUNGER STUDENTS
LESSON 1

LESSON OVERVIEW

The purpose of this first lesson is to develop the students' background knowledge of persuasive writing, discuss the strategies, and establish partners for help transferring the strategies to other areas of writing. The teacher will review the POW strategy and introduce the TREE strategy. (NOTE: If POW has not been introduced, refer to the WWW story-writing strategy for introduction.) It will be important to establish the students understanding of the term *opinion essay*.

STUDENT OBJECTIVES

The students will orally state what makes a good opinion essay. The students will be able to find essay parts in an essay read in class. The students will orally state the meaning of *transfer*.

MATERIALS

One copy for each student:
- POW + TREE Mnemonic Chart for Younger Students
- POW + TREE Graphic Organizer for Younger Students

- Transition Words
- Transfer sheet
- Essay Samples for Younger Students
- Paper, pencils, and scratch paper

SET THE CONTEXT FOR STUDENT LEARNING

Tell the students that they will be learning a new writing trick that will help them write a paper that tells the reader what they believe or what they think about a certain topic. This is called an *opinion essay*. Discuss the words *opinion* and *essay* to ensure that the students understand the meanings of the terms.

DEVELOP THE STRATEGY AND SELF-REGULATION

Step 1: Develop Background Knowledge

- Review POW. Put out the POW + TREE mnemonic chart so that only POW shows. Ask the students to tell you what POW represents, and remind them that POW gives them power when they write stories and can give them power when they are writing their opinion.

  P = *P*ick my Idea

  O = *O*rganize my Notes

  W = *W*rite and Say More

- Describe and discuss what makes writing an opinion powerful. The students may not be familiar with this concept. Tell the students that

  1. An opinion essay is powerful when it tells a reader what the writer believes, gives a reader at least three reasons why he or she believes it, and has an ending sentence. (You will be practicing this with them, so at this point, you just want to be sure they have the idea.)

160

2. A powerful opinion essay makes sense and has several parts. Tell the students that they will learn a trick for remembering the parts of writing a good opinion essay.

Step 2: Introduce TREE

Uncover the rest of the chart. Say, *"Let's look at the important parts of a powerful opinion."* Go over each part of TREE and how it relates to a living TREE.

T: The *topic* sentence is like the trunk. It is strong and every part of the tree is connected to it.

R: The *reasons* are like the roots. They support the trunk. The more roots—or reasons—a tree has, the stronger the trunk will be.

E: The ending is like the *earth.* It wraps around the tree (like wrap it up).

E: The last part of TREE is *examine.* Say, *"Look at the picture of the girl. She is looking carefully at the tree with a telescope, making sure all the parts are there.* Spend some time discussing the word examine. *"To examine something means to look at it closely. For instance, you can examine something closely using a magnifying glass or microscope. We will be looking closely—examining—with our eyes."*

Step 3: Find Parts in an Opinion Essay

• Tell the students that you will read and examine a previously written opinion essay (see essay samples) to find out if the writer used all of the parts (e.g., What I believe, at least three reasons why, an ending sentence). Display the TREE chart where the students can see it.

• Give each student a copy of the first opinion essay. Ask them to read along silently while you read the paper aloud. Tell them to raise their hands when they hear what the writer believes, each reason why, and an ending sentence.

• Give each student a pencil. When they have identified the topic sentence, have them underline it.

• Tell the students that you will be looking for *transition* words—the words the writer has used to show that a reason is being given. Show them the list of transition words and have them locate the ones in the paper. Have the students circle the transition words. Reinforce that the transition words help you find the reasons in the paper. Spend some time discussing this. Label each reason with a number.

• Tell the students to locate the ending sentence and underline it.

• Tell the students to examine the parts and decide if they are all there.

Step 4: Introduce the Organizer

Show the students how to write the parts they have found in the sample essay in note form on the organizer. Make sure you number the reasons as you are doing this. The parts need not be found in order, so it is all right to move around the chart out of order. Call on students as they raise their hands, ensuring that all students have a turn. When all the parts have been identified, complete the last step—examine—by checking the *yes* space.

Step 5: Practice TREE

Practice the TREE mnemonic and review what each letter represents. Turn over the chart and the students' papers. Ask each student to explain the TREE parts mnemonic and what each letter represents, and then have them write this information down on their scratch paper. If students have trouble, turn the chart back over and allow them to look at it. Keep doing this until all students can explain the mnemonic and write it on paper from memory.

Step 6: Find Parts in a Second Essay

Read the second opinion essay. Be sure to collect the students' pencils so they do not start underlining and circling. Leave out the mnemonic chart and the transition words list. As before, remind the students to raise their hands when they hear a part. Be sure each part is identified. Write parts on the graphic organizer. Do not underline or circle words this time. Be sure to point to the transition words when finding the reasons, to write in note form, and to number parts. Examine parts collaboratively. Check yes when all parts are found.

Step 7: Establish Writing Partners

- Tell the students that you want them to use POW + TREE in all of their other classes and outside of school where they can, and that they will act as partners to help each other.

- Tell the students that they have two goals for next time.

  1. Goal 1: The next time, the students should use all or parts of POW + TREE in other classes for other writing tasks. Brainstorm together some classes or other writing tasks where they could use both POW + TREE; be sure to note that they should use POW whenever they use TREE. Other ideas could include letters to friends, reports on special topics, articles for a school newsletter, letters to a leader, like the principal or the president, or any writing task where they want to tell someone their opinions or convince someone they are right. Briefly note that for some tasks, all parts of the TREE trick might not be appropriate to use. In such cases, they should change TREE to fit the kind of paper they need to write and not use all TREE parts if they do not make sense in that situation.

     Tell the students to report back to you on using all or any parts of POW or TREE next time. Review the "I transferred my strategies/I helped my partner" chart and tell them that you will write down and put a star next to each time they tell you about using all or any part of POW or TREE outside of this class. Briefly review the word *transfer,* saying that it means *to move.* Emphasize that you want them to transfer what they learn about POW + TREE from this class to other classes and writing tasks.

  2. Goal 2: Tell the students to help each other by pointing out situations when they might transfer POW or TREE. Tell them to report back on times they helped each other transfer by reminding their partner. Explain that you will write down and put a star next to each time they tell you about helping their partner transfer all or any part of POW or TREE.

WRAP-UP

Announce that there will be a test (no grade) during the next session. The students will write out POW + TREE and explain what each represents from memory. Have each student keep his or her scratch paper with POW and the TREE mnemonic on it with them for practice.

LESSON 2

LESSON OVERVIEW

POW + TREE are reviewed in this lesson. The students will look for the parts of TREE in their previously written essay. They will graph the correct number of parts on charting paper. The teacher will say that although the essay may contain a certain part, that part can be made better.

STUDENT OBJECTIVES

The students will write the POW + TREE mnemonic and state what each represents. They will identify parts in an essay read in class and locate essay parts in a previously written essay.

MATERIALS

One copy for each student:
- POW + TREE Mnemonic Chart for Younger Students
- POW + TREE Graphic Organizer for Younger Students
- Cue cards for Younger Students
- Cue cards for Older Students

- Transition Words
- Transfer sheet
- Essay Rockets Graph for Younger Students
- Essay Samples for Younger Students
- Students' previously written essays
- Paper, pencils, and scratch paper

SET THE CONTEXT FOR STUDENT LEARNING

Test to see if the students remember POW + TREE. Also, review the definitions of the words *opinion* and *essay*. On a piece of scratch paper, have the students write POW and then ask them what each letter stands for. If the students have trouble remembering POW, continue to practice it. Then ask them to write TREE on the scratch paper and explain what each letter stands for. Alternate review practice so that each student has an opportunity to answer several times. Cue cards may be used to practice TREE.

It is essential that each student memorize the mnemonic. If some students are having trouble with this, spend a few minutes practicing it. Tell the students that you will test them each day to make sure they understand it. Remind them that they can practice memorizing it.

Ask the students to report back on how they used all or parts of POW and/or TREE in other classes or for other writing tasks. Brainstorm ideas together. Ask the students how they helped one another remember to transfer. Record student responses on the transfer sheet and encourage them in their efforts.

DEVELOP THE STRATEGY AND SELF-REGULATION

Step 1: Find Essay Parts

Display the TREE mnemonic chart, graphic organizer, and transition chart. Go through two more essay samples for younger students and have the students verbally identify the paper parts (i.e., what the writer believes, at least three reasons, the ending sentence). Be sure to model writing in note form. Ask the students if they can think of more reasons that could be included in these papers. Number and write the reasons on the graphic organizer. Ask the students what transition words could be used with the additional reasons. BE SURE TO EXAMINE PARTS! Ask the students if all the parts are there and check the yes space.

Step 2: Look at Current Writing Behavior

- Hand out the students' previously written essays.

- Tell the students to read their essays and see which parts they have. Beforehand, you should have identified which parts the students had and which were missing; for opinion essays, the total can be five or more (e.g., What I believe, at least three reasons why, and an ending).

- Briefly note with each student which parts they have and which are missing. As a group, briefly note the common missing parts.

- Note also that although a part may be included, it is possible to make that part better next time. This will make the paper more fun to write and more fun to read. Discuss examples of how the students can do each of these things, using either their essays or the essays you have previously read.

  - Make the topic sentence more interesting.

  - Give more than three reasons.

  - Use transition words.

  - Make the ending sentence more interesting.

  - Use good word choices or *million-dollar words.*

Step 3: Graph Current Level of Performance and Establish Goal

- Hand out the Essay Rockets graphs and have the students fill in the graph for the number of parts they had in their previously written essays. Be positive; remind them that they are just now learning the trick of writing good opinion essays. Explain that if they have more than three reasons, they can *bust the rocket.* If they bust the rocket, they can color a star for each extra reason.

- Explain the goal, which is to write better opinion essays. Remind the students that a good and powerful opinion essay tells the reader what the writer believes, gives at least three reasons why, and has an ending sentence. Good opinion essays are fun to write, fun for others to read, and make sense.

 Say, *"Our goal is to have all of the parts and better parts the next time we write an opinion essay."*

WRAP-UP

- Remind the students that there will be a POW + TREE test again during the next class.

- Remind the students to transfer POW + TREE.

- If the students are still having trouble finding the parts in the papers you have read, plan to read another paper aloud at the beginning of the next lesson.

LESSON 3

LESSON OVERVIEW

The teacher models the way to use POW + TREE for writing an opinion essay. The teacher models the use of self-statements during the process. The students write personal self-statements. If the students have not developed self-statements in prior lessons, the teacher will refer to the POW + WWW essay writing strategy for instructions. The teacher will provide additional practice with essays for any student who needs practice locating essay parts.

STUDENT OBJECTIVES

The students will orally recite the mnemonic for POW + TREE and state what each letter represents. The students will attend to the teachers modeling lesson and locate essay parts in a previously written essay. They will write self-statements for the POW + TREE writing strategy.

MATERIALS

One copy for each student:

- POW + TREE Mnemonic Chart for Younger Students
- POW + TREE Graphic Organizer for Younger Students
- Transition Words
- Transfer sheet

- Essay Rockets Graph for Younger Students
- My Self-Statements
- Essay prompt
- Essay Samples for Younger Students (if necessary)
- Paper, pencils, and scratch paper

SET THE CONTEXT FOR STUDENT LEARNING

Test to see if the students remember POW + TREE. Also, review the definitions of the words *opinion* and *essay.* On a piece of scratch paper, ask the students to write down POW and then ask them what the letters represent. If the students have trouble remembering POW, continue to practice it. Ask them to write out TREE on the scratch paper and to explain what each part of TREE represents. Alternate practice so each student has the opportunity to answer several times.

It is essential that each student memorize the mnemonic. If some students are having trouble with this, spend a few minutes practicing it. Tell the students that you will test them on the mnemonic each day to make sure they understand it. Remind the students that they can practice memorizing it.

Ask the students to report back on how they used all or parts of POW and/or TREE in other classes or for other writing tasks. Brainstorm ideas together. Ask the students how they helped one another remember to transfer. Record student responses on the transfer sheet and encourage them in their efforts.

If the students are still having trouble finding the essay parts as you read aloud, use this time to read another essay sample or two aloud.

DEVELOP THE STRATEGY AND SELF-REGULATION

Step 1: Model the Strategy

Pick My Idea

Lay out a copy of the POW + TREE graphic organizer. Then say, *"Remember that the first letter in POW is P for Pick my idea. We will now practice how to write an opinion essay."* Review the definition of *opinion* if necessary. Say, *"To do this, we must be creative and think free."*

Read a practice essay prompt (see essay prompt) out loud: *toys.* Tell the students the things you say to yourself when you want to think of good paper ideas or parts. Be sure to tell them the examples ("I have to let my mind be free," "Take my time; a good idea will come to me," "Think of new, fun ideas"). Discuss the things you say to yourself to help you work. Note that it's not always necessary to think aloud and that the students can think these ideas in their heads.

Organize My Notes

Say, *"The second letter in POW is O for Organize my notes. I will write an opinion essay today with your help. I will use POW + TREE to help me organize and plan my essay. I will use this graphic organizer to make and organize my notes; you will do this, too, the next time you write a paper."* Point out the parts of an opinion essay on the graphic organizer. Review the important points (e.g., "What should my goal be?" "A good opinion essay has all the parts"). Remind the students that a good and powerful opinion essay tells the reader what the writer believes, gives at least three reasons why, and has an ending sentence. Also, good opinion essays are fun to write and for others to read and they make sense.

• Model writing a paper using POW + TREE; the students can help as much as they like.

  1. Display the POW + TREE graphic and the transition words list.

  2. Model the entire process for writing an opinion essay using the practice prompt. Be sure to use problem definition, planning, self-evaluation, and self-reinforcement self-statements as you go. Model how to include *million-dollar words.* Follow these steps and statements, filling in ad lib statements where indicated. Ask the students to help you with ideas and the writing, but be sure that you remain in charge of the process.

• Say, *"What do I have to do? I have to write an opinion essay. My paper needs to make sense and have all the parts. Remember P in POW—Pick my idea. Let my mind be free."* Pause. *"Take my time. What I believe and good reasons why will come to me."*

• Say, *"Now I can do O in POW—Organize my notes. This helps me plan my paper. I can write down ideas for each part. I can write down ideas in different parts of this graphic organizer as I think of them."* Be sure to model moving out of order during your planning. *"First, I need to ask, What do I believe and what do I want to tell the reader I believe?"* Talk this out and fill in notes for the topic sentence. *"Good! I like this idea! Now I need to come up with at least three reasons why I believe this. Let my mind be free so I can think of good ideas."* Talk this out and briefly write notes for at least three reasons. DO NOT WRITE FULL SENTENCES. Use coping statements at least twice. Be sure to number your reasons. Say,*"What do I need to do next? I need*

to wrap it up and write notes for my ending sentence." After you have generated notes for all the paper parts, say, *"Now I can look back at my notes and see if I can add more notes for my paper parts."* Actually do this. Model it and use coping statements. *"I can also look for ideas for good choices as well as million-dollar words."* Do this and then model examining the notes for all parts and checking the yes space.

Write and Say More

- Continue modeling the last step—"W" in POW.

 Say, *"Now I can do W in POW—Write and say more. I can write an opinion essay, think of more good ideas, and use transition and million-dollar words as I write."* Talk yourself through writing the paper; the students can help. Use a clean piece of paper and print. Start by saying, *"How shall I start? I need to tell the reader what I believe. I need a topic sentence."* Pause and think, and then write out the sentence. Be sure to add one or two more ideas and *million-dollar words* on your plan as you write. Model how to select and use transition words. Don't hurry, but don't slow it down unnaturally. Ask yourself at least twice, *"Am I using good parts? Am I using all of my parts so far?"* Use coping statements. Also ask yourself, *"Does my paper make sense? Will the reader believe my reasons?"* Model writing the ending sentence. Model how to examine the paper for all parts. When the paper is done, say, *"Good work. I'm done. It will be fun to share my paper with others."*

Step 2: Graph Essay Parts

Graph the parts in this paper on the Essay Rockets graph. Ask the students, *"Does this paper have at least five parts?"* Fill in the graph, coloring stars for each reason over the required three.

Step 3: Develop the Students' Self-Statements

- Ask the students if they remember 1) the things you said to yourself to get started, 2) the things you said while you worked, and 3) the things you said to yourself when you finished.

- Give each student a self-statements sheet. Ask the students to write some things they could say to themselves as they work. Be sure to note that these should be in their own words.

  1. Things to say to get started; these phrases I can be along the lines of "What do I have to do? I have to write an opinion essay using POW + TREE."

  2. Things to say while you work; these phrases can be along the lines of "I can use transition words."

  3. Things to say when you are finished; these phrases can be along the lines of "Do I have at least five parts?"

WRAP-UP

- Remind the students that there will be a POW + TREE test again during the next class.

- Remind the students to transfer POW + TREE.

LESSON 4

LESSON OVERVIEW
The students and teacher will collaboratively write an opinion essay using POW + TREE.

STUDENT OBJECTIVES
The students will orally recite the mnemonic for POW + TREE and what each letter represents. The students will collaboratively write an opinion essay with the teacher and orally identify parts of the essay that is written.

MATERIALS

One copy for each student:
- POW + TREE Mnemonic Chart for Younger Students
- POW + TREE Graphic Organizer for Younger Students
- Transition Words

- Transfer sheet
- Essay Rockets Graph for Younger Students
- Paper and pencils
- Essay prompts
- My Self-Statements

SET THE CONTEXT FOR STUDENT LEARNING

Test to see if the students remember POW + TREE. Also, review the definitions of the words *opinion* and *essay.* On a piece of scratch paper, ask the students to write down POW and then ask them what the letters represent. If the students have trouble remembering POW, continue to practice it. Ask them to write out TREE on the scratch paper and to explain what each part of TREE represents. Alternate practice so that each student has the opportunity to answer several times.

It is essential that each student memorize the mnemonic. If some students are having trouble with this, spend a few minutes practicing it. Tell the students that you will test them on it each day to make sure they understand it. Remind the students that they can practice memorizing it.

Ask the students to report back on how they used all or parts of POW and/or TREE in other classes or for other writing tasks. Brainstorm ideas together. Ask the students how they helped one another to remember to transfer. Record student responses on the transfer sheet and encourage the students in their efforts.

DEVELOP THE STRATEGY AND SELF-REGULATION

Step 1: Collaborative Writing—Support It

- Display the POW + TREE mnemonic chart and the transition words list. Give each student a blank graphic organizer and their self-statements list. Display a practice prompt. This time, let the students lead as much as possible but prompt and help as much as needed. Go through each of these processes. The students can share and use the same ideas, but each student should write an opinion essay using his or her own notes.

 Say, *"Remember that the first letter in POW is P—Pick my idea."* Refer the students to their self-statements for creativity or thinking free. Help the students decide what they believe and start to think of good reasons why they think this way.

- Say, *"The second letter in POW is O—Organize my notes. I will use TREE to help me organize and plan my paper. I will use this graphic organizer to make and organize my notes."* Review the important points (e.g., "What should my goal be?" "I need to write an opinion essay," "Good and powerful opinion essays tell the reader what the writer believes," "I must give at least three good reasons why I believe this, and have an ending sentence. Also, a good opinion essay is fun for me to write as well as for others to read, and makes sense"). After the students have generated notes for all the paper parts say, *"I have to remember to look back at my notes and see if I can add more notes for my paper parts."* Help the students actually do this. Remind them to look for more ideas for good word choices or million-dollar words. Make sure that they examine the parts of TREE in their notes and check off yes on the organizer if they have them all.

- Say, *"The last letter in POW is W—Write and say more."* Remind them to use the transition words list to find transition words for their papers. Encourage and remind them to start by saying, *"What do I have to do here? I have to write an opinion essay. A good opinion essay has all the parts and makes sense. I can write my paper and think of more good ideas or million-dollar words as I write."* Help the students as much as is necessary, but try to let them do as much as they can alone. Encourage them to use other self-statements of their choice while they write. If the students do not finish writing during this class time, they can continue during the next lesson.

Step 2: Graph the Essay

Have the students graph their papers on their Essay Rockets graph. Ask them to determine if their papers have at least five parts, and then fill in the graph. For each reason over the required three written, they may color in a star. Reinforce them for reaching five or more.

WRAP-UP

- Remind the students that there will be a POW + TREE test again during the next class.

- Remind the students to transfer POW + TREE.

The students will be weaned off the TREE graphic organizer. If the teacher feels that the students are not ready to move on to writing with scratch paper for notes instead of the graphic organizer, the class should repeat Lesson 4 with other practice prompts. Lesson 4 can be repeated as often as necessary.

LESSON 5

LESSON OVERVIEW

The students continue to practice the POW + TREE strategies for writing opinion essays. The focus of this lesson is to wean the students off the graphic organizer.

STUDENT OBJECTIVES

The students will develop an organizer for an opinion essay and write an essay that includes at least five parts.

MATERIALS

One copy for each student:
- POW + TREE Mnemonic Chart for Younger Students
- Transition Words
- Transfer sheet

- Essay Rockets Graph for Younger Students
- Paper and pencils
- Essay prompts
- My Self-Statements

SET THE CONTEXT FOR STUDENT LEARNING

Test to see if the students remember POW + TREE. Do this aloud to save time. It is essential that all the students memorize the mnemonic. If some students are having trouble with this, spend a few minutes practicing it. Tell the students you will test them on it each day to make sure they understand it.

Ask the students to report back on how they used all or part of POW and/or TREE in other classes or for other writing tasks. Brainstorm ideas together. Ask the students how they helped one another remember to transfer. Record student responses on the transfer sheet and encourage them for their efforts.

If you feel the students are not ready to move on to writing with scratch paper for notes instead of the graphic organizer, repeat Lesson 4 with other practice prompts and go on to this lesson when they are ready. You can repeat Lesson 4 more than once.

DEVELOP THE STRATEGY AND SELF-REGULATION

Step 1: Wean Off Graphic Organizer

Explain to the students that they won't usually have a TREE organizer page with them when they have to write, so they can make their own notes on blank paper. Review the way to write down the mnemonic at the top of the page.

POW

TREE

Make a space on the paper for notes for each part.

Step 2: Collaborative Writing—Support It

- Ask each student to get out his or her self-statements list. Display two practice prompts. Each student can select one about which to write. Let the students lead as much as pos-

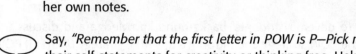

sible, but prompt and help as much as is necessary. The students can make notes on the paper on which they wrote the mnemonic. Go through each of these processes. The students can share ideas, but each student should write his or her own essay using his or her own notes.

Say, *"Remember that the first letter in POW is P—Pick my idea."* Refer the students to their self-statements for creativity or thinking free. Help each student decide what he or she believes and think of good reasons why.

- Say, *"The second letter in POW is O—Organize my notes. I will use my TREE mnemonic to help me organize and plan my paper. I will use this graphic organizer to make and organize my notes. What should my goal be? I want to write an opinion essay. A good and powerful opinion essay tells the reader what the writer believes, gives at least three good reasons why, and has an ending sentence. Also, good opinion essay papers are fun for me to write as well as for others to read, and they make sense."* After the students have generated notes for all TREE parts, say, *"I must remember to look back at my notes and see if I can add more notes for my paper parts."* Help the students actually do this. Remind them also to look for more ideas for good word choices or million-dollar words. Remind them to examine the parts. They can make a check-mark or write yes or no next to the last E in TREE.

- The last letter in POW is W—Write and say more. Encourage and remind the students to start by saying, *"What do I have to do? I have to write an opinion essay. A good opinion essay has all the parts and makes sense. I need to use transition words for my reasons. I can write my paper and think of more good ideas or million-dollar words as I write."* Help the students as much as is necessary, but try to let them do as much as they can alone. Make suggestions if parts can be improved or better choices can be used. Encourage them to use other self-statements of their choice while they write.

Step 3: Share Writing and Graph Performance

Have the students read and graph their essays aloud. Ask each student to determine if his or her paper has at least five parts. Let them fill in their graphs. They can color in stars for more than three reasons. Reinforce them for reaching five or more.

WRAP-UP

- Remind the students that there will be a POW + TREE test again during the next class.
- Remind the students to transfer POW + TREE.
- Repeat this lesson as often as necessary.

LESSONS FOR OLDER STUDENTS
LESSON 1

LESSON OVERVIEW

The purpose of this first lesson is to develop students' background knowledge and discuss the strategies. The teacher will review the POW strategy and introduce the TREE strategy (NOTE: If POW has not been introduced, refer to the WWW story-writing strategy for introduction to POW. It will be important to establish the students' understanding of the terms *opinion* and *essay.*)

STUDENT OBJECTIVES

The students will orally state the qualities that make a good opinion essay. The students will be able to find essay parts in an essay read in class.

MATERIALS

One copy for each student:
- POW + TREE Mnemonic Chart for Older Students
- POW + TREE Graphic Organizer for Older Students

- Essay Samples for Older Students
- Paper, pencils, and scratch paper

SET THE CONTEXT FOR STUDENT LEARNING

Tell the students that they will be learning a new writing trick that will help them write a paper that tells the reader their opinions about specific subjects. This is called an *opinion essay.* Describe and discuss both words to be sure that the students understand the definitions of the words *opinion* and *essay.*

DEVELOP THE STRATEGY AND SELF-REGULATION

Step 1: Develop Background Knowledge

- Review POW. Display the POW + TREE mnemonic chart so that only POW is revealed. Ask the students to tell you what the letters in POW represent and remind them that POW gives them *power* when they write.

- Describe and discuss what makes a good opinion essay. Some students may not be familiar with this. Be sure to tell the students that

  1. A good opinion essay tells a reader what the writer believes, gives a reader at least three reasons why, provides an explanation for each reason, and has an ending sentence. (You will be practicing this with them, so be sure they have the idea here.)
  2. Good opinion essays make sense and have several parts. Tell the students that they will learn a trick for remembering the parts of a good opinion essay.

Step 2: Introduce TREE

 Uncover the rest of the mnemonic chart to reveal TREE. Say, *"Let's look at the parts that make up a good opinion essay."* Go over each part of TREE, describing how it relates to a living TREE.

T: The *topic* sentence is like the trunk. It is strong, and every part of the tree is connected to it.

R: The *reasons* are like the roots. They support the trunk. The more roots (or reasons) a tree has, the stronger the trunk will be.

E: The next part of TREE is *explain. Explain* means to tell more about your reason. The more explanations, the stronger the reasons and the stronger the trunk.

E: The ending is like the *earth.* It wraps around the tree, as in wrap it up.

Step 3: Find Parts in an Essay

- Tell the students that they will read an opinion essay to find out if the writer used all of the parts (e.g., What I believe, at least three reasons why, an explanation for each reason, an ending sentence). Display the TREE mnemonic chart where the students can see it.

- Lay out a TREE graphic organizer. Point out the TREE mnemonic at the top and review what the letters represent.

- Give each student a copy of the first opinion essay; have the students read along silently while you read the essay aloud. Tell them to raise their hand when they hear what the writer believes, each reason why, an explanation, and an ending sentence. Each time you find a reason why, discuss with the students which words the writer uses to show that a reason is being given. Also, note how the writer gives the reason and then tells more about the reason (expands on the reason). You can move the chart around out of order as you find the parts. As the students identify each part, you should write each in the appropriate space on the graphic organizer. Do not use full sentences. Use note form.

Step 4: Practice TREE

Practice the TREE mnemonic and ask the students what each letter means. Turn over the chart and the students' papers. Ask each student to tell you the opinion essay parts mnemonic, and what each letter represents. Then have the students write the mnemonic on scratch paper. If the students have trouble, turn the chart back over and allow them to look. Keep doing this until all the students can recall the mnemonic and write it on paper from memory.

Step 5: Find Parts in a Second Essay

Read the second opinion essay as before. Display the chart. Again, remind the students to raise their hand when they hear a part. Be sure that each part is identified. Do not write them out this time. Point to—or ask the students to point to—the places where the parts go on the chart.

WRAP-UP

Announce a test for the next session. The students will not be graded. Tell them that they will write out POW + TREE and explain what they mean from memory. Have the students keep their scratch paper with POW and the TREE mnemonic on it with them for practice.

LESSON 2

LESSON OVERVIEW

POW + TREE are reviewed in this lesson. The students will look for TREE parts in an essay read in class, as well as in an opinion essay they had previously written. They will graph the correct number of parts on charting paper. It will be important for the teacher to point out that although a part may be included, that part can usually be improved. The students should be given the opportunity to share how they would make their essays better.

STUDENT OBJECTIVES

The students will write the POW + TREE mnemonic and state what each letter represents. The students will identify parts in an essay read in class, as well as in one of their own previously written essays.

MATERIALS

One copy for each student:
- POW + TREE Mnemonic Chart for Older Students
- POW + TREE Graphic Organizer for Older Students

- Essay Rockets Graph for Older Students
- Essay Samples for Older Students
- Students' previously written essays
- Paper and pencils

SET THE CONTEXT FOR STUDENT LEARNING

Test to see if the students remember the POW + TREE mnemonic. Also, review the definition of the term *opinion essay*. Give the students some scratch paper, have them write down POW, and ask them what the letters represent. If the students have trouble remembering POW, continue to practice it. Have the students write out TREE on scratch paper and ask them what each part of TREE represents. Alternate review between the students so that each student has an opportunity to answer several times.

(NOTE: It is essential that every student memorize the mnemonic. If some students are having trouble with this, spend a few minutes practicing it. Tell the students that you will test them on it each day to make sure they understand it. Remind them that they can practice memorizing it.)

DEVELOP THE STRATEGY AND SELF-REGULATION

Step 1: Find Essay Parts

Go through two more essay samples for younger students and have the students verbally identify the essay parts (e.g., what the writer believes, at least three reasons why, an ending sentence). For each of these essays, ask the students if they can think of more reasons and explanations.

POW + TREE

Step 2: Look at Current Writing Behavior

- Hand out the students' previously written essays.

- Tell the students to read their essays and see which parts they have. Work out ahead of time which parts they had and which ones were missing; for opinion essays, the total can be eight or more (e.g., "What I believe," at least three reasons why, at least one explanation for each reason, an ending).

- Briefly note with each student which parts they have and which are missing. As a group, briefly note common missing parts.

- Note also that even though a part is present, that part can be made even better next time. This makes the essay more fun to write and more fun to read. Discuss examples of how the students could do each of the following using either their essays or the essays you read in the previous step:

  - Give more than three reasons

  - Use good word choices, or *million-dollar words*

  - Use an interesting first sentence

  - Use an interesting ending sentence

Step 3: Graph Current Level of Performance and Set Goals

- Give each student a Essay Rockets graph. Have the students fill in the graph for the number of parts they had in their pretest essays. Be positive by reminding them that they are just now learning the trick of writing good essays. Explain that they fill in one space for each step in TREE—one for topic, one for each reason, one for each explanation, and one for wrap-up. Explain that if they have more than three reasons or explanations, they can *bust the rocket*. If they *bust the rocket*, you will write the total number of parts (eight or more) above the rocket.

- Explain the goal, which is to write better opinion essays. Remind the students that good opinion essays tell the reader what the writer believes, give at least three reasons why, give an explanation for each reason, and have an ending sentence. Also, good opinion essays are not only fun for them to write, they are fun for others to read and they make sense.

- The class goal is to have all of the parts and *better* parts the next time they write an opinion essay.

WRAP-UP

Remind the students that there will be a POW + TREE test again at the next session.

LESSON 3

LESSON OVERVIEW

The teacher models how to use POW + TREE for writing an opinion essay. The teacher models the use of self-statements during the process. The students write personal self-statements. If the students have not developed self-statements in prior lessons, refer to the POW + WWW—a story writing strategy—for instructions. (NOTE: Additional practice with essays may be included in this lesson for any student who needs practice in locating parts.)

STUDENT OBJECTIVES

The students will orally say the mnemonic for POW + TREE and state what each letter stands for. The students will attend to the teachers modeling lesson. The students will locate essay parts in a previously written essay if needed. The students will write self-statements for the POW + TREE writing strategy.

MATERIALS

One copy for each student:
- POW + TREE Mnemonic Chart for Older Students
- POW + TREE Graphic Organizer for Older Students

- Essay Rockets Graph for Older Students
- My Self-Statements
- Paper and pencils
- Essay prompts

SET THE CONTEXT FOR STUDENT LEARNING

Test to see if the students remember POW + TREE. Do this aloud to save time. It is essential that each student memorizes these. If the students have trouble with this, spend a few minutes practicing it. Tell the students that you will test them on it each day to make sure they understand it.

DEVELOP THE STRATEGY AND SELF-REGULATION

Step 1: Revisit Locating Essay Parts

If any student is still having trouble finding the essay parts as you read aloud, do another essay or two aloud at this time.

Step 2: Model the Strategy

Pick My Idea

 Lay out a copy of the TREE graphic organizer. Say, *"Remember that the first letter in POW is P for Pick my idea. We will practice how to write a good opinion essay."* Review what that means if necessary. Say, *"To do this, we must be creative and think free."*

- Read aloud the practice prompt: *toys.* Explain to the students the kinds of things you say to yourself when you want to think of good essay ideas or parts. Be sure to say, *"I have to let my mind be free,"* *"Take my time. A good idea will come to me,"* and *"Think of new, fun ideas."*

- Say, *"The things you say to yourself help you to work."* Note that its not always necessary to think aloud and that they can think these things in their heads.

Organize My Notes

Say, *"The second letter in POW is O, which stands for* Organize my notes." Tell the students that today you are going to write an opinion essay with their help. Say, *"I will use POW + TREE to help me. I will use this page to make and organize my notes; you will do this, too, the next time you write an essay."* Briefly review—point at—the parts of a good essay on the graphic. Review "What should my goal be? To write better opinion essays." Remind them that good opinion essays tell the reader what you believe, give at least three reasons why you believe it, give an explanation for each reason, and have an ending sentence. Also, good opinion essays are fun for me to write and for others to read, and they make sense.

- Model the entire process for *Organize my notes.* Use problem definition, planning, million-dollar words, self-evaluation, and self-reinforcement self-statements as you go. Follow the steps and statements, filling in ad lib statements where indicated. Ask the students to help you with ideas as well as the writing, but be sure you remain in charge of the process.

- Say, *"What do I have to do? I have to write a good opinion essay. My essay needs to makes sense and have all the parts. Remember P in POW—Pick my idea. Let my mind be free. Take my time and think about what I believe and some good reasons why will come to me."*

- Say, *"Now I can do O in POW, which stands for Organize my notes. I can write down ideas for each part. I can write ideas down in different parts of this page as I think them."* Be sure to model moving out of order during your planning. Say, *"First, what do I believe? What do I want to tell the reader I believe?"* Talk out and fill in notes for the *topic sentence.* Say, *"Good! I like this idea! Now I need to come up with at least three reasons and give an explanation for each reason. Let my mind be free. Think of good ideas."* Talk out and briefly write notes for at least three reasons in note form. Use coping statements at least twice. After generating notes for all essay parts say, *"Now I can look back at my notes and see if I can add more notes for my essay parts."* Model this action using coping statements. Say, *"I can also look for ideas for good choices or million-dollar words."*

Write and Say More

Say, *"Now I can do W in POW, which stands for Write and say more. I can write my opinion essay and think of more good ideas or million-dollar words as I write."* Talk yourself through writing the essay; the students can help. Use a clean piece of paper and print. Start by saying, *"How shall I start? I need to tell the reader what I believe, so I'll need a topic sentence."* Pause and think, and then write out the sentence. Be sure to add one or two more ideas and million-dollar words on your plan as you write. Don't hurry, but don't slow down unnaturally. Also, ask yourself at least twice, *"Am I using good parts? Am I using all of my parts so far?"* Use a coping statement. Ask yourself, *"Does my essay make sense? Will the reader believe my reasons?"* Model writing the ending sentence. When you have completed the essay, say, *"Good work! I'm done. It'll be fun to share my essay with others."*

Step 3: Self-Statements

- Ask the students if they can remember 1) things you said to yourself to get started, 2) things you said while you worked, and 3) things you said to yourself when you finished.

- Ask the students to write some things they could say to themselves on the self-statements sheet:

  - What to say to get started; this must be along the same lines as "What do I have to do? I have to write an opinion essay using TREE." Be sure the students use their own words.

  - Things to say while working; self-evaluation, coping, self-reinforcement, and any others in the students' own words

  - Things to say when finished in the students' own words

  - Note that the students don't always have to think these things aloud; once they learn them, they can think them in their heads or whisper them to themselves.

Step 4: Graph the Essay

Graph this essay on the Essay Rockets graph. Ask, *"Does this essay have at least eight parts?"* Fill in the graph.

WRAP-UP

Remind the students that there will be a POW + TREE test again at the next session.

LESSON 4

LESSON OVERVIEW

The students and the teacher will collaboratively write an opinion essay using POW + TREE.

STUDENT OBJECTIVES

The students will orally state the mnemonic for POW + TREE and what each letter represents. The students will collaboratively write an opinion essay with the teacher and orally identify parts of the essay.

MATERIALS

One copy for each student:
- POW + TREE Mnemonic Chart for Older Students
- POW + TREE Graphic Organizer for Older Students

- Essay Rockets Graph for Older Students
- My Self-Statements
- Paper and pencils
- Essay prompts

SET THE CONTEXT FOR STUDENT LEARNING

Test to see if the students remember POW + TREE. Do it aloud to save time. It is essential that each student memorizes these. If the students have trouble with this, spend a few minutes practicing it. Tell the students that you will test them on it each day to make sure they understand it.

DEVELOP THE STRATEGY AND SELF-REGULATION

Step 1: Collaborative Writing—Support It

- Give each student a blank graphic organizer and have everyone get out their self-statements sheets. Display practice prompts. Let the students lead as much as possible, but prompt and help as much as needed. Go through each of the processes. The students can share and use the same ideas, but each student should write an opinion essay using his or her own notes.

Say, *"Remember that the first letter in POW is P, which stands for Pick my idea."* Refer the students to their self-statements for creativity or thinking free. Help each student decide what he or she believes and start to think of good reasons why.

- Say, *"The second letter in POW is O, which stands for Organize my notes. I will use TREE to help me. I will use this graphic organizer to make and organize my notes."* Review the goal, which is to write better opinion essays. Say, *"Good opinion essays tell the reader what you believe, give at least three good reasons why, give an explanation for each reason, and have an ending sentence. Also, good opinion essays are fun to write and for others to read, and they make sense."* After the students have generated notes for all essay parts say, *"I have to look back at my notes and see if I can add more notes for my essay parts."* Remind them to also look for more ideas for good choices or million-dollar words.

- Say, *"The last letter in POW is W, which stands for Write and say more."* Encourage and remind the students to start by saying, *"What do I have to do here? I have to write a good essay. A good essay has all the parts and makes sense. I can write my essay and think of more good ideas or* million-dollar words *as I write."* Help the students as much as necessary, but try to let them do as much as they can alone. Encourage them to use other self-statements of their choice while they write. If the students do not finish writing during this session, they can continue at the next lesson.

Step 2: Graph the Essay

Have the students graph their essays. Ask the students to determine if their essays have at least eight parts. Let them fill in the graph. Reinforce them for reaching eight or more.

WRAP-UP

Remind the students that there will be a POW + TREE test again at the next session. In the next lesson, the students will be weaned off the TREE graphic organizer. If you feel the students are not ready to move on to writing with scratch paper for notes rather than the graphic organizer page, repeat Lesson 4 with other practice prompts. Repeat Lesson 4 as often as necessary.

LESSON 5

LESSON OVERVIEW
The students continue to practice the POW + TREE strategies for writing opinion essays. The focus of this lesson is to wean the students off the graphic organizer.

STUDENT OBJECTIVES
The students will develop an organizer for an opinion essay, which they will write with at least eight essay parts.

MATERIALS
One copy for each student:
- POW + TREE Mnemonic Chart for Older Students
- Essay Rockets Graph for Older Students

- My Self-Statements
- Paper and pencils
- Essay prompts

SET THE CONTEXT FOR STUDENT LEARNING

Test to see if the students remember POW + TREE. Do this aloud to save time. It is essential that each student memorizes these. If the students have trouble with this, spend a few minutes practicing it. Tell the students that you will test them on it each day to make sure they understand it.

DEVELOP THE STRATEGY AND SELF-REGULATION

Step 1: Wean Off Graphic Organizer

Explain to the students that they won't usually have a TREE mnemonic chart with them when they have to write opinion essays, so they can make their own notes on blank paper. Discuss and model how to write down the POW + TREE mnemonic at the top of the page, leaving space on the paper to insert notes for each part.

Step 2: Collaborative Writing—Support It

- Ask the students to get out their self-statements sheets. Display two practice essay prompts. Each student can select one to write about. Let the students lead as much as possible, but prompt and help as much as needed. The students can make notes on the paper on which they have written the mnemonic. Go through each of the following processes. The students can share ideas, but each student should write his or her own essay using his or her own notes.

Say, *"Remember that the first letter in POW is P, which stands for Pick my idea."* Refer the students to their self-statements for creativity or thinking free. Help each student decide what he or she believes and start to think of good reasons why.

- Say, *"The second letter in POW is O, which stands for Organize my notes. I will use my TREE mnemonic to help me. I will use this graphic organizer to make my notes and organize my notes."* Review the goal, which is to write better opinion essays. Say,

"Good opinion essays tell the reader what you believe, give at least three good reasons why, give an explanation for each reason, and have an ending sentence. Also, good opinion essays are fun to write and for others to read, and they make sense." After the students have generated notes for all essay parts say, *"I need to look back at the notes and see if I can add more notes for my essay parts."* Remind them to also look for more ideas for good choices or *million-dollar words.*

- The last letter in POW is W, which stands for *Write and say more.* Encourage and remind them to start by saying, *"What do I have to do here? I have to write a good essay. A good essay has all the parts and makes sense. I can write my essay and think of more good ideas or million-dollar words as I write."* Help the students as much as necessary, but try to let them do as much as they can alone. If parts can be improved or better choices can be used, you can make suggestions. Encourage them to use other self-statements of their choice while they write.

- Have the students graph their essays. Ask them to determine if their essays have at least eight parts. Let them fill in the graph. Reinforce them for reaching eight or more.

WRAP-UP

Celebrate student learning!

POW + TREE Mnemonic Chart for Younger Students

POW
Pick my idea.
Organize my notes.
Write and say more.

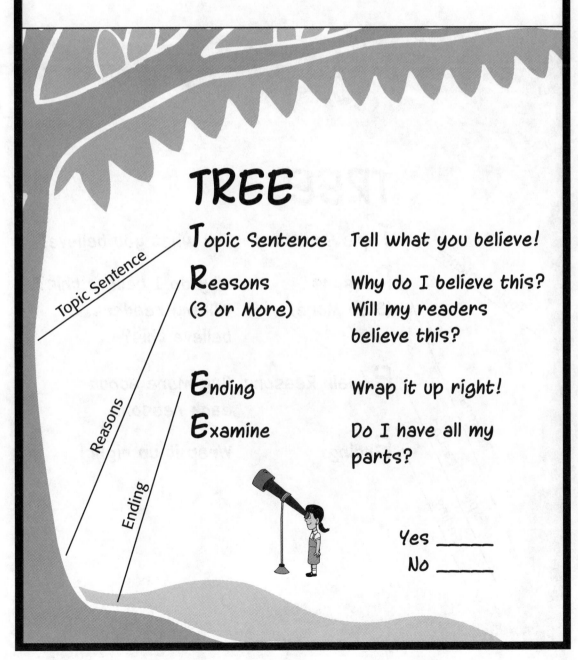

TREE

Topic Sentence	Tell what you believe!
Reasons (3 or More)	Why do I believe this? Will my readers believe this?
Ending	Wrap it up right!
Examine	Do I have all my parts?

Yes _____
No _____

183

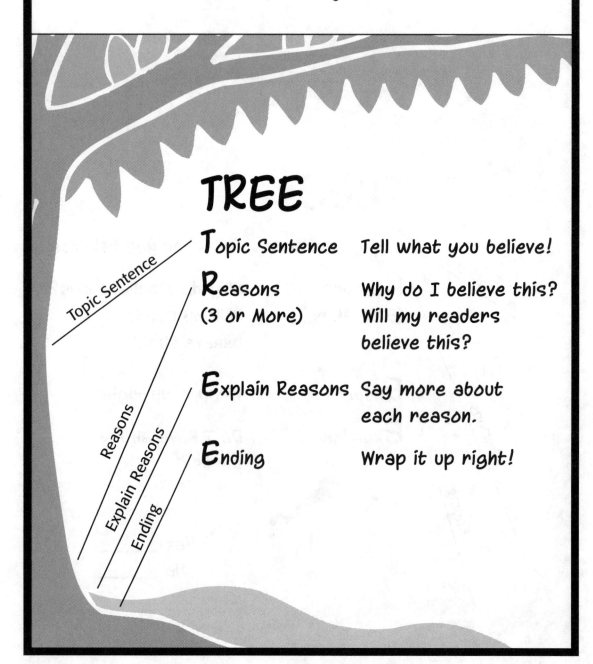

POW + TREE Mnemonic Chart for Older Students

POW

Pick my idea.

Organize my notes.

Write and say more.

TREE

Topic Sentence	Tell what you believe!
Reasons (3 or More)	Why do I believe this? Will my readers believe this?
Explain Reasons	Say more about each reason.
Ending	Wrap it up right!

Topic Sentence

Reasons

Explain Reasons

Ending

Graphic Organizer for Younger Students

Topic Sentence   Tell what I believe!

_____

_____

_____

Reasons—3 or More   Why do I believe this?
Will my readers believe this? Number my reasons.

_____

_____

_____

_____

_____

_____

Ending   Wrap it up right!

_____

_____

Examine
Do I have all my parts?

Yes _____

No _____

Graphic Organizer for Older Students

T	**Topic Sentence: Tell what you believe.**
R **E**	**Reasons (3 or more). Explain each reason further.** 1. Reason: Explanation: 2. Reason: Explanation: 3. Reason: Explanation:
E	**Ending: Wrap it up right.**

I Transferred My Strategy	I Helped My Partner

Essay Rockets Graph for Younger Students

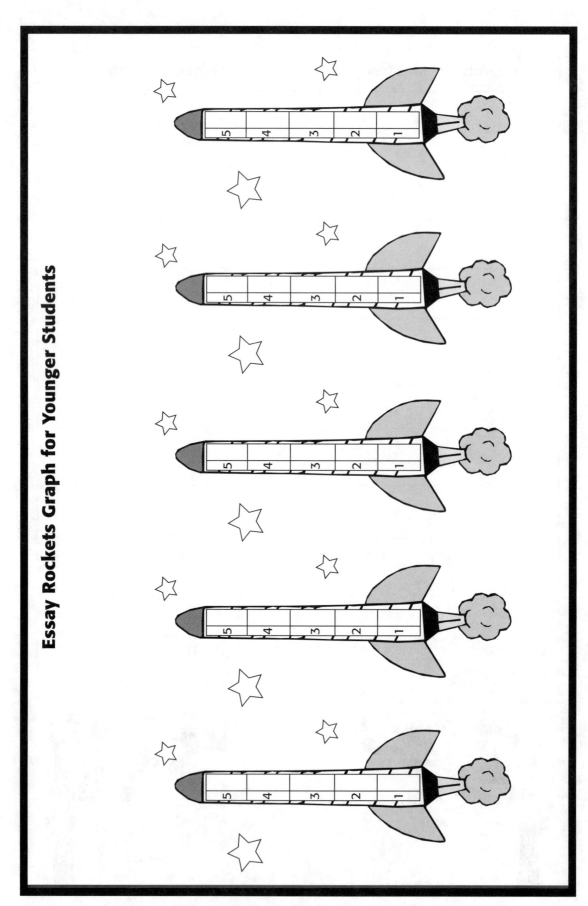

Essay Rockets Graph for Older Students

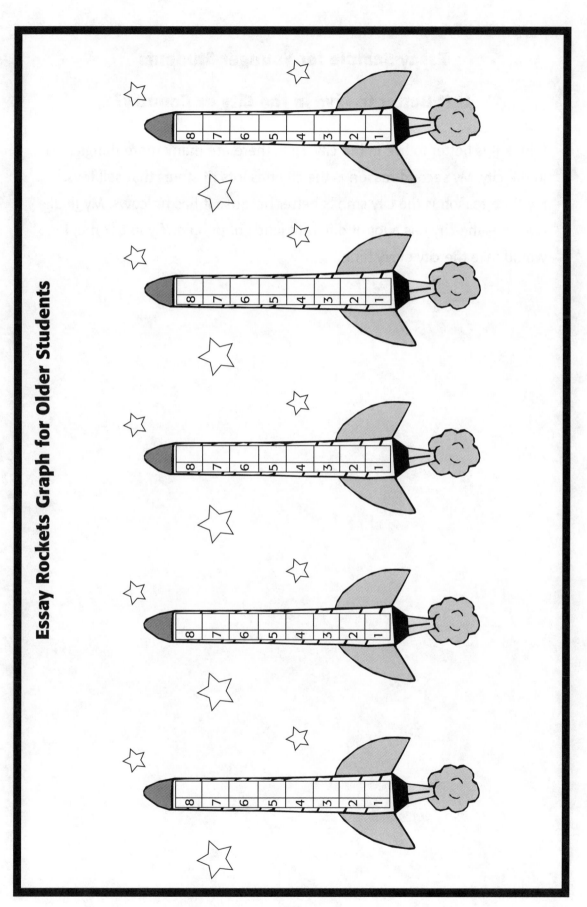

Essay Sample for Younger Students

Is It Better to Live in the City or Country?

I think it is better to live in the city. First, there are many more things to do in the city. My second reason is the city has lots of stores that sell toys. My third reason is the city smells better because it has no cows. My final reason is the city has a lot of different kinds of people. If you ask me, I would take the city every time.

Essay Sample for Younger Students

Is It Better to Live in the City or the Country?

The city and the country are both good places, but the country is better. First, the people in the country are nicer. Second, you can go fishing in the country. Third, you can play outside in the country. Finally, there is not as much traffic in the country. When you think about it, the country is much better than the city.

Essay Sample for Younger Students

Should Children Have to Go Outside for Recess?

Not everyone likes to play outside for recess. First, some kids get sick when they go outside. Second, some kids need recess time to finish their homework. Third, it is no fun to go outside when it is raining or is too cold. Fourth, there are a lot of games to play inside. Fifth, recess is longer when you are inside because you don't waste time in the hallway. All in all, it is better if it is up to the kid. Some kids will go outside and others will not.

Essay Sample for Younger Students

Should Children Have to Go Outside for Recess?

Everyone should have to go outside for recess. One reason why everyone should go outside is because children need to move their bodies. Another reason for going outside is that it is hard to sit in one place all day. Another good reason for going outside is that you get to meet kids from different grades and classes. A final reason for going outside is to play sports. These are the reasons why I believe kids should go outside for recess.

Essay Sample for Younger Students

Should All Children Learn How to Use a Computer?

I do not think that all children should have to learn how to use a computer. There are three reasons why I believe this. First, some kids do not have a computer at home. Second, some kids have trouble with typing. Third, some computers are always breaking down. So, please, don't make all children learn how to use a computer.

Essay Sample for Younger Students

Should All Children Learn How to Use a Computer?

I think that everyone should learn how to use a computer. The main reason why I think that kids should learn to use the computer is because it can help them at school. Another good reason for learning to use the computer is to play games. My final reason is that the computer is a good way to send messages and write to other kids. So if you ask me, everyone needs to learn how to use the computer. The sooner they start, the better.

Essay Sample for Older Students

Is It Better to Live in the City or the Country?

I think it is better to live in the country than the city. First, country living is fun because you can play in the fields and woods. Second, when you live in the country you get to work with the animals. Third, the country has clean air. You do not get sick. Finally, the country is so quiet at night you can hear the bugs sing. The country is where I would live because then I would have more fun, feel better, and get to be with the animals.

Essay Sample for Older Students

Should Children Have to Go to School?

Kids need to go to school. One reason why it is important to go to school is because at school you make friends who live outside your neighborhood. Another reason why school is important is because this is where you learn to read and write; for example, you learn about science and history. One more reason why kids should go to school is because school can be a lot of fun, especially during special activities and field trips. I know that some kids might say, "No school." But I disagree. I say, "School is fun, it helps you make new friends, and teaches you what you need to know."

Transition Words

First
Second
Third
Fourth
Fifth

Another
Also
A different
One more
Next
My final
Finally

Cue Cards for Younger Students

Reasons—3 or More

Why do I believe this?
Will my readers believe this?

Examine

Do I have
all my parts?

Topic Sentence

Tell what you believe!

Ending

Wrap it up right!

Cue Cards for Older Students

Topic Sentence
Tell what you believe!

Reasons-3 or More
Why do I believe this?
Will my readers believe this?

Explain Reasons
Say more about each reason.

Ending
Wrap it up right!

Essay Prompts

Should students give some of their toys to children who do not have toys?

Should students your age have to do chores at home?

Should students be allowed to eat snacks in the classroom?

Should students have to go to school in the summer?

Should students be allowed to chew gum at school?

My Self-Statements

To think of good ideas:

_____

_____

_____

_____

_____

_____

While I work:

_____

_____

_____

_____

_____

_____

To check my work:

_____

_____

_____

_____

_____

_____

CERTIFICATE
of Achievement

Congratulations to

_____

POW
+
TREE

Writing Self-Statements

Chapter 9

STOP and DARE

This chapter is adapted from the STOP and DARE lesson plans developed by
Steve Graham, Vanderbilt University, and Susan De La Paz, University of Maryland.

S = Suspend Judgment

T = Take a Side

O = Organize Ideas

P = Plan More as You Write

D = Develop Your Topic Sentence

A = Add Supporting Ideas

R = Reject Arguments for the Other Side

E = End with a Conclusion

MATERIALS
STOP and DARE Mnemonic Chart
STOP and DARE Directions
STOP and DARE Checklist
Brainstorming Sheet
Linking Words
Cue Cards
Essay Topics
Transfer Sheet
My Self-Statements
STOP and DARE Certificate
Bulletin Board:
- Self-Statements Stop Signs
- Writing Paper

LESSON 1

LESSON OVERVIEW

The essay planning strategy and essay parts reminder will be introduced in this lesson. The teacher will introduce the parts of the persuasive/opinion essay planning strategy called STOP:

S: *Suspend judgment*

T: *Take a side*

O: *Organize ideas*

P: *Plan more as you write*

Collaboratively, the teacher and students will brainstorm, discuss, and list the parts of a well-written essay: for example, good essays have a topic sentence. The teacher will describe the reminder for the four essay parts called DARE:

D: *Develop your topic sentence*

A: *Add supporting ideas*

R: *Reject possible arguments*

E: *End with a conclusion*

The students and teacher will establish goals for using STOP and DARE—namely, "To write better essays with four parts."

STUDENT OBJECTIVES

The students will orally recite the parts of the essay planning strategy called STOP. The students will orally recite the essay parts reminder called DARE. The students will identify essay parts in an essay read in class, as well as in their personal essay previously written in a prior class session at school. The students will graph the number of parts found in an essay.

MATERIALS

One copy for each student:
- STOP and DARE mnemonic chart
- STOP and DARE Checklist
- Sample essays for identifying parts (see essay samples in chapter 8)

- Chart paper or chalkboard
- Pencils
- Students' previously written essays
- Transfer sheet

SET THE CONTEXT FOR STUDENT LEARNING

This introduction to the strategy emphasizes the qualities that make a good essay. Explain to the students that for this writing class they will learn how to compose good essays. They will learn that good essays can persuade someone to change her or his point of view, that good writers plan before they write, and that good essays have several parts.

Why should students learn to write essays? The basic ideas in essays are found everywhere (e.g., on TV, on the radio, in newspaper editorials, at government meetings and political rallies, in letters to the editor, at home). People who can write good essays know how to convince and persuade others of their opinions. The students can share examples of their trying to convince their parents, teachers, or friends to believe their side of an issue and what that issue was.

DEVELOP THE STRATEGY AND SELF-REGULATION

Step 1: Describe and Discuss the Strategy STOP

Discuss the writing process with the students, emphasizing that most *expert* writers plan before starting to compose.

- Give each student a copy of the STOP and DARE mnemonic chart. The chart should be covered so that only the first step, Suspend Judgment, shows. Ask the students if they know what the word *suspend* means. Analogies such as a policeman stopping traffic could be used. Clarify that in this case the word *judgment* means the formation of an opinion after hearing both sides of an argument. Explain that during this step, they will brainstorm ideas for and against the assigned topic.

- Uncover *Take a Side.* Tell the students that in this step, they will evaluate what they have brainstormed up to this point. Spend a few minutes discussing an important part of planning—deciding which side to believe. Explain that once that decision has been made, they will try to convince whoever reads their essay to agree with them.

- Uncover *Organize Ideas.* The third step will help the students to select ideas they feel will support their beliefs and to select at least one argument against the ideas that they can refute. Arguments both for and against the ideas must be stated to make a strong essay. Arguments that the writer does not agree with must be countered or dealt with in some way or they will actually weaken the essay. Discuss ways to refute an argument such as thinking of a contrasting reason or a condition that would make an exception to the argument. After the students select ideas and the side or an argument to agree with, they will number the ideas in the order in which they will be used. Deciding the numbered order of ideas is similar to using a map. Explain that when travelers use maps, they first look for the final destination and then choose a route that will take them there. Taking a side is like deciding a destination, and the essay will guide others to accept the side that the writer supports.

- Uncover *Plan More as You Write.* Emphasize that this means *to continue planning as you compose,* and remember to include the four essay parts in DARE.

Step 2: Parts of an Essay

The teacher and students will brainstorm parts of a good essay.

- Ask the students to state the parts of a good essay. Respond positively to all student answers; write down any answers that correspond with the vital essay parts (i.e., main idea, reasons, examples, arguments, end).

- Tell the students to use the terms *topic sentence, supporting ideas, argument(s),* and *conclusion* for the essay parts. Write these parts on the chart paper or chalkboard. Note any essay parts that the students have previously generated.

Step 3: Essay Parts Reminder—DARE

This step will introduce the students to the essay parts reminder DARE.

- Pass out copies of sample essays (selected from Chapter 8 materials or one you have developed) to each student. Ask the students to read along silently while you read the essay aloud; tell them to raise their hand when they hear the topic sentence, supporting ideas, arguments, and conclusion. All the students should have a turn locating an essay part. Be sure to be encouraging and positive throughout.

- After the students find all of the essay parts, ask for another example of each part for the same topic (i.e., an opposing premise). All the students should have a turn generating one essay part. Write down student responses on chart paper or chalkboard. Tell the students that they will learn a reminder for the four essay parts as they practice writing essays. Uncover the essay parts reminder DARE:

    D *D*evelop your topic sentence.

    A *A*dd supporting ideas.

    R *R*eject arguments for the other side.

    E *E*nd with a conclusion.

- Ask the students if they have heard of DARE in another context. They may recall the Drug and Alcohol Resistance Education program although they need not know what the letters represent. Tell them that they will be able to remember the word DARE because they have heard it before.

Step 4: Chart Current Level of Performance

The students' current level of performance will be reviewed in this step. The students will set goals for writing a good essay. If time is running short, proceed to Step 5 and complete Step 4 during the next writing class.

- Remind the students of previously written essays. Hand out the previously written essays.

- Tell the students to read their essays and see which essay parts they have. Work out ahead of time which parts they have and which ones are missing.

- Briefly note which parts each student has and which are missing.

    - As a group, briefly note common missing parts. Note also that even if a part is present, the students may be able to make that part better the next time. For example,

        - It could tell the writer's point of view.

        - It could have several reasons.

        - It could give examples.

        - It could consider an argument.

        - It could reject an argument by countering it or dealing with it in some way.

        - It could have a clear ending.

- Spend a few minutes explaining the checklist. Give each student a checklist and ask him or her to mark the number of essay parts written in their essays in the DARE section of the list.

- Explain the goal: to write better essays. Remind the students that good essays have all the STOP and DARE parts and that good essays make sense. The goal is to have all the parts and *better* parts the next time. Using all steps of STOP and DARE will help them do this.

Step 5: Practice STOP and DARE

In each lesson, the students will practice the mnemonics and parts of STOP and DARE. This will continue until the teacher is certain that both the mnemonic and the parts are remembered automatically.

- Practice the essay planning strategy STOP. Turn over the mnemonic chart and ask each student to recall the essay planning strategy mnemonic. After they respond, "STOP," explain again what each letter represents. Ask each student to write the mnemonic on paper. If the students have trouble, turn the chart over and allow them to look. Keep doing this until all the students can recite the reminder and explain each letter from memory.

- Practice the essay parts. Ask each student to explain the parts. Turn over the chart and ask the students to recall the essay parts reminder (DARE). Ask each student to write the reminder on paper. If the students have trouble, turn the chart back over and allow them to look. Help the students as needed. Continue to do this until you feel sure that each student has learned all the parts.

WRAP-UP

Announce that the students will take a non-graded test at the beginning of the next writing class, at which time they will be asked to recall the essay planning and essay parts reminder.

NOTE: If you want to establish "transfer" partners, do so in this or the following lesson. See the transfer sheet and refer to instructions in Chapter 8, Lessons for Younger Students.

LESSON 2

LESSON OVERVIEW

The essay planning strategy and essay parts reminder will be reviewed in this lesson. The teacher and students will collaboratively identify parts and elaborations in an essay that is read in class. The teacher will model using the strategy with cue cards. The students will rehearse the strategy using the cue cards.

STUDENT OBJECTIVES

The students will verbally state the parts of the essay planning strategy STOP and the parts of the essay parts reminder DARE. The students will demonstrate an understanding of how to use the cue cards.

MATERIALS

One copy for each student:
- STOP and DARE mnemonic chart
- STOP and DARE Directions
- STOP and DARE Checklist
- Linking Words
- Brainstorming Sheet
- Cue Cards

- Sample essays for identifying parts (see essay samples in Chapter 8)
- Chart paper or chalkboard
- Pencils
- Essay Topics
- STOP and DARE Self-Statements

SET THE CONTEXT FOR STUDENT LEARNING

Test the students to see if they remember the word that will help them remember how to plan an essay (STOP). Give them a piece of paper and tell them to write down the word. Ask the students to tell you what each word/phrase in STOP means. Help as necessary. Test to see if they know the word that will help them remember the parts of a good essay (DARE). Tell them to write down that word. Ask the students to explain what each word/phrase in DARE means. Help as necessary.

DEVELOP THE STRATEGY AND SELF-REGULATION

Step 1: Identify Essay Parts and Elaborations

Pass out the STOP and DARE mnemonic chart, directions sheet, and a sample essay to each student. Ask the students to read along as you read the essay aloud. Tell them to raise their hands when they hear each essay part. All the students should have a turn locating an essay part. After reading the essay, go back and ask for other examples of each essay part. Point out that examples, conditions, and so forth often elaborate reasons, topic sentence, argument, and conclusions. These elaborations provide support for the reasons, arguments.

Step 2: Model the Strategy

In this step, the teacher will model how to use the strategy to plan and write a good essay. For this lesson you will need to select a prompt from Essay Topics. It is important that the teacher has memorized the procedure so that it will be fluent. A sample script for modeling this strategy is provided below.

- Put the STOP and DARE mnemonic chart and directions sheet to the side. You will use cue cards during modeling.

 Say, *"I am going to show you how to use STOP and DARE together to plan and write a good essay. I will talk aloud as I go. You might be able to help me, but what I really want you to do is to listen and watch me work. It is my turn to work and your turn to relax!"*

- Model the entire process using the cue cards and the linking words. Follow the steps and statements, using ideas generated for the model essay.

- Say, *"First, I need to suspend judgment. That means I won't make up my mind about the topic yet. I need to brainstorm ideas for and against my topic."*

- Write two or three ideas for one side and one or two ideas for the other side on the brainstorming sheet.

- Introduce the cue cards for Step 1. Say, *"I have three cue cards for Step 1 to help me plan, and they all say 'Suspend Judgment.' Cue Card #1 says, 'Did I list ideas for both sides? If not, do this now.' Let me see . . . I did that! This is easy to do."*

- Say, *"What does Cue Card #2 say? 'Can I think of anything else? Try to write more.' All right, I need to think of more reasons."* Add at least one idea to each side of the brainstorming sheet, pause to think, and then add another idea to one side.

- Say, *"Cue Card #3 says, 'Another point I haven't yet considered is . . . . Think of possible arguments.' Do I have any arguments? Yes, I do."* Pause to think and then ask, *"Are there any points I haven't considered yet? This is hard because I have so many ideas already. I need to take my time and think of something someone else would say."* Add at least one idea to the brainstorming sheet, preferably on the "For" side.

- Say, *"That's great. I'm finished with Step 1, and I have done so much good work. Now I need to do Step 2, which has only one cue card: Cue Card #4. This cue card says, 'Take a side.' That means I have to pick one side as my argument. Which one do I really be-lieve?"* Provide an answer.

- Say, *"This cue card also says, 'Place a "+" at the top of one box to show the side you will take in your essay.' This card is the same as the chart where it says 'Take a side.' I can remember this card right away because it is on the Brainstorming sheet."*

- Say, *"Step 3 says that I should 'Organize Ideas.' I need to decide which ideas are strong and which ideas are not as strong that I can dispute. This means I should think about all of the ideas I have for my argument."* Read each idea that is on the side you have chosen (the "For" side) and decide if it is a good idea. You should note at least one idea that is not strong and decide aloud to skip it.

- Say, *"I now have strong ideas for my argument. I need to decide which ideas I can dis-pute. That means I need an argument that I can reject—one that I can easily say why I do not agree with it."* Choose one argument from the "Against" side of the brainstorming sheet and then think of one more argument. *"I have to choose my arguments carefully so my reader doesn't get confused about which side I am on. I'm really doing well with this plan. I like my ideas. Let me look at the three cards for Step 3. The first card, Cue Card #5, says, 'Put a star next to the ideas you want to use.' I need to choose at least three ideas to use.*

- Say, *"What does the second card for Step 3 say? Cue Card #6 says, 'Did I star ideas on both sides? Choose at least ___ argument(s) that you can dispute.' I decided that I had two arguments that I can dispute. The last card for Step 3, Cue Card #7, says, 'Number your ideas in the order you will use them.' I'd better think about this. What makes sense?"*

- Bring in the map analogy here. Say, *"Doing things in the correct order, like following directions on a map, will help me guide the reader to agree with what I believe."* Reflect aloud about an order that seems logical to you based on the ideas you have generated.

- Say, *"This will be a good essay. I'm really taking my time to plan it out. The last step is, 'Plan more as you write. Remember to use all four essay parts and continue planning.' That means I should still think of ideas as I write my essay."*

- Say, *"I'm ready for the card for Step 4. It has the essay parts reminder D–A–R–E written on it. I know what that means."* Read the card. *"I'm ready to write my essay. I'll just think of DARE as I go."*

- Verify each part that you write by explaining that you have your topic sentence, and so forth. Point out that you can add supporting ideas after you reject your argument for what this means. Use cohesive words sparingly at key places, such as when you refute an argument or with a group of related ideas.

- Be sure to elaborate on two or three ideas as you write, and try to revise something as you go. Give a strong, summative conclusion by restating your premise using different words.

- After you finish, compliment yourself for the work you have done and then demonstrate how to use the checklist. Mark the checklist for each part and write down the number of ideas selected on the line under the column. If you have met a goal of more than three, you *busted* the chart and can draw a star on top of the column. Thank the students for their help—which may have simply been to pay attention.

Step 3: Rehearsal of STOP and DARE

- The students should verbally rehearse STOP and DARE until mastery has been achieved. The students must be able to recite all steps and essay parts from memory. Wording doesn't have to be exact, but an understanding of the meaning should be apparent.

- Review the four steps. Read STOP off the chart using cue cards as you go. Tell the students that they must memorize steps.

- Have the students practice in any way you think will be helpful. Read with the STOP and DARE mnemonic chart and cue cards facing up. Turn the chart and cards over, write, cover, say, repeat, and so forth.

- The students can paraphrase the four steps and DARE from memory.

- The students can paraphrase at least half of the cue cards from memory. Tell them that they will be able to memorize all the cards after they get a chance to compose an essay during the next session.

WRAP-UP

Remind the students that you will check to see if they can remember on their own the essay planning strategy (STOP) and the essay parts reminder (DARE) at the next session.

NOTE: You may establish the students' individual self-statements during this or the next lesson. Use the My Self-Statements sheet and refer to directions in Chapter 6.

LESSON 3

LESSON OVERVIEW

The students will be given the opportunity to collaboratively write an essay using the essay planning strategy and the essay parts reminder. The linking words list will be explained in this lesson. The teacher will work individually with the students, assisting them in establishing personal goals for writing good essays.

STUDENT OBJECTIVES

The students will verbally state the parts of the essay planning strategy STOP and the parts of the essay parts reminder DARE. The students will engage in collaborative practice, writing an essay using STOP and DARE. Using this essay and their previously written essay evaluated in Lesson 1, the students will set a goal for writing essays.

MATERIALS

One copy for each student:
- STOP and DARE mnemonic chart
- STOP and DARE Directions
- Brainstorming Sheet
- Cue Cards
- Linking Words

- Sample essays from Lessons 1 and 2
- Students' previously written essays
- Paper and pencils
- STOP and DARE Checklist
- Essay Topics

SET THE CONTEXT FOR STUDENT LEARNING

Test the students to see if they remember the planning steps and essay parts. Ask if they've been thinking about what they have learned. Have the students tell you about times they have used or thought about using STOP and DARE.

DEVELOP THE STRATEGY AND SELF-REGULATION

Step 1: **Introduce Linking Words**

- Tell the students that you will show them some words that will make their ideas go together. Give each student a list of linking words.

- Have the students retrieve the previously read sample essays from Lessons 1 and 2 and locate linking words in sample essays. Tell them to think of different or better examples of linking words.

Step 2: **Criterion Setting**

- Have the students retrieve the checklist from their folders. Explain that you will write an essay together and that this essay will be put on the checklist.

 Say, *"Before we start on the essay, we want to set a goal for ourselves. Remember, we will use everything we have learned to help us. What will our goal be?"*

- Look at the students' checklists. Set the goal as having all four parts, plus more than three ideas. Talk with the students about what they think is reasonable. *Hint:* Set the collaborative goal to be appropriate for the middle student in your class.

Step 3: Collaborative Practice

- Explain that planning and composing one essay will be completed together. Get out the essay topics, mnemonic chart, directions, cue cards, and brainstorming sheet.

- As a group, select one topic quickly.

 Ask the students, *"What is the first thing you have to say to yourself?"* They should answer, "Plan my essay," or an equivalent response.

- Say, *"Now we start the steps. What is Step 1 in STOP?"* The students should say, "Suspend Judgment."

- Ask, *"How do we suspend judgment?"* The students should say, "Brainstorm ideas for and against the topic." Get each student to brainstorm one idea. Write ideas on the brainstorming sheet. Direct the students through the cue cards for this step. Make sure that each student reads his or her own set of cards as you go.

- Ask, *"What is Step 2 in STOP?"* The students should say, "Take a Side." You will lead discussion here, gaining group consensus for the side they will take. If the students disagree, you decide and tell them that they will get a chance to write their own essay next time from the other point of view then.

- Ask, *"What is Step 3 in STOP?"* The students should say, "Organize Ideas." Again, lead the discussion, selecting strong ideas for the selected point of view and one or two arguments. Direct the students to use the cue cards. Ask the students to suggest an order, allowing each student to give you an order first, and then you select best order. Remind them of the map analogy by saying, "Deciding the order will help lead the reader to agree with our point of view." Also stress the logic behind the order (i.e., not jumping back and forth).

- Ask, *"What is Step 4 in STOP?"* The students should say, "Plan More as You Write." Read the cue card with DARE and tell the students to keep this card in front of them as they compose. Tell the students that they will take turns thinking of sentences for the essay. Ask for a volunteer for the first sentence. If the student doesn't create a topic sentence, refer to the D in DARE, and then prompt him or her to create a topic sentence. Continue generating sentences, referring to DARE and linking words.

Step 4: Review Essay and Chart Performance

Have each student fill in a checklist. Note that this essay is better than their previously written essay examined in Lesson 1. Compare the two essays. If needed, discuss whether the students' goals were appropriate (i.e., if they set the goal too high, a new goal should be set).

Step 5: Verbal Rehearsal

 Say, *"We will memorize the cue cards along with the planning steps and essay parts."*

- To help the students memorize the planning steps and essay parts, teach them an exercise called *rapid fire*. This is called *rapid fire* because the steps are to be named as rapidly as possibly. Tell the students that they may look at the chart or cue cards if they need to, but they shouldn't rely on them too much because the cards will be put away after several rounds of rapid fire. Allow the students to paraphrase but be sure that intended meaning is maintained.

- Do rapid fire with planning steps, adding appropriate cue cards as they occur. If the response is correct, make a brief positive comment; if it is incorrect, prompt the student by pointing to the information.

- Do rapid fire without cues. If a student does not know a step, you should provide it.

- After rapid fire, explain to the students that they must be able to name all the steps, cue cards, and essay parts in an oral quiz. Give them time to rehearse.

- When the students indicate that they have learned the steps, ask them to recite them orally, including information from the cue cards. Describe the information the students have omitted or named out of sequence.

WRAP-UP

Remind the students that you will check to see if they can remember on their own the essay planning strategy (STOP) and the essay parts reminder (DARE) at the next session.

LESSON 4

LESSON OVERVIEW

The students will practice writing an essay independently using STOP and DARE. It is crucial that the teacher provide continuous feedback during the writing process.

STUDENT OBJECTIVES

The students will verbally state the parts of the essay planning strategy STOP and the parts of a good essay as in DARE. The students will independently practice writing an essay using STOP and DARE. Using their individual previously written essay, the students will set a goal for writing the essay.

MATERIALS

One copy for each student:
- STOP and DARE mnemonic chart
- STOP and DARE Directions
- Brainstorming Sheet
- Cue Cards

- Linking Words
- Students' previously written essay
- Essay Topics
- Paper and pencils

SET THE CONTEXT FOR STUDENT LEARNING

Using the rapid fire method, test the students to see if they remember the planning steps and essay parts. Ask if they've been thinking about what they've learned. Have the students tell you about times they have used or thought about using STOP and DARE.

DEVELOP THE STRATEGY AND SELF-REGULATION

Step 1: Criterion Setting

Set goals with the students individually for two or three times the initial level of their previously written essays. Be sure to include all four parts and the understanding that the essay must make sense.

Step 2: Independent Practice with Feedback

- Give each student two essay topics and a brainstorming sheet.

- Tell the students to use their cue cards, list of linking words, directions, and chart when they are planning.

- Make sure the students plan before composing. Provide assistance only when a student skips a step or does it incorrectly. You may need to help the students whose order can lead to an illogical essay. Encourage them to use at least one word from the list of linking words if they fail to do so on their own.

Step 3: Review Essay and Graph

- After each student finishes, review each essay as a group. Have the students read their essays aloud; identify the parts, pointing out elaborations as well as the topic sentence, reasons, arguments, and conclusion, if they are present.

- If any parts are missing, discuss how and where they could be added. Completely review one essay before going on to the next. The students should help each other think of parts that are better or to make the order better for next time.

- Have each student fill in a checklist. Note that they reached their goal if they have done so.

- Discuss the goal for next time, which will be to use all four essay parts and two to three times more parts than on essays written before learning STOP and DARE.

WRAP-UP

Remind the students that you will check to see if they can remember on their own the essay planning strategy (STOP) and the essay parts reminder (DARE) at the next session.

LESSON 5

LESSON OVERVIEW

The students will learn to create their own brainstorming sheets in this lesson. By this lesson, the students should set goals for writing and composing essays independently.

STUDENT OBJECTIVES

The students will verbally state the part of the essay planning strategy STOP and the parts of a good essay as in DARE. The students will create a brainstorming sheet for writing the essay and will independently write an essay using STOP and DARE. The students will set a goal for writing an essay.

MATERIALS

One copy for each student:
- STOP and DARE mnemonic chart
- STOP and DARE Directions
- Cue Cards

- Linking Words
- Students' previously written essays
- Essay Topics
- Paper and pencils

SET THE CONTEXT FOR STUDENT LEARNING

Using the rapid fire method, test the students to see if they remember the planning steps and essay parts. Ask if they've been thinking about what they've learned. Have the students tell you about times they have used or thought about using STOP and DARE. Tell them they will learn a way to use the strategy without the brainstorming sheet. Be sure to emphasize that by planning themselves, they can use STOP and DARE any time they want to write a good essay.

DEVELOP THE STRATEGY AND SELF-REGULATION

Step 1: Create a Brainstorming Plan Sheet

- Show the students how to create their own planning brainstorming sheet by taking paper, writing STOP at top, drawing a vertical line down the page, and writing DARE at the bottom. Model how to cross out letters in each word as they complete the steps.

- Briefly model a plan for an essay with a topic that the students had used during collaborative practice or independent practice. Do this quickly, but emphasize the steps that the students haven't yet mastered, such as making the order of ideas logical. If they have been doing this well, model a different organization than they have been using.

Step 2: Goal Setting

Set goals with the students individually for two or three more parts as in previously written essay, and include all four parts of DARE without using the brainstorming sheet.

Step 3: Independent Practice with Feedback

- Give each student two essay topics. Tell the students that they will need to make and write their own brainstorming sheet. Remind the students to use a new piece of paper for writing their essay. Make sure they plan before composing. Be sure to check each student's plan! Provide assistance only when a student skips a step or does it incorrectly.

• Tell the students they can use their list of linking words if they want or need to.

Step 4: Review Essays and Graph

• When the students have finished working, review each essay as a group. Have the students read their own essays aloud; identify the parts, pointing out elaborations as well as the topic sentence, reasons, arguments, and conclusion, if they are present.

• If any parts are missing, discuss how and where they could be added.

• Have each student fill in the checklist. Note that they reached their goal if they have done so.

WRAP-UP

The students should repeat Lesson 5 until they reach a criterion performance of two or three times as many essay parts as in their previously written essays.

STOP

Suspend Judgment

Take a Side

Organize Ideas

Plan More as You Write

- Did I list ideas for each side?
- Can I think of anything else? Try to write more.
- Another point I haven't considered yet is . . .
- Put a star next to ideas you want to use.
- Put an X next to arguments you want to dispute.
- Number your ideas in the order you will use them.

DARE

Develop Your Topic Sentence

Add Supporting Ideas

Reject Arguments for the Other Side

End with a Conclusion

STOP and DARE Directions

1. **S**uspend Judgment

Consider each side before taking a position. Brainstorm ideas for and against the topic. When you can't think of more ideas, see the first three cue cards:
   - (a) Did I list ideas for each side? If not, do this now;
   - (b) Can I think of anything else? Try to write more ideas; and
   - (c) Another point I haven't considered yet is . . .

2. **T**ake a Side

Read your ideas. Decide which side you believe in or which side can be used to make the strongest argument. Place a "+" on the side that shows your position.

3. **O**rganize Ideas

Choose ideas that are strong and decide how to organize them for writing. To help you do this, see the next three cue cards:
   - (a) Put a star next to the ideas you want to use. Choose at least ____ ideas;
   - (b) Choose at least ____ argument(s) to refute; and
   - (c) Number your ideas in the order you will use them.

4. **P**lan More as You Write

Continue to plan as you write. Use all four essay parts (see the last cue card if you can't remember DARE):

   Develop Your Topic Sentence

   Add Supporting Ideas

   Reject Arguments for the Other Side

   End with a Conclusion

STOP and DARE Checklist

Suspend Judgment Did I list ideas for both sides?						
Can I think of anything else? Try to write more.						
Another point I haven't yet considered is . . . Think of possible arguments.						
Take a Side Place a "+" at the top of one box to show the side you will take in your essay.						
Organize Ideas Put a star next to ideas you want to use. Choose at least _____ ideas that you will use.						
Plan More as You Write						
Use DARE						
Develop Your Topic Sentence						
Add Supporting Ideas						
Reject Arguments for the Other Side						
End with a Conclusion						

Brainstorming Sheet

Suspend Judgment. Brainstorm ideas for and against the topic.

_____ (for)	_____ (against)
1.	1.
2.	2.
3.	3.
4.	4.
5.	5.
6.	6.
7.	7.

Take a Side. Place a "+" at the top of the box that shows the side you will take.

Organize Ideas. Decide which ideas are strong and which ideas you can dispute.

Plan More as You Write. Remember to use all four essay parts and continue planning.

Now write your essay on another piece of paper.

Linking Words

First
Second
Third
Fourth
Fifth

Another
One more
Also
Additionally
Furthermore
Likewise
Besides
Still
In fact

Cue Cards

STOP · STEP 1 · Suspend Judgment

Cue Card #1

Did I list ideas for both sides?
If not, do this now.

STOP · STEP 1 · Suspend Judgment

Cue Card #2

Can I think of anything else?
Try to write more.

STOP · STEP 1 · Suspend Judgment

Cue Card #3

Another point I haven't yet considered is... Think of possible arguments.

STOP · STEP 2 · Take a Side

Cue Card #4

Place a "+" at the top of one box to show the side you will take in your essay.

STOP · STEP 3 · Organize Ideas

Cue Card #5

Put a star next to ideas you want to use.
Choose at least ____ ideas that you will use.

STOP · STEP 3 · Organize Ideas

Cue Card #6

Did I star ideas on both sides?
Choose at least ____ argument(s) that you can dispute.

STOP · STEP 3 · Organize Ideas

Cue Card #7

Number your ideas in the order you will use them.

DARE · STEP 4 · Plan More as You Write

Cue Card #8

Develop your topic sentence.
Add supporting ideas.
Reject possible arguments.
End with a conclusion.

Essay Topics

1. Do you think children should have to go to school in the summer?

2. Do you think teachers should give students homework?

3. Are school rules necessary?

4. Do you think children should be required to clean their rooms?

5. Do you think children should be allowed to pick which movies they can see?

6. Do you think parents should decide who their children's friends should be?

7. Do you think children should be allowed to eat whatever they want?

8. Do you think children should be allowed to have their own pets?

9. Should parents give their children money for getting good grades on their report cards?

10. Do you think children should be allowed to choose their own bedtime?

11. Do you think the school day should be shorter?

12. Should students be able to choose the subjects they study in school?

13. Should children be punished when they do something wrong?

14. Do you think children should be allowed to choose which television shows they can watch?

15. Is it better to be an only child or to have brothers and sisters?

16. Should children be required to learn how to use computers?

17. Should parents coach their children's sports teams?

18. Do you think children your age should be allowed to go to the mall alone?

19. Should boys and girls be taught in separate classes in school?

20. Do you think sports stars should be treated as heroes?

21. Do you think children your age should be able to vote?

22. Should children your age be allowed to have paying jobs after school?

23. Should children give some of their toys to children who do not have toys?

24. Should students be required to wear uniforms at school?

25. Should students be graded on their schoolwork?

I Transferred My Strategy	I Helped My Partner

My Self-Statements

To think of good ideas:

_____
_____
_____
_____
_____
_____

While I work:

_____
_____
_____
_____
_____

To check my work:

_____
_____
_____
_____
_____
_____

STOP and **DARE**   **STOP** and **DARE**

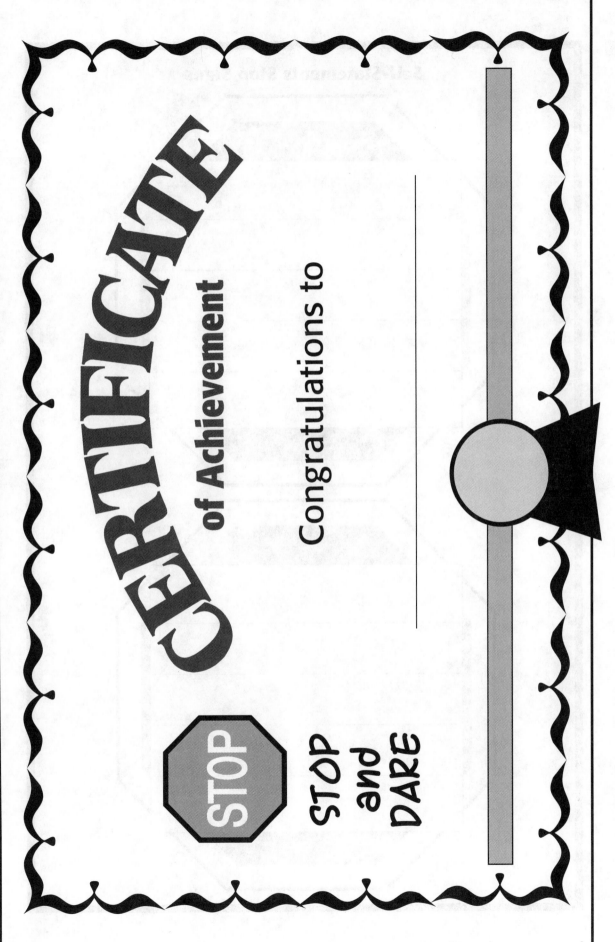

CERTIFICATE

of Achievement

Congratulations to

STOP

STOP
and
DARE

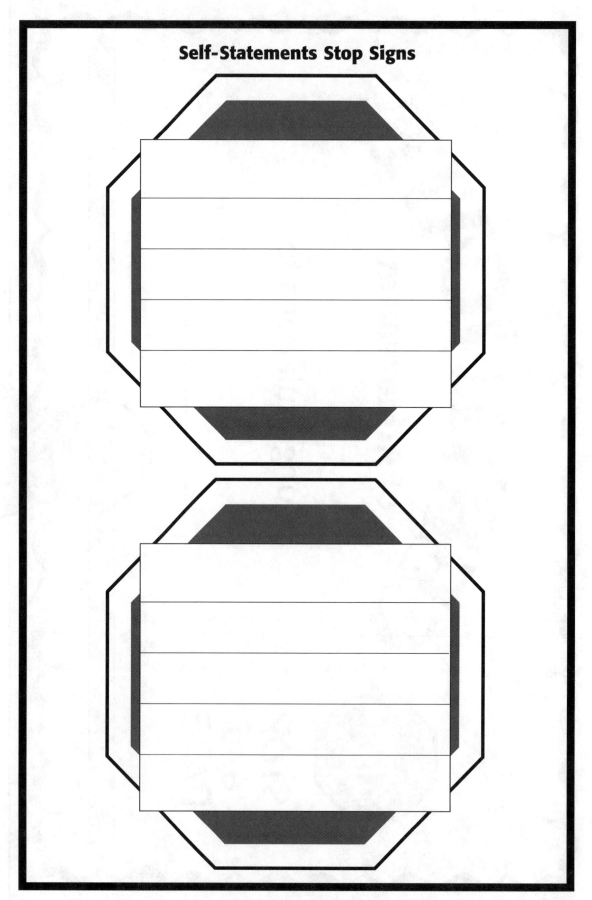

Self-Statements Stop Signs

STOP
and
DARE

Chapter 10

Report Writing

MATERIALS
Report Writing Strategy
Report Writing Web

LESSON 1

NOTE: Skills for brainstorming, webbing, reading to locate information, interviewing, and conceptualizing and categorizing information as main ideas and details should be taught prior to introducing the students to Report Writing.

NOTE: This chapter is significantly different from the other chapters in this book. The Report Writing strategy was developed for teachers who already had experience using the SRSD instructional approach, and thus the Lesson Plans are not detailed in terms of the method of instruction. Therefore, we encourage teachers to either use another strategy before attempting this one or to at least carefully read a chapter (e.g., Chapter 8, POW + TREE) that gives detailed Lesson Plans for how to conduct the instruction. In addition, we note that PLAN & WRITE (Chapter 16) is most appropriate for informational text with an explicit text structure, while TWA + PLANS (Chapter 17) is more appropriate for teaching students how to pull information out of text.

LESSON OVERVIEW

The teacher will introduce the Report Writing Strategy parts in this lesson. Collaboratively, the teacher and students will brainstorm, discuss, and list the parts of a well-written report. The teacher will describe the Report Writing Strategy steps.

STUDENT OBJECTIVES

The students will orally state the parts of the Report Writing Strategy.

MATERIALS

One copy for each student:
- Transparencies and handouts:
  - Report Writing Strategy chart
  - Report Writing Web

- Paper and pencils

SET THE CONTEXT FOR STUDENT LEARNING

Introduce the Report Writing Strategy. This introduction to the strategy emphasizes what makes a good report. Explain to the students that for this writing class, they will learn how to compose good reports. Good writers plan before they write. Good reports have many parts.

DEVELOP THE STRATEGY AND SELF-REGULATION

Step 1: Describe and Discuss Brainstorming

Uncover the first step on the Report Writing Strategy chart. Tell the students that the first thing they will need to do is to *brainstorm.* Then they will write a list of what they already know about their report topic and at least five things they would like to know about it.

Step 2: Describe and Discuss Organizing Information

- Uncover the second step on the Report Writing Strategy chart.

- Show the students the Report Writing Web. Tell the students that they will use this web to start organizing information for their report. Discuss how ideas will be organized into main ideas and details on the web. Provide examples.

Step 3: **Describe and Discuss Gathering New Information and Revising**

- Uncover the third step on the Report Writing Strategy chart.

Tell the students that they will now be gathering information about the topic. This part of information gathering can take several class periods. Tell the students how much time you will allot for information gathering. Say, *"You will need to ask yourself three questions during information gathering."*

1. What do I want to know?

2. What is the main point of this section?

3. Is this information on my web?

Step 4: **Describe and Discuss Using the Web as You Write**

- Uncover the fourth step on the Report Writing Strategy chart.

- Say, *"Once your map is complete, you will number the sections in the order that you want to write. You will then begin to write your report."*

Step 5: **Describe and Discuss Continuing to Plan as You Write**

- Uncover the fifth step on the Report Writing Strategy chart.

- Tell the students that they can continue to plan and look for information while writing.

Step 6: **Describe and Discuss Checking the Web**

- Uncover the sixth step on the Report Writing Strategy chart.

- Tell the students that the last thing you will do is go back to your web and place a check mark next to each section that is written in the report.

WRAP-UP

Give each student a copy of the Report Writing Strategy chart and the Report Writing Web.

REMAINING LESSONS

Report Writing is a complex task, and it will often take many weeks to write one report. This lesson can be extended in the following ways:

1. Reteach skills such as brainstorming, webbing, reading to locate information, interviewing, and conceptualizing and categorizing information as main ideas and details as needed.

2. Have the students read a *model* report and identify its attributes.

3. Model how to use the strategy, and be sure to include the students in all steps.

4. Write a collaborative class report.

5. Have the students work in pairs to write a report.

Report Writing Strategy

- Brainstorm what you know and what you want to learn

- Organize your information on a web

- Gather new information and revise your web

- Use the web as you write

- Keep planning as you write

Report Writing Web

Web of What I Know and What I Want to Learn

Chapter 11

PLANS

P = Pick Goals

L = List Ways to Meet Goals

A = And

N = Make Notes

S = Sequence Notes

MATERIALS
Learning Strategies Contract
PLANS Mnemonic Chart
PLANS Worksheet
PLANS Goals Chart
PLANS Cue Cards
My Self-Statements
PLANS Rehearsal Checklist
PLANS Certificate
Self-Statements Bull's-Eyes

LESSON 1

LESSON OVERVIEW

The students and teachers will discuss current performance in writing an essay and/or story. Individual student goals will be established for improved writing performance. The teacher will explain that writing performance can be improved by learning a strategy.

STUDENT OBJECTIVES

The students will commit to improving writing performance by signing the Learning Strategies Contract.

MATERIALS

One copy for each student:
- Student folders
- Learning Strategies Contract
- PLANS mnemonic chart

- Students' previously written essays and/or stories
- Paper and pencils

SET THE CONTEXT FOR STUDENT LEARNING

Give each student a Learning Strategies Contract. Explain that you are going to help them learn a strategy for improving their writing. Establish a criterion for student performance. For example, if the students have written stories, brainstorm together how many parts a story should include to be considered a *good* story.

DEVELOP THE STRATEGY AND SELF-REGULATION

Step 1: Review Current Writing Performance

Ask, *"Do you remember the story/essay you wrote the other day that asked _____?"*

- Ask the students to read their stories/essays and see which parts from previously established criteria they have included.

- Collaboratively with the students, note in a matter-of-fact way which parts they have and which parts are missing. Also note that even parts that are included can be improved next time. For example, in a persuasive essay, including more reasons, good reasons, and believable reasons can make the essay more convincing.

- Have the students count the number of words they wrote. Ask if they could have written more words. Ask, *"Was there more that you could have told the reader?"*

Step 2: Establish a Goal to Learn the Strategy

- Tell the students that you will teach them a procedure to help them write better essays, stories, descriptions, and so forth. Tell the students that although you will practice the procedure with only one form of writing now (persuasive essays), the procedure can be used for other forms of writing such as story writing and report writing, as well as writing to inform your friends about something.

- Given their pretest performance, ask the students to review the Learning Strategies Contract indicating their commitment to learning a strategy for writing better papers.

- The students and teacher should sign the contract.

 Say, *"Once you have completed the Learning Strategies Contract and learned to use the procedure, I will send a note home to your parents telling them what a good job you have done. Also, you will share your best essay with the principal, your teacher, and your parents, and, as we mentioned earlier, some of your papers will be shared with your friends in class."*

WRAP-UP

Ask the students to put their materials for the day in their folders. If time permits, do not do wrap-up at this point but instead go on to Lesson 2. Remember to do wrap-up at the end of the lesson. Ask yourself the following questions:

- Will any of my students' papers need modifications?

- Should I add a homework component?

- Do I want to enhance this strategy in any way?

LESSON 2

LESSON OVERVIEW
Give the students a copy of the PLANS mnemonic chart, which will be explained in detail to them. The students will begin to memorize the steps in PLANS.

STUDENT OBJECTIVES
The students will identify goals for writing essays using the PLANS strategy. They will verbally state the steps in PLANS as they begin to memorize the strategy.

MATERIALS
One copy for each student:
- Student folders
- Learning Strategies Contract
- PLANS mnemonic chart

- PLANS Worksheet
- PLANS Goals Chart
- PLANS Cue Cards
- Paper and pencils

SET THE CONTEXT FOR STUDENT LEARNING

 Ask the students if they know the meaning of the word *plan.* Discuss how planning helps improve writing. Give examples such as how planning helps the writer to organize his or her paper and to make the paper longer. Say, *"I will teach you the steps for planning and writing a paper. Although we will learn how to use the steps to write essays, you can use the steps for other types of writing as well. For example, you could use the steps to help you write stories or reports in class."*

DEVELOP THE PLANS STRATEGY AND SELF-REGULATION

Step 1: P for Pick Goals

- Give each student a PLANS mnemonic chart. They'll need to look at each step on their PLANS mnemonic chart as you talk about them.

 Cover your PLANS mnemonic chart so that only the first step shows. Say, *"The first thing you need to do when you write a paper is to figure out what you want to do. In other words, you must Pick Goals for what you want your paper to say. The goals that you set for your paper should direct what you do.*

"For example, if your teacher has given you a prompt with the question, 'Should boys and girls play sports together?' and has asked you to write a paper or an essay on what you think about that, the first thing you should do is set goals for the purpose of your paper. I might pick a goal to write a paper that will convince my friends that I am right. Can you think of any other types of goals that I might set?"

- Brainstorm ideas for goals. Say, *"As you can see, there are many types of goals that will help me write my paper. I can set goals for how much I want to say, for the types of things I want to include, for the types of words I want to use, and so on. Also, the type of goals that I pick will depend on the type of paper I am writing. Some of my goals for an essay will be different from my goals for a story. To help you pick your goals for your paper, I will give you a PLANS Goals Chart with sample goals. You are to keep this PLANS Goals Chart in your writing folder or desk, and you can use it anytime you are asked to write a paper. The goals on the PLANS Goals Chart can be used when writing essays, stories, or reports."*

- Review each of the goals on the PLANS Goals Chart. Read each goal to the students and have them orally repeat it.

- Say, *"When using the PLANS Goals Chart, we pick one goal from each section—A, B, and C."*

- Say, *"Now, let's return to our PLANS mnemonic chart. If I had to write a paper on whether boys or girls should play sports together, my first step would be to pick my goals."* Point to this on the PLANS chart. *"I would do this by looking at my PLANS Goals Chart and picking one goal from the A, B, and C sections. Then I would write my goals on a PLANS Worksheet."* Show the students the PLANS Worksheet. *"For instance, I would pick . . ."* Select "convince my friend," "essay that has all the parts," and "60 words or longer," and explain why you picked each. *"Next, I would write each of my goals down on the PLANS Worksheet so that I remember them. Then, I would put a star by the most important one (e.g., 'convince my friends'). Similarly, if you were asked to write a story about a girl on skis, which three goals would you pick?"* The students should select "fun for my friend to read," "story that has all the parts," and any under section C. If they select a goal that does not work for the prompt, ask the students to justify their selection and then explain why the response was incorrect. Ask, *"Which would be the most important goal? Fun to read."* Correct the selection, if necessary, and ask the students to justify their selection.

Step 2: L for List Ways to Meet Goals

Uncover the second step on the PLANS mnemonic chart. Say, *"Once I have written down my goals, I need to think about how I will meet or accomplish the goals. Next to each goal on the PLANS Worksheet, I would list one or more things that I can do to meet my goals. For example, if I am writing a paper on whether boys or girls should play sports together, and one of my goals is to write a paper that will convince my friends that I am right (point to goal on the PLANS Goals Chart), one way I might be able to successfully meet this goal is by examining my reasons to see if my readers might accept them. For example, if I believed that boys and girls should play sports together, and one of my reasons for supporting this belief is that girls are just as strong as boys, I would ask myself, 'Would my reader believe this?' If the answer is yes, I would keep it; if the answer is no, I would try to think of a better reason."*

Step 3: A

Point out that the A in PLANS doesn't mean anything; it is just a filler letter used to make a word (mnemonic) that will help with remembering the strategy.

Step 4: N for Make Notes

Say, *"Once I have finished picking my goals and listing ways to meet those goals, I would make notes about the kinds of things that I might use in my paper."* Uncover Step 4. *"If I were writing an essay, this might include a statement as to what I believed, possible reasons for that belief, key words I might use, and so forth. If I were writing a*

story, I might make an outline of who the characters are, where the story takes place, what happens, and how the story ends."

Step 5: S for Sequence Notes

Say, *"When I finished making all of my notes, I would think about what I wanted to come first in my paper, then second, third, and so forth."* Uncover Step 5. *"I would put a '1' by what I wanted first, a '2' by what I wanted second, a '3' by what I wanted third, and so forth."*

Step 6: Write and Say More

Say, *"Once I had finished PLANS, I would be ready to write."* Uncover Step 6. *"My notes would be my plan, and my plan would guide what I would write. However, as I write, I may think of other things to say, and I want to be sure to include them as well. To help me do this, I will remind myself to say more as I write and to remember my goals."*

Step 7: Test Goals

Uncover Step 7. Say, *"The final step is to test to see if I met my goals. To do this, I would read my paper again and check to see if I met all of the goals that I had set. For example, if I set a goal to write 60 words, I would count the number of words written, write the number next to my goal, and write Yes if I met my goal and No if I did not. For the parts of an essay, I would check to see if I included each part; if so, I would write Yes next to my goal. If I were missing parts, I would write the parts I had left out. For my goal to write a convincing paper, I would ask myself if my paper would convince my friends. If I believed that it would, I would write Yes next to my goal; otherwise, I would write No next to it. If I did not meet any of my goals, I would think about how I might meet those goals on my next writing assignment or revise this paper."*

- Work with the students on identifying or reading goals. They can paraphrase. It is important that the students can recognize each goal and can write it out in their own words.

Step 8: Practice PLANS

If time permits, tell the students that they will work on memorizing the steps for planning and writing. Give each student a set of PLANS Cue Cards. Say, *"To help you remember the steps, we will do an exercise called* rapid fire. *We will take turns saying the steps. This is called rapid fire because you are trying to name the steps as rapidly as you can. If you need to look at the cue card, you may; however, don't rely on the card too much because I will put it away after several rounds of rapid fire."* Allow the students to paraphrase, but be sure the intended meaning is maintained. Do this with and without the cue card. If the students' responses are correct, make a brief positive comment. If they are incorrect, prompt by pointing to the cue card.

WRAP-UP

- Have the students put all materials in their folders or desks.
- Remind the students that you will check to see if they remember PLANS steps and goals at the next session.

LESSON 3

LESSON OVERVIEW

The teacher will model the PLANS steps for writing an essay, which include the use of detailed self-statements. A detailed script for modeling has been provided in the lesson plan. After the teacher has modeled the steps, the students will develop personal self-statements to help them when using the strategy.

STUDENT OBJECTIVES

The students will attend to the teacher's modeled lesson. The students will write personal self-statements. The students will verbally state the parts of the PLANS strategy.

MATERIALS

One copy for each student:
- Student folders
- Learning Strategies Contract
- PLANS mnemonic chart
- PLANS Worksheet

- PLANS Goals Chart
- PLANS Cue Cards
- PLANS Self-Statements sheet
- Paper and pencils

SET THE CONTEXT FOR STUDENT LEARNING

Test the students to see if they remember the steps. Have them write down the steps on a piece of paper. Prompt them as necessary. Ask the students to tell you what each step means. Ask them to read each goal on the PLANS Goals Chart. Help as necessary.

DEVELOP THE STRATEGY AND SELF-REGULATION

Step 1: Introduce Modeling

 Say, *"Today, I will show you how to use PLANS to write a good essay. Please remember that we could use the PLANS for other types of writing, too, like stories."*

- Say, *"As I show you how to use PLANS to write an essay, I will talk aloud. The things we say to ourselves while we work are very helpful."*

- Model the entire process using the PLANS steps. Use problem definition, planning, self-evaluation, and self-reinforcement self-statements as you model the procedure. Give the students the sentence, "Should boys and girls play sports together?" on a card. Also, have a copy of the same card in front of you. Display your PLANS mnemonic chart so that the students can see it and you can point to each step as you initiate it. Follow the steps and statements provided, contributing ad lib statements where indicated or necessary. Say, *"What do I have to do? I have to write an essay about 'Should boys and girls play sports together?' First, I will do PLANS."* Point to this on the sheet.

Step 2: PLANS

Say, *"To help me do PLANS, I will write the steps on this piece of paper. This will help me remember each step of PLANS. Also, I will use the PLANS Worksheet when I write my goals, when I decide the ways to meet my goals, and when I make my notes. Now that I have written PLANS on my paper, I will do the first step of PLANS, which is Pick my goals. I will pick one goal from each section."* Point to each section on the PLANS Goals Chart. *"As I pick a goal, I will write it in abbreviated form at the top of my paper, and I will leave a little space in between each one so I can* List *ways to meet goals.*

"I have to write a paper on 'Should boys and girls play sports together?' I want to be sure that I pick goals that will be right for this type of paper. This paper will be an essay.

"First, I will read all of the goals under A. Now I have to select a goal for my paper. Which goal should I select? I should select the goal: 'I will convince my friends.'" Write this down. *"I am selecting this goal because I will be writing an essay, and essays are used by writers to convince others that they are right. I am going to write an essay that will convince my friends that I am right. I want to be sure my essay will be convincing."* Repeat this procedure with the goals under B. You must, however, select the wrong goal—the one for a story. Model how to correct yourself and then self-reinforce; write the correct goal under goal from A. Be sure to leave some space between them. Finally, be sure that you point out why it is important to include all of the parts such as the topic sentence, so that the reader will know what you believe; the reasons, so that the reader will know why you believe it; and the conclusion, so that you can wrap up your paper.

Repeat procedures for section C. Say, *"Now I need to select a goal for how long my paper will be."* Read all of the goals. *"My last paper was 42 words long. I would like to write a longer paper this time. Which goal should I select?"* If a student picks 100 words, moderate that by saying, *"Let's try 60 or 80. That is more than we wrote last time. If I write a longer essay, I will be able to say more."* Write down the goal: I will write a longer paper. *"Good, I have selected three very good goals that will help me write a better essay. These goals will guide what I do. I will write an essay that will convince my friends that what I believe is right, that will have all the parts, and that will be _____ words long. Which of these three goals is the most important? That's right, the first one: to convince my friends, that what I believe is right. Let's put a star by it to remind us that this is the most important goal. Great, I've done a good job."*

Say, *"Now that I have written my goals, I need to list ways to meet them."* Point to the step and say, *"For each goal, I list at least one way to meet that goal."* Listing is done in note form. *"My first goal is to convince my friends that what I believe is right. What are some things that I can do to meet this goal? One thing that I can do is be sure that I give good reasons for what I believe. How can I be sure that my reasons are good? I can test each reason I write.*

"When making notes, I can ask myself, 'Will my friends buy this reason?' If not, I won't use that reason. So, one way I can meet my first goal is to test my reasons." Write this next to the goal. *"Let me ask you a question: Which do you think would be a better essay—a paper with one good reason or a paper with five good reasons? Yes, a paper with five good reasons would be better."* Next to the goal, write Try to think of five good reasons. *"Great, we have thought of some good ways to help us meet our first goal."*

Point to the second goal. Say, *"Let's think of some ways to meet our second goal. Can you think of any ways that I can be sure my essay has all the parts?"* Use any viable recommendation the students offer and reinforce. Be sure that you select one way each part is an included in notes and papers. This can be checked by using an essay mnemonic chart (e.g., the POW + TREE mnemonic chart in Chapter 8).

Point to the third goal. Say, *"We need to think about how we will meet our third goal, which is to write a paper _____ words long. Can you think of any ways that I can be sure that my paper is _____ words long?"* Use any viable recommendations the students offer. Be sure that includes *count words* and *add more detail to his paper* (e.g., examples, explanations). *"Great, we have done a good job of thinking of ways to meet our goals."*

Say, *"I need to make some notes for what my paper will say. When making my notes, I want to remember my goals. I will want to first think about what I believe—Should boys and girls play sports together?—and think of good reasons and a good conclusion."* Model the process of writing down notes, using strategies, and using self-statements. *"When thinking of reasons, be sure to say to yourself 'Let my mind be free. Good ideas will come to me. I first need to take my time.'"*

Say, *"I now need to sequence my notes, which means I must decide what will come first, second, third, and so forth. What do you think should come first? Yes, what I believe."* Put a circled "1" next to that note. Continue sequencing until you are finished. Make corrections and reinforce yourself.

Step 3: Model How to Write the Paper

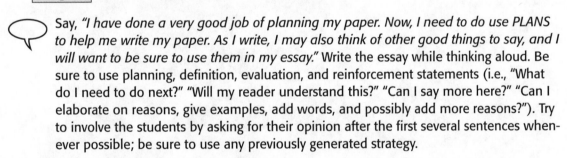

Say, *"I have done a very good job of planning my paper. Now, I need to do use PLANS to help me write my paper. As I write, I may also think of other good things to say, and I will want to be sure to use them in my essay."* Write the essay while thinking aloud. Be sure to use planning, definition, evaluation, and reinforcement statements (i.e., "What do I need to do next?" "Will my reader understand this?" "Can I say more here?" "Can I elaborate on reasons, give examples, add words, and possibly add more reasons?"). Try to involve the students by asking for their opinion after the first several sentences whenever possible; be sure to use any previously generated strategy.

Step 4: Test Goals

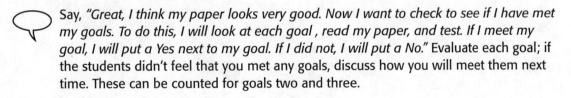

Say, *"Great, I think my paper looks very good. Now I want to check to see if I have met my goals. To do this, I will look at each goal, read my paper, and test. If I meet my goal, I will put a Yes next to my goal. If I did not, I will put a No."* Evaluate each goal; if the students didn't feel that you met any goals, discuss how you will meet them next time. These can be counted for goals two and three.

- Ask the students if they have any questions.

Step 5: Self-Statements

Say, *"When I showed you how to use PLANS to write a paper, I talked aloud. The things I said to myself helped me write a better essay. For example, when I was trying to think of reasons, what did I say to help me? That's right. I told myself to 'take my time' and*

'to let my mind be free.' These things helped me think of ideas." Record these on a PLANS Self-Statements Sheet.

- Say, *"Can you think of other things that you might say to yourself that would help you write better papers?"* Try to get self-statements related to definition, planning, evaluation, and reinforcement. If the students give you negative ideas or statements (i.e., "I'm not good at thinking of reasons."), briefly discuss how some things we say to ourselves can get in our way. Record the students' self-statements on a self-statements sheet. Be sure to include "Let my mind be free" and "Take my time." Put the self-statements in the students' own words.

- Say, *"We don't have to say these things aloud; once we learn them, we can think them in our heads or whisper to ourselves."*

WRAP-UP

- Have the students put all of their work in their folders or desks.

- Remind the students that you will test them for memorization of the three steps and goals.

- Ask the students to think about what they say to themselves and how they say it can help them learn.

PLANS

LESSON OVERVIEW

It is important that the students memorize the strategy at this point. This lesson focuses on practicing the strategy until the students can fluently recite the steps.

STUDENT OBJECTIVES

The students will record their performance in memorizing PLANS on a PLANS Rehearsal Checklist.

┌─ **MATERIALS** ──┐

One copy for each student:
- Student folders
- Learning Strategies Contract
- PLANS mnemonic chart
- PLANS Worksheet

- PLANS Goals Chart
- PLANS Cue Cards
- PLANS Self-Statements sheet
- PLANS Rehearsal Checklist
- Paper and pencils

└──┘

SET THE CONTEXT FOR STUDENT LEARNING

Ask the students if they have been thinking about how the things they say to themselves can help them to work. Briefly discuss any times they have used self-statements in class.

DEVELOP THE STRATEGY AND SELF-REGULATION

Step 1: Rapid-Fire Practice

Say, *"Today you are going to memorize the PLANS steps. If you know these steps, you will be able to tell yourself what to do when you write. To help you memorize PLANS, we will do an exercise called rapid fire. We will take turns saying the steps. You will then take turns with a partner saying the steps. This is called rapid fire because you are trying to name the steps as rapidly as you can. You may look at the PLANS Cue Cards if you need to, but don't rely on the card too much because I'm going to put it away after several rounds of rapid fire."* Allow the students to paraphrase but be sure that the intended meaning is maintained.

- Do rapid fire with the PLANS Cue Cards. If a student's response is correct, make a brief positive comment; if it is incorrect, prompt the student by pointing to the step on the cue card.

- Do rapid fire without the PLANS Cue Cards. If a student does not know a step, you can provide it.

- After verbal rehearsal, explain to the students that they must be able to name all the steps in an oral quiz. Give them time to rehearse steps. They can use the PLANS Cue Cards.

- When the students indicated that they have learned the steps, ask them to list the steps orally. Record their performance on the PLANS Rehearsal Checklist. Show each student his or her performance. Describe the steps the student has omitted or named out of sequence. Continue to do this until all of the students can name all steps with no assistance twice in a row.

Step 2: Review and Practice Goals

Have the students get out their PLANS Goals Chart and make sure they can read or paraphrase each goal; practice as necessary.

Step 3: Review Self-Statements

Have the students get out their PLANS Self-Statements sheet. Briefly review the types of things they can say to themselves.

WRAP-UP

Remind the students that you will test them to see if they remember the PLANS steps at the next session.

LESSON 5

LESSON OVERVIEW
The students will have the opportunity to practice the steps in PLANS collaboratively with the teacher.

STUDENT OBJECTIVES
The students, along with the teacher, will collaboratively write an essay.

MATERIALS

One copy for each student:
- Student folders
- Learning Strategies Contract
- PLANS mnemonic chart
- PLANS Worksheet

- PLANS Goals Chart
- PLANS Cue Cards
- PLANS Self-Statements sheet
- PLANS Rehearsal Checklist
- Paper and pencils

SET THE CONTEXT FOR STUDENT LEARNING

Ask the students to verbally rehearse the steps for PLANS. Let them know that this is a test. Record their performance on the PLANS Rehearsal Checklist. If their performance is below 100% on any of the procedures, return to practice procedures in Lesson 4. Do not go to controlled practice until the students meet 100% mastery. Ask the students to read the goals and practice as necessary.

DEVELOP THE STRATEGY AND SELF-REGULATION

Step 1: Collaborative Writing

Say, *"For the next several days, you will practice using PLANS to write essays."*

- Have the students get out their PLANS mnemonic chart, Worksheet, and Self-Statements sheets. Also, have them take out the PLANS Goals Chart. Give each student a card with one writing topic (see essay prompts in Chapter 9). Read the card to the student.

- Tell the students that together you will write an essay using PLANS.

- Collaboratively, develop an essay using PLANS; let the students do as much of the work as possible.

WRAP-UP

- Tell the students that you will review their performance in writing the essay with them the next time.

- Have the students put all work in their folders or desks.

LESSON 6

LESSON OVERVIEW

The students will begin to write essays or stories independently. The teacher will provide as much support as necessary for student success.

STUDENT OBJECTIVES

The students will write an essay or story using PLANS.

MATERIALS

One copy for each student:
- Student folders
- Learning Strategies Contract
- PLANS mnemonic chart
- PLANS Worksheet

- PLANS Goals Chart
- PLANS Cue Cards
- PLANS Self-Statements sheet
- PLANS Rehearsal Checklist
- Paper and pencils

SET THE CONTEXT FOR STUDENT LEARNING

Ask the students to recite the steps in PLANS. Describe the students' performance on the essay they wrote in the previous session. Describe this in same terms you used in Lesson 1.

DEVELOP THE STRATEGY AND SELF-REGULATION

Step 1: Guided Practice

Say, *"Today you will practice using the PLANS steps. You will be writing an essay."*

- Give the students a sentence prompt for an essay.

- Say, *"I want you to write this essay using PLANS. If you need to look at the cue cards, you may, but rely on them only when you need to. I will be here to make sure that you use the procedures correctly and to provide help when you need it."*

- Direct the students to begin practice. Prompt and provide as much assistance as necessary (e.g., "What is the first step?"). When you provide corrective feedback

   1. Tell the student what he or she has done incorrectly.

   2. Have the student correct the work.

   3. Be positive and encouraging.

WRAP-UP

Tell the students that you will review their performance in writing the essay with them during the next session. Decide if the students need another day of controlled practice. If they do, repeat Lesson 6. If the students are able to use the procedures independently, go to Lesson 7. This determination is based upon amount of assistance needed and the quality of the essay. If a student needs virtually no assistance and his or her essay has all the parts, he or she is ready for final lesson.

LESSON 7

LESSON OVERVIEW

The teacher will foster generalization and maintenance of strategy use.

STUDENT OBJECTIVES

The students will brainstorm ways in which they can use the PLANS strategy to improve writing.

MATERIALS

- Learning Strategies Contract
- Student folders
- Paper and pencils

SET THE CONTEXT FOR STUDENT LEARNING

Ask the students to tell you steps in PLANS. Describe each student's performance on the essay in same manner as in Lesson 6.

DEVELOP THE STRATEGY AND SELF-REGULATION

Say, *"You have done a good job of learning how to use PLANS to help you write papers. This means you have a tool for helping you write papers, and such a tool is like money in the bank. However, if you keep this procedure stored away in your brain and do not use it, it will never help you write better."*

- Say, *"Obviously, you can use this procedure to help you write essays. You can also use PLANS to help you with other types of writing in your classroom."*

- Collaboratively, brainstorm and discuss how the students could use the procedure in writing stories or reports. Ask them how they could use it with classroom assignments. Prompt as necessary. Be sure that they understand that when writing stories or reports, they should use all three steps but pick different goals. Discuss which goals would be appropriate for stories and which would work for reports.

- Collaboratively, brainstorm and discuss types of writing assignments you would not use, such as writing notes.

WRAP-UP

Tell the students that they have done an excellent job learning the procedures. Make sure that each student has all of his or her material. Complete the contract and tell them you will be giving them a note to take home to their parents telling them what a good job they have done. Also, tell them you will be picking an essay to share with the principal, their teachers, and their parents. You may give them a book that contains all of their essays.

Learning Strategies Contract

STRATEGY _____

Student _____ Date _____

Teacher _____

Target Completion Date _____

Goal_____

_____

_____

_____

How to meet this goal_____

_____

_____

_____

Signatures:

Student _____

Teacher _____

- -

_____ has successfully completed

instructions in the _____ Strategy and

agrees to use it in _____

_____

_____

Date _____

Student _____

Teacher _____

PLANS

1. Do **P** Pick Goals

   L List Ways to
   Meet Goals

   A And

   N Make Notes

   S Sequence Notes

2. Write and Say More

3. Test Goals

PLANS Worksheet

PICK GOALS:

1.   2.   3.

LIST WAYS TO MEET GOALS:

1.   2.   3.

AND, MAKE **N**OTES (on your own paper):

SEQUENCE NOTES (on your own paper):

PLANS Goals Chart

A. _____ Write a paper that will *convince* my friends that I am right.

_____ Write a paper that will be *fun* for my friends to read.

_____ Write a paper that will *teach* my friends something new.

B. _____ Write an essay that has all the parts.

_____ Write a story that has all the parts.

_____ Write a report that has all the parts.

C. _____ Write a paper that is 40 words or longer.

_____ Write a paper that is 60 words or longer.

_____ Write a paper that is 80 words or longer.

_____ Write a paper that is 100 words or longer.

PLANS Cue Cards

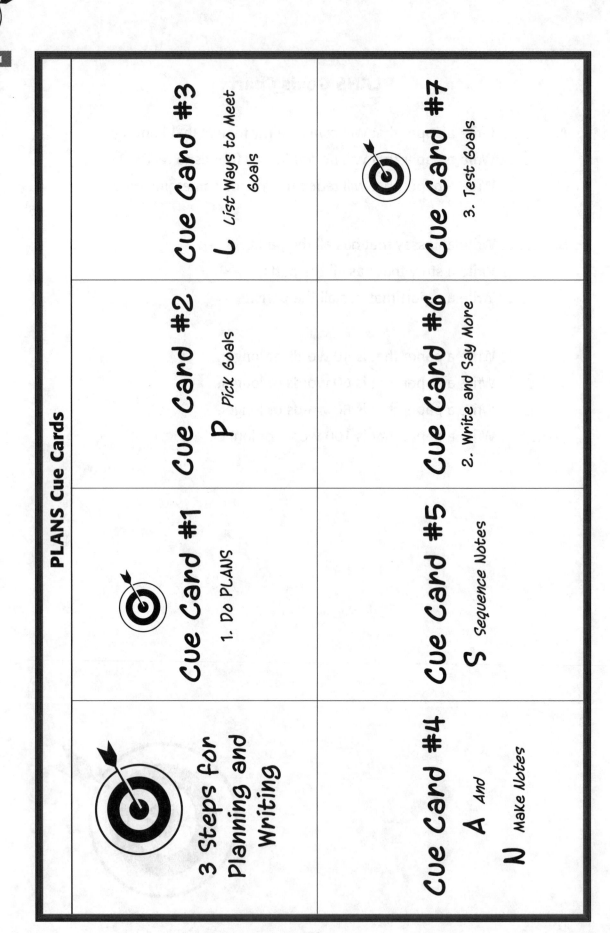

3 Steps for Planning and Writing

Cue Card #1

1. Do PLANS

Cue Card #2

P Pick Goals

Cue Card #3

L List Ways to Meet Goals

Cue Card #4

A And

N Make Notes

Cue Card #5

S Sequence Notes

Cue Card #6

2. Write and Say More

Cue Card #7

3. Test Goals

My Self-Statements

To think of good ideas:

_____
_____
_____
_____
_____
_____

While I work:

_____
_____
_____
_____
_____
_____

To check my work:

_____
_____
_____
_____
_____
_____

PLANS Rehearsal Checklist

Student's Name: _____

	Attempts	1	2	3	4	5	6
1. Do *P Pick* Goals		__	__	__	__	__	__
L List Ways to Meet Goals		__	__	__	__	__	__
A And							
N Make *Notes*		__	__	__	__	__	__
S Sequence Notes		__	__	__	__	__	__
2. *Write* and *Say More*		__	__	__	__	__	__
3. *Test Goals*		__	__	__	__	__	__

CERTIFICATE

of Achievement

Congratulations to

_____

PLANS

Self-Statements Bull's-Eyes

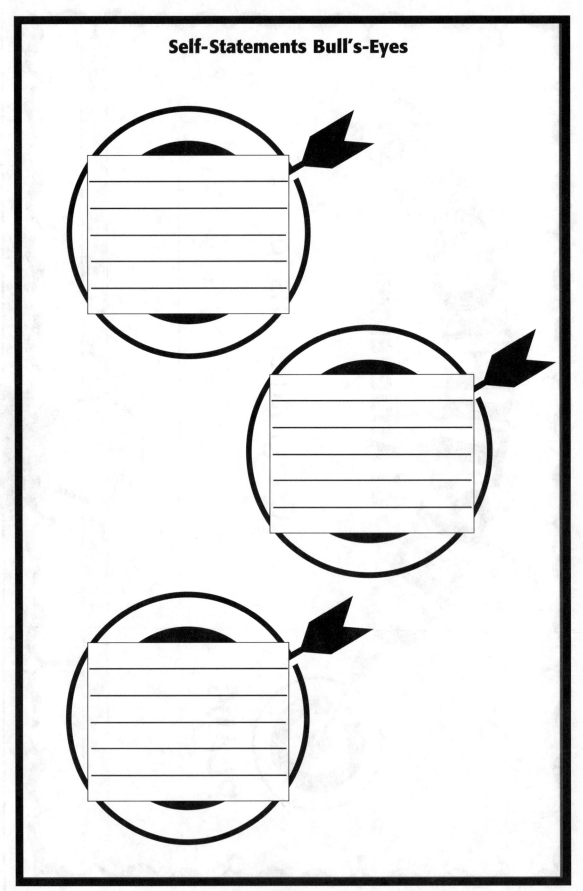

Section IV

Strategies for Revising

Chapter 12

SCAN

S = Does it make **S**ense?

C = Is it **C**onnected to my belief?

A = Can you **A**dd more?

N = **N**ote errors?

MATERIALS
Six Steps for Revising Checklist
SCAN Checklist
Six Steps Cards with Prompts
Six Steps Cards without Prompts
SCAN Cue Cards
My Self-Statements
Bulletin Board:
  • Writing Paper

LESSON 1

NOTE: These lessons and materials are written for revising a persuasive or opinion essay.

LESSON OVERVIEW

The students will examine a persuasive or opinion essay they have previously written. The students and teachers will discuss each student's current level of performance on revising. The teacher will introduce the Six Steps for Revising and SCAN as strategies for improving revision skills.

STUDENT OBJECTIVES

The students will orally brainstorm ways to improve revising efforts. The students will write a goal for revising. The students will orally practice the Six Steps for Revising and SCAN strategies.

MATERIALS

One copy for each student:
- Copy of each student's previously written essay
- Six Steps for Revising Checklist

- SCAN Checklist
- Six Steps Cards with Prompts, Six Steps Cards without Prompts, or SCAN Cue Cards

NOTE: See below. You will need to select the set of cards that best suits your students' needs.

SET CONTEXT FOR STUDENT LEARNING

Ask the students if they remember the essay previously written and revised during the previous class. Describe to the students how they are currently performing in regard to revising their essays. Point out some examples of revision selected from the individual essays. Describe each student's performance in a matter-of-fact way. Tell the students that you will teach them a way to make more and better revisions. Explain that by making more revisions when they rewrite their assignments, they can improve their grades.

INSTRUCTIONAL DELIVERY

Step 1: A Commitment to Learn the Strategy

Using their pretest performance as a guide, ask the students to write a goal indicating a commitment to learning a strategy or procedure for revising essays. Each student should write a personal goal on a blank piece of paper (e.g., "I want to learn how to revise my essays"). The teacher should also sign the goal statement.

Step 2: Describe the Strategy

Ask the students if they know what the word *revising* means? Say, *"When you revise something, you change it. How will revising help you when you write? It will make your writing better."*

- Show the students the six steps checklist. Cover all the steps, uncovering them one by one as you explain each.

- Show the students the SCAN checklist. Uncover each step as you explain it.

Step 3: Practice the Strategy

- Give each student a set of the six steps cards. Three sets of cards are provided; select the set that best suits your students' needs. The students may paraphrase the instructions provided in each step, but it is important that the intended meaning is maintained.

- Give the students time to orally practice the steps without the steps cards. If a student's response is incorrect, prompt him or her by pointing to the step on the card. If a student does not know a step, you can provide it.

WRAP-UP

- Give each student a copy of the six steps checklist, the SCAN checklist, and the steps cards.

- Tell the students that you will check next time to see if they can remember the six steps and the SCAN strategy on their own.

EVALUATION

Ask yourself

- Do I need to make modifications for any student?

- Should I create a revision bulletin board?

- Do I need to enhance or extend instruction with homework?

LESSON 2

LESSON OVERVIEW

The teacher will model the use of the Six Steps for Revising and the SCAN strategies. While modeling, the teacher should use all types of self-instructions (e.g., problem definition, planning, coping, strategy use, self-evaluation, self-reinforcement). A script for modeling has been provided as an example of the process.

STUDENT OBJECTIVES

The students will attend to the teacher's modeled lesson. The students will make additional revisions to one of their essays. The students will create a list of self-statements to use while revising.

MATERIALS

One copy for each student:
- Copy of each student's previously written essay
- Six Steps for Revising Checklist

- SCAN Checklist
- SCAN Cue Cards
- Self-Statements sheet

SET THE CONTEXT FOR STUDENT LEARNING

Ask the students to explain the steps for revising, the steps for SCAN, and the rationale for each. This review is to familiarize them with the steps learned in the previous lesson. Use the cue cards as necessary. Memorization will come later.

INSTRUCTIONAL DELIVERY

Step 1: Modeling

- Show the students a previously written and revised essay. This essay could be displayed on checklist paper, the chalkboard, or overhead projector. Be sure the students can easily see both the essay and the upcoming revisions. Tell them that you will model how to use the six steps and the SCAN strategies to improve their ability to revise their work. Let them know that you will be talking aloud to show them the things you say to yourself when using the strategies and revising.

- Model the entire process. Use problem definition, planning, coping, strategy use, self-evaluation, and self-reinforcement self-statements as you model the procedure. The steps and statements below are a guide for the modeling process. Fill in ad lib statements where indicated or where necessary.

 Say, *"What is it I have to do? I have to revise this essay. I will use my six steps checklist to help me revise my essay. Okay, the first thing I need to do is read the essay."* Point to the first step. Read the essay out loud and direct the students to read along silently. As you read, make several comments to yourself (e.g., "I really liked that sentence . . . I need to change that word . . . Another reason I can add is . . ."). When you finish reading say, *"That's pretty good but I can make it better. The second thing I need to do is look at the sentence that states what I believe."* Point to the step. With your finger, locate that sentence and underline it. *"Will other people know what I believe? Is it clear?"* Read the sentence out loud. If it is very clear, say so and move to the next step. If not,

point out how it can be made clearer. Cross out the old sentence and write a new one. *"Now, the third thing I need to do is add at least two more reasons why I believe what I do."* Point to this step. *"If I add more reasons that will make my essay stronger. What are some more reasons to support my belief?"* Give reasons that you noted during Step 1 while you were reading the essay out loud. Write them down saying them out loud. Before writing, make comments out loud about where you will put the reason (e.g., "I think it will go best here. . . That looks good and makes my essay stronger. . . Okay, I need to add another reason. . . What is another reason for [state belief]. . . Okay, I'll take my time and let my mind be free. An idea will come to me"). Propose one idea and then reject it; propose another and reinforce yourself for the good idea. Talk about where to put it and then write it in. Say, *"I am now ready to do Step 4."* Point to Step 4. *"When I do Step 4, I will SCAN."* Pull out the SCAN cue cards. *"I will look at this first sentence on my paper and ask myself if it is clear. Is it connected? Should I add more?"* Model and point to the steps on the steps cards. *"I will now make my changes on the paper copy and note any errors."* Model how to look for capitalization, punctuation, and spelling errors. Involve the students in the process whenever possible.

 Say, *"Now that I have completed Step 4, I need to do Step 5."* Point to Step 5 on the steps card. *"Now that I have completed Step 5, I need to do Step 6. I will reread my essay and make any final changes. This will make my essay more polished."* Model the procedures for making changes and additions. Involve the students in the process whenever possible. *"Now that I have finished making revisions, my essay looks much better."*

- Ask the students to write down some things they can say to themselves while they are revising. They can write these on the SCAN Self-Statements sheet or on a blank piece of paper.

- Ask the students if they have any questions.

WRAP-UP

- Briefly review the six steps and SCAN strategies.

- Tell the students that next time they will try the revision strategies for themselves.

- Remind the students that you will check to see if they remember the six steps and SCAN strategies during the next class.

LESSON 3

LESSON OVERVIEW
The students will memorize the six steps and SCAN components.

STUDENT OBJECTIVE
The students will memorize the steps and components listed on the various steps cards.

MATERIALS

One copy for each student:
- Copy of each student's previously written essay
- Six Steps for Revising Checklist

- SCAN Checklist
- SCAN Cue Cards
- Self-Statements sheet

SET THE CONTEXT FOR STUDENT LEARNING

Ask the students to explain the Six Steps for Revising and the SCAN strategies, as well as the rationale for each. Use the SCAN Cue Cards as necessary.

INSTRUCTIONAL DELIVERY

Step 1: Verbal Rehearsal

 Say, *"Today, we will memorize the Six Steps for Revising and SCAN. If you know the steps well, you will be able to tell yourself what to do when you are revising an essay."*

- Say, *"To help you memorize the six steps, we will do an exercise called rapid fire. We will take turns saying the steps. This is called rapid fire because you are trying to name the steps as rapidly as you can. You may look at the cue cards if you need to, but don't rely on them too much because I will put the cards away after several rounds of rapid fire."* Allow the students to paraphrase the steps, but ensure that the intended meaning is maintained.

- The students should practice rapid fire with the cue cards. If a response is correct, make a brief positive comment. If a response is incorrect, prompt the student by pointing to the correct step on the card.

- The students should practice rapid fire without the cue cards. If a student does not know a step, you can provide it.

Step 2: Rehearsal

- After verbal rehearsal, explain to the students that they must be able to name all the steps in an oral quiz. Give them time to rehearse the steps (they can use cue cards).

- When the students indicate that they have learned the steps, ask them to list the steps orally. Record each performance on the six steps checklist.

- Show each student his or her performance. Describe the steps each student omitted or named out of sequence.

Step 3: **Repeat Steps 1 and 2 with SCAN**

• Once the students can name the six steps with no assistance, repeat Steps 1 and 2 with SCAN. Emphasize and use the letters of the strategy as an aid to memory. Use the SCAN Checklist to record each student's progress.

• Once both have been mastered individually, test to determine if the students know both.

Step 4: **Revise Self-Statements**

Ask the students to revise and add to their Self-Statements sheets based on this lesson.

WRAP-UP

Remind the students that they will be tested to see if they can remember the six steps and SCAN strategies.

LESSON 4

LESSON OVERVIEW

The students will have an opportunity to use the six steps and SCAN strategies for revising essays they had previously written. It is important that the teacher provide as much help as is necessary at this stage of instruction.

STUDENT OBJECTIVES

With teacher guidance, the students will use the six steps and SCAN strategies to revise a previously written essay.

MATERIALS

One copy for each student:
- Copy of each student's previously written essay
- Six Steps for Revising Checklist

- SCAN Checklist
- SCAN Cue Cards
- Self-Statements sheets

SET THE CONTEXT FOR STUDENT LEARNING

Ask the students to verbally rehearse the six steps and SCAN strategies. Let them know that this is a test. If they recall less than 100% of either strategy, return to the practice procedures used in Lesson 3. Use the six steps checklist and SCAN Checklist to record each student's performance. Do not go to controlled practice until each student meets 100% mastery.

INSTRUCTIONAL DELIVERY

Step 1: Controlled Practice

- Tell the students that for the next several days you will practice using the revision procedure. The students will be revising their previously written essays.

- Give each student a copy of an essay written previously and make sure that it is not one that has been used during the SCAN lessons.

 Say, *"I want you to revise this essay using the six steps and SCAN strategies. You may look at the cue cards or self-statements if you need to. I will be here to make sure that you use the revision procedures correctly and to provide help when you need it."*

- Direct the students to begin practice. Provide as much assistance and prompt as necessary (e.g., "What is the first step?"), but try to let the students work on their own. When you provide corrective feedback

  1. Tell the student what was done incorrectly.

  2. Have the student correct the work.

  3. Be positive and encouraging.

WRAP-UP

Remind the students that they will be tested to see if they can remember the six steps and SCAN strategies.

LESSON 5

LESSON OVERVIEW

The students will be provided with another opportunity to practice the revision strategies. Teacher assistance should be given as needed.

STUDENT OBJECTIVES

The students will use the six steps and SCAN strategies while revising an essay or story.

MATERIALS

One copy for each student:
- Copy of each student's previously written essay
- Six Steps for Revising Checklist

- SCAN Checklist
- SCAN Cue Cards
- Self-Statements sheets

SET THE CONTEXT FOR STUDENT LEARNING

Ask the students to verbally rehearse the six steps and SCAN strategies. Provide corrective feedback if necessary. Describe their performance on the essays they revised during the previous session. Point out how many revisions they made and compare that with their performance discussed in Lesson 1. Present this data visually on a graph to highlight each student's improvement.

INSTRUCTIONAL DELIVERY

Step 1: Controlled Practice

- Tell the students that they will practice using the revision procedure. The students will be revising a previously written essay.

Give each student a copy of a previously written essay (the initial draft) and make sure that it is not one that has been used during the SCAN lessons. Say, *"I want you to revise this essay using the six steps and SCAN strategies. You may look at the cue cards and your self-statements. I will be here to make sure that you use the revision procedures correctly and to provide help when you need it."*

- Direct the students to begin practice. Provide as much assistance and prompt as necessary (e.g., "What is the first step?"), but try to let the students work on their own. When you provide corrective feedback

   1. Tell the student what was done incorrectly.

   2. Have the student correct the work.

   3. Be positive and encouraging.

WRAP-UP

Tell the students that you will review their performance in revising the essay with them during the next class.

EVALUATION

Decide if a student needs another day of controlled practice. If more practice is necessary, go to Lesson 6. If the student is able to use the procedures independently, go to Lesson 7. This determination is based upon the amount of assistance the student needs. If the student needs virtually no assistance, he or she is ready to use the strategies independently.

LESSON 6

LESSON OVERVIEW

The students will be provided with another opportunity to practice the revision strategies. Teacher assistance should be provided as needed.

STUDENT OBJECTIVES

The students will use the six steps and SCAN strategies while revising an essay.

MATERIALS

One copy for each student:
- Copy of each student's previously written essay
- Six Steps for Revising Checklist

- SCAN Checklist
- SCAN Cue Cards
- Self-Statements sheets

SET THE CONTEXT FOR STUDENT LEARNING

Ask the students to verbally rehearse the six steps and SCAN strategies. Provide corrective feedback if necessary. Describe their performance on the essays they revised during the previous session. Point out how many revisions they made and compare that with their performance on the essays revised during the last lesson. Present this data visually on a graph to highlight each student's improvement.

INSTRUCTIONAL DELIVERY

Step 1: Controlled Practice

- Tell the students that they will now practice using the revision procedure. The students will be revising a previously written essay.

Give each student a copy of an essay and make sure that it is not one that has previously been used during the SCAN lessons. Say, *"I want you to revise this essay using the six steps and SCAN strategies. You may look at the cue cards and self-statements. I will be here to make sure that you use the revision procedures correctly and to provide help when you need it."*

- Direct the students to begin practice. Provide as much assistance and prompt as necessary (e.g., "What is the first step?"), but try to let the students work on their own. When you provide corrective feedback

    1. Tell the student what was done incorrectly.

    2. Have the student correct the work.

    3. Be positive and encouraging.

WRAP-UP

Tell the students that you will review their performance in revising the essay with them during the next class.

LESSON 7

LESSON OVERVIEW

The students will be provided with the opportunity to discuss ways to revise essays that are written in different settings, for different subjects, and in different formats (e.g., an essay written on a computer).

STUDENT OBJECTIVES

The students will make cue cards to help them generalize the revision skills to new settings and/or subject material.

MATERIALS

One copy for each student:
- Copy of each student's previously written essay
- Six Steps for Revising Checklist

- SCAN Checklist
- SCAN Cue Cards
- Self-Statements sheets

SET THE CONTEXT FOR STUDENT LEARNING

Ask the students to verbally rehearse the strategies for the six steps and SCAN. Provide corrective feedback if necessary. Describe their performance on the essays they revised during the previous session. Tell them how many revisions they made and compare that with their performance on the previously revised essays and stories. Present data visually on a graph to highlight each student's improvement.

INSTRUCTIONAL DELIVERY

Step 1: Transferring Revision

Say, *"You have done a good job of learning how to use this revision procedure to help you revise your persuasive or opinion essays. This means you now have a tool for helping you revise essays, and such a tool is like money in the bank. However, if you keep this procedure stored away in your brain and do not use it, it will never help you write better essays."*

- Say, *"Obviously, you can use this revision procedure to rewrite essays that you wrote with pen and paper. You can also use this revision procedure to rewrite essays that you write on a computer. However, you will need to alter or change the revision procedure somewhat if you plan to use it to revise an essay that was written on a computer."*

- Have the students take out their cue cards. Ask them to suggest ways of changing the cards so that the six steps can be used when they are writing an essay on a computer (e.g., "I might want to write initial draft on every other line and change the fifth step to type my essay with the new changes added"). Go through the six steps strategy step by step.

- Have each student make a new cue card for the "Six Steps for Revising (Computer)."

- Ask the students if it is necessary to change or alter the procedures for SCAN when revising computer-written essays. Point out that it is not necessary to revise these steps.

WRAP-UP

- Tell the students that they have done an excellent job learning the procedures.

- Complete the contract paper written and signed in the first lesson. Tell the students that you will be giving them a note to take home to their parents telling them what a good job they have done. Also, as appropriate, tell them you will be picking an essay to share with the principal, their teacher, and their parents.

Six Steps for Revising Checklist

Steps	Attempts					
1. Read your essay.						
2. Find the sentence that tells what you believe. Is it clear?						
3. Add *two* reasons why you believe it.						
4. Scan each sentence.						
5. Make changes.						
6. Read your essay and make final changes.						
Date:						

SCAN Checklist

Steps						
Attempts						
1. **S** – Does it make Sense?						
2. **C** – Is it Connected to my belief?						
3. **A** – Can you Add more?						
4. **N** – Note errors? (Use COPS)						
Date:						

Six Steps Cards with Prompts

Third,
Add two reasons
why you believe it.

Sixth,
Reread your
essay and make
final changes.

Second,
Find the sentence
that tells what
you believe.
Is it clear?

Fifth,
Make changes.

First,
Read your
essay.

Fourth,
SCAN each
sentence.

Six Steps Cards without Prompts

Read your essay.

Find the sentence that tells what you believe. Is it clear?

Add two reasons why you believe it.

SCAN each sentence.

Make changes.

Reread your essay and make final changes.

SCAN Cue Cards

Is it **Connected** to my belief?

Note errors? (Use COPS)

Does it make **Sense**?

Can you **Add** more?

My Self-Statements

To think of good ideas:

_____

_____

_____

_____

_____

While I work:

_____

_____

_____

_____

_____

To check my work:

_____

_____

_____

_____

_____

Chapter 13

Compare, Diagnose, Operate

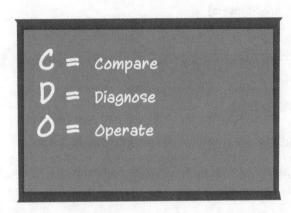

C = Compare
D = Diagnose
O = Operate

MATERIALS
CDO Mnemonic Chart
CDO Revising Strategy Directions
My Self-Statements
CDO Memorization Flash Cards
CDO Diagnose Cards
CDO Operate Cards

LESSON 1

LESSON OVERVIEW

The students and teacher will discuss current performance in revising an essay or story. Student tasks and goals for each day of instruction will be established. The teacher will explain that revising can be improved by learning how to revise the work of others as well as one's own work.

STUDENT OBJECTIVES

The students will revise by adding detail to an essay.

MATERIALS

- Overhead of essay for modeling
- Essays previously written by other
- students (boys and girls in different grade levels)

SET THE CONTEXT FOR STUDENT LEARNING

Establish the context for the Compare, Diagnose, Operate (CDO) revising lessons. Say, *"For the next several days, we will practice revising essays written by other students. These students were in _____ grade, and they include both boys and girls. We will practice revising the essays that these students wrote so that you learn how to revise your own essays better."*

Discuss 1) how revising leads to good writing, which can help the students earn better grades in school; 2) that a first draft will get their ideas down on paper, but that the paper will not yet be finished; 3) that readers sometimes have a hard time understanding what the writers have written unless they go back to fix their ideas; 4) that good writers revise their work; and 5) that good writing can help the students persuade other people to agree with their point of view.

Say, *"Each day you work with me, we will do the same kinds of things. Each day I will start our lesson by showing you one way, or method, for making changes to an essay. I will tell you what method we are going to cover each day, and then I will show you how to make changes on one essay using that method. The first thing I will do is demonstrate how to make changes to an essay.*

"The second activity will be to read and decide how to make changes for a poorly written essay using the same method that I covered. We will read an essay together, and you and I will make changes for the student who wrote the essay as if we were teachers or newspaper editors. If you need help, I will tell you what kind of changes to make and where you should try to make them. This activity should help you revise your own essays because if you can find problems in someone else's essay, you can probably find problems in your own essay too.

"The last thing you will do each day is make your own revisions on a short essay using the same revision method. You can ask questions, and I will provide help if you need it. It is important that you become independent in making revisions, so I will encourage you to try making changes on your own before asking me for help."

DEVELOP THE STRATEGY AND SELF-REGULATION

Step 1: Model *Add*

 Say, *"I will read this essay, and you can follow along. I will show you how to add information to an essay. The revising method for today is to add words, phrases, or sentences to our essay."*

- Read the essay completely and then go back and talk aloud about where and why to add information to each sentence in the essay.

- Say, *"I need to add information to the first sentence,"* *"I need to add something in this next sentence for the whole essay to make sense,"* *"There are too few ideas in this essay"* and *"Use the caret symbol (^) before each location you want to add content."*

- Model on the overhead how to insert a caret to make the change, and then go on to find others to make carets and further changes. Say, *"Something is missing here. I need to add another word, phrase, or idea."*

Step 2: Collaborative Changes

 Say, *"You did a good job following how I was adding to the essay sentences. Now we will look at a poorly written essay, sentence by sentence, and make it better using the same method, which for today is to add. We must read the essay first. What do you think needs to be changed? You can make the changes directly on the paper, or you can tell me what changes to make. As we read the essay, remember that the students don't always write what they intend to say. They may have been thinking of different ideas or different ways to express those ideas than what you actually see now."*

- Read the essay sentence by sentence and then ask the students to tell or show you what they would change. You can write the changes or let the students do the writing. Make sure they make a minimum of two changes.

- If the students need help getting started, say, *"Something does not sound right here. Can you add to this?"* Also, if a student cannot make a change based on knowing where to focus his or her attention, be sure to suggest specific changes, such as adding, so that the essay has at least two revisions. Give constructive feedback, such as "That's fine. You need to make another addition to the essay to make it better." You want the students to do more than simply watch you model the revising element, but at the same time, they may need your help to ensure that the changes make sense. Say, *"Let me know if this is hard to do!"*

- Tell the students that they have one more task for today.

Step 3: Practice Revising

 Say, *"Now this time I will show you a short essay and ask you to work on your own. You need to make changes directly on this essay, sentence by sentence, in your own writing, so I cannot do the writing for you. If you have a question about what to do or how to make a change, you can ask me for help."*

- Remind the students to read the essay completely before trying to make any changes and tell them that today you worked on *adding* to sentences.

- Give the students whatever help they need after they try to make changes independently. You can and should comment on the accuracy of what each student does. Make sure they make a minimum of two changes (e.g., spelling, punctuation, single word). If the students don't think anything needs to be changed, tell them that this essay has room for improvement and encourage them to add to it. If they maintain that nothing needs to be revised, tell them where to make the change and offer suggestions (e.g., "Should you add this word or that word to this sentence?") so that each student is successful.

WRAP-UP

Record notes about the students with limited ability to revise during the last independent activity. Thank the students for working hard and for trying something new.

LESSONS 2–4

Compare, Diagnose, Operate

LESSON OVERVIEW

The students and teachers will review previous steps learned for revising an essay sentence by sentence. Student tasks and goals for the day of instruction will be established. The teacher will explain that revising can be improved by learning how to delete, change, or rewrite the work of others as well as one's own work. (NOTE: These three lessons repeat the same format as Lesson 1 each day with a different revising task.)

STUDENT OBJECTIVES

The students will revise by deleting, moving, or rewriting sentences to improve essay content.

MATERIALS

- Essays previously written by other students (boys and girls in different grade levels)
- Overhead of essay for modeling

SET THE CONTEXT FOR STUDENT LEARNING

Review the revising step taught during the previous session. Say, *"Today we will practice [deleting/moving/rewriting] sentences in an essay. First, we will practice together, and then you will make changes on your own."*

DEVELOP THE STRATEGY AND SELF-REGULATION

Step 1 (Lesson 2): **Model *Delete***

Tell the students that the method for today is to *delete.* Be sure to read through the essay completely first. Use the same basic procedures as in the *add* model essay. Say something like, "This idea tells the same information as an earlier idea," "This information is off-topic," "This sentence is redundant," "This doesn't sound like it is needed," "The writer is getting away from his or her main point," or "This is a weak or incomplete idea." Highlight the word, phrase, or sentence. Draw a single line through the content to be deleted to make this change more explicit. You are highlighting the problem and then striking through the material that you want to eliminate. Remind the students that you want to be able to see whatever the original material was, so they should not cross it out completely.

Step 1 (Lesson 3): **Model *Change***

Tell the students that the method for today is to *change* or *move.* Use the same basic procedures as in the previous model essays. Be sure to read through the essay completely first. Say something like, "The order of this word, phrase, idea, sentence does not make sense," or "Part of the essay isn't in the right order." Then say, *"I want to move this word, phrase, idea, sentence to a different place. First, I will highlight what I want to move, and then I will draw an arrow to show where it should go."* Again, you are highlighting the problem, and then showing how to make the revision.

| **Step 1 (Lesson 4):** | **Model *Rewrite*** |

Tell the students that the method for today is to *rewrite*. Use the same basic procedures as in the previous model essays. Be sure to read through the essay completely first. Say something like, "Something is wrong here. I am not sure the writer meant to write what we are reading in this essay," or, "This doesn't sound quite right," "People may not understand what the writer means," or "This is a weak idea." Then say, *"I think it would be better to rewrite this* [word/phrase/idea/sentence] *to make the idea clearer. I will change _____ to _____* (fill in the appropriate content)." Write the new content either directly above the material that has been highlighted, or use an asterisk (*) to show the change somewhere that is legible (e.g., in the margins, below the sample essay).

| **Step 2:** | **Collaborative Changes** |

Say, *"You did a good job following how I was* [deleting/changing/rewriting] *sentences in the essay. We will now look at an essay with poor sentences and together we will make it better using the same method, which for today is to* (delete, move, rewrite). *We must read the essay first. What do you think needs to be changed? Either you can make the changes directly on the paper or you can tell me what changes to make. As we read the essay, remember that the students don't always write what they intend to say. They may have been thinking of different ideas or different ways to express those ideas than what you actually see now."*

- Read the paper and ask the students to tell or show you what they would change sentence by sentence You can write the changes or let the students do the writing. Make sure they make a minimum of two changes.

- If the students need help getting started, say, *"Something does not sound right here. Can you* [delete/move/rewrite] *to fix this?"* Also, if a student cannot make a change based on knowing where to focus his or her attention, suggest specific changes, such as deleting, moving, or rearranging text, so that the essay has at least two revisions. Give constructive feedback to the student, such as, "That's fine. You need to make another addition to this sentence to make it better," or "I know you wanted to delete something, but you got rid of something that is really important. The sentence won't make sense if you delete that idea." You want the students to do more than simply watch you model the revising element, but at the same time, they need your help to ensure that the changes make sense. Say, *"Let me know if this is hard to do!"*

- Tell the students that they have one more task for today.

| **Step 3:** | **Practice Revising** |

Say, *"This time I will show you a short essay and ask you to work on your own. You need to make changes directly, sentence by sentence, on this essay, in your own writing, so I cannot do the writing for you. If you have a question about what to do or how to make a change, you can ask me for help."*

- Remind the students to read the essay completely before trying to make any changes, and tell them that today you have been working on *adding, deleting, moving,* or *revising,* if needed.

- Give the students whatever help they need after they try to make changes independently. You can and should comment on the accuracy of what the student does. Make sure the students make a minimum of two changes (e.g., spelling, punctuation, single word or sentence, and so forth). If a student says he or she doesn't think anything needs to be changed, point out that this essay has room for improvement and encourage the student to (delete, move, or rewrite). If a student maintains that nothing needs to be revised, demonstrate where to make a change, and, if necessary, give the student suggestions (e.g., "Should you delete this word or that word?") so that he or she is successful.

WRAP-UP

Be sure to make notes about the students with limited ability to revise during the practice activity. Thank the students for working with you and for trying something new.

LESSON 5

LESSON OVERVIEW
The teacher will model the CDO (Compare, Diagnose, Operate) revising strategy.

STUDENT OBJECTIVES
The students will revise an essay using the steps in the CDO strategy.

MATERIALS

One copy for each student:
- Overhead of essay for modeling
- CDO mnemonic chart
- CDO Revising Strategy Directions
- My Self-Statements

- CDO Diagnose Cards
- CDO Operate Cards
- CDO Memorization Flash Cards (if needed for memorization practice)

SET THE CONTEXT FOR STUDENT LEARNING

Say, *"Today we will do something new that builds on the work we have done together in previous lessons."* Briefly review what the students have learned. *"I will show you a strategy, or several steps, that will help you make better revising decisions. The strategy is called CDO–Compare, Diagnose, Operate."* Give the students a mnemonic chart.

DEVELOP THE STRATEGY AND SELF-REGULATION

Step 1: Describe CDO

Say, *"Each letter of CDO tells you to do something specific, or a series of specific things. CDO is a mnemonic, or a reminder, for the revising strategy. I will ask you to memorize what each letter represents after we go over it a few times together."*

- Say, *"The first step of the strategy is to read your essay sentence by sentence aloud softly. As you read, you will try to find places where your sentences need changes. If you find a place where a change needs to be made, you should highlight the word or words in the sentences that you want to change. You should also ask yourself if you need more ideas. You will use a caret (^) to show where you want to add something.*

- *"The next step of the strategy is to diagnose what the problems are in your essay sentences. The word* diagnose *means to identify or decide something. How can you diagnose the problem? I have a set of CDO Diagnose Cards for you to use as you try to decide what is wrong with each sentence."* Read each card and explain any statements that the students do not understand.

- *"The third letter in CDO is O, which stands for operate. The third step in the CDO revising strategy is to select a CDO Operate Card for making changes. I have a set of CDO Operate Cards for you to use as you decide what changes to make to each sentence.*

- *"The fourth step in the revising strategy is to make your revisions. That means you actually try to add, delete, rewrite, or move something. In the diagnose step, you are trying to figure out what the problems are, and in the operate step, you are trying to decide what to do to fix the problems. You then actually make your revision based on what you have decided."*

Step 2: Model

Say, *"I will now show you how to use the CDO strategy using the mnemonic chart, which has all the steps and directions, the diagnose and operate cards, and an essay I wrote yesterday. I want to show you how everything fits together before we try to revise an essay together."*

- This is where the teachers need excellent acting skills, a good memory, and some practice. You must be believable when you model the CDO revising strategy, and you must make it look easy. It is a good idea to plan what to say, especially because you must reflect, monitor, and congratulate yourself as you think aloud. Also, don't forget to set a goal for yourself before you start the actual revisions. This is a fun part of teaching as long as you are prepared. Be sure to model six types of self-statements in the process.

Step 3: Self-Statements

Ask the students to record the things they can say to themselves while comparing, diagnosing, and operating to revise an essay on the self-statements sheet.

Step 4: Memorization

Each day, until the students have memorized the strategy, ask them to complete a strategy quiz. Take out a sheet of lined notebook paper. Write down the numbers 1 through 3, but be sure to skip two lines between each number to allow plenty of room for your answers. Ask, *"What is the first step in the revising strategy?"* (Answer: Read your sentence.) *"What is the next step?"* (Answer: Diagnose: Select the best diagnose card.) *"What are the third and fourth steps?"* (Answer: Operate: Select an operate card, and Operate: Make your revision.) *"Go back to the first step, which is* [tell the students if they missed it] *'What two things do you do when you read your essay aloud softly?'"* (Answer: Highlight places where you want to make changes and use a caret [^] to show where you will add, delete, move, or rewrite something.) *"Go to the second step, which is diagnose. Name two of the diagnose cards."* The students can tell you more if they know them (e.g., "This doesn't sound quite right," "People may not understand what I mean," "This is good," and so forth). *"Go to the third and fourth steps and name the operate cards."* (Answer: Rewrite, Change the wording, Add more, Leave this part out.) Ask what *implement the changes* means if the students did not clarify before.

- Once the students have a good start on memorizing, you can do this verbally. Use rapid-fire practice with the flash cards if needed.

WRAP-UP

Be sure to make notes about the students with limited ability to revise during the practice activity. Thank the students for working with you and for trying something new.

LESSON 6

LESSON OVERVIEW

The students will practice the CDO strategy, first collaboratively with the teacher and then independently. This lesson is repeated until the students have memorized the steps of CDO and have learned to apply the steps toward revising their own essays.

STUDENT OBJECTIVES

The students will revise an essay using the CDO strategy.

MATERIALS

- Overhead of essay for modeling
- CDO mnemonic chart
- My Self-Statements
- CDO Diagnose Cards
- CDO Operate Cards
- CDO Memorization Flash Cards

SET THE CONTEXT FOR STUDENT LEARNING

Briefly review with the students the CDO steps. Have each student place a mnemonic chart, a self-statements sheet, and diagnose and operate cards on his or her desk.

DEVELOP THE STRATEGY AND SELF-REGULATION

Step 1: Collaborative Practice

After reviewing the CDO strategy, the students will engage in one collaborative essay. If you finish this collaborative essay and still have time, go on to the independent practice in the same day. Basically, you are working together in a way that is similar to the previous lessons. The difference is that you will ask "What is the first step?" and so on, in addition to ensuring that the answer is correct before actually engaging in that step. Be sure to give error corrections that fully state the original content. "That's not quite right. *Diagnose* means to identify the problem and then decide what to do to fix it. We need to use the diagnose and operate to do this step." You can also help as much as is necessary for the students to successfully revise their essays.

Step 2: Independent Practice

Tell the students that you hope they will be able to use the CDO strategy when you finish working together to help them revise essays in the future. To reach this goal, you want to encourage the students to try to use the CDO strategy on their own and to ask questions when they get stuck. You will also remind and provide support to the students if they forget any steps or make mistakes in using any of the steps. Finally, you will try to give the students less help as time goes on so that they can really do this on their own. Reminder: On the last day, you will have to teach the students to underline text they have highlighted because highlighters are not available at all times.

Step 3: Memorization

Try to practice memorizing the mnemonic for about 5 minutes each day. Use the flash cards for drill and practice if needed. A good time to do this is between essays when you are revising two essays in one day.

WRAP-UP

Be sure to make notes about the students with limited ability to revise during the practice activity. Thank the students for working with you and for trying something new.

CDO

Compare: Read the sentence.

Diagnose: Select the best diagnose cards.

Operate: Select an operate card.

Operate: Make your revision.

CDO Revising Strategy Directions

Step 1. **C**ompare: Read the sentence.

Step 2. **D**iagnose: Select the best diagnose cards.
- This doesn't sound quite right.
- This is not what I intended to say.
- Part of the essay isn't in the right order.
- People may not understand what I mean.
- I'm getting away from my main point.
- This is a weak or incomplete idea.
- The problem is _____.

Step 3. **O**perate: Select an operate card.
- Add: Include more information, examples, details, and so forth.
- Leave this part out: Take something (a word, phrase, sentence) out.
- Rewrite: Say it (a word, phrase, sentence) in a different way.
- Change the wording: Rearrange information (a word, phrase, sentence).

Step 4. **O**perate: Make your revision.

My Strategy Self-Statements

Things to say when I compare:

_____

_____

_____

_____

_____

_____

Things to say when I diagnose:

_____

_____

_____

_____

_____

_____

Things to say when I operate:

_____

_____

_____

_____

_____

_____

_____

CDO Memorization Flash Cards

Step 1. Compare: Read the sentence.

Step 2. Diagnose: Select the best diagnose cards.

- This doesn't sound quite right.
- This is not what I intended to say.
- Part of the essay isn't in the right order.
- People may not understand what I mean.
- I'm getting away from my main point.
- This is a weak or incomplete idea.
- The problem is _____.

Step 3. Operate: Select an operate card.

- Add: Include more information, examples, details, and so forth.
- Leave this part out: Take something (a word, phrase, sentence) out.
- Rewrite: Say it (a word, phrase, sentence) in a different way.
- Change the wording: Rearrange information (a word, phrase, sentence).

Step 4. Operate: Make your revision.

CDO Diagnose Cards

Diagnose each sentence **This doesn't sound right.**	Diagnose each sentence **People won't believe this part.**
Diagnose each sentence **This is not what I intended to say.**	Diagnose each sentence **People may not understand this part.**
Diagnose each sentence **This is not useful to my paper.**	Diagnose each sentence **People won't be interested in this part.**
Diagnose each sentence **This is good.**	

CDO Operate Cards

Operate:

Rewrite

Operate:

Change the wording

Operate:

Add more

Operate:

Leave this part out

Chapter 14

REVISE

R = Read

E = Evaluate

V = Verbalize

I = Implement

S = Self-Check

E = End

MATERIALS
REVISE Mnemonic Chart
Evaluate Cards
Verbalize Cards
Self-Check Cards
REVISE Directions
My Self-Statements

LESSON 1

LESSON OVERVIEW

The students and teachers will discuss current performance in revising an essay. (NOTE: This strategy can be adapted to story revision.) Student tasks and goals for each day of instruction will be established. The teacher will explain that revising can be improved by learning how to revise the work of others as well as one's own work.

STUDENT OBJECTIVES

The students will revise essays by adding detail.

MATERIALS
- Overhead of an essay for modeling
- Essays previously written by students

SET THE CONTEXT FOR STUDENT LEARNING

Establish the context for REVISE lessons. Say, *"Do you remember when we revised essays together? For the rest of this week and most of next week, we will practice revising essays written by other students. These students—boys and girls—were in _____ grade at the time they composed these essays. We will practice revising their essays so you can learn how to better revise your own essay.*

"Do you understand why this goal is important? Let's talk more about how learning to revise can help you in school."

Discuss the following points:

1. Revising leads to good writing, which can help the students earn better grades.

2. A first draft will get the students' ideas down on paper, but the essay is usually not yet finished.

3. Readers sometimes have a hard time understanding what is written unless writers go back to fix their ideas.

4. Good writers revise their work.

5. Good writing can help students persuade other people to agree with their point of view.

Say, *"Each day that we work together, we will do the same kinds of things. Every day, I will start our lesson by showing you one way, or one method, for making changes to an essay. I will tell you what method we are going to cover each day, and then I will show you how to make changes on one essay using that method. The first thing I will do is demonstrate how to make changes to an essay.*

"The second activity will be to read and decide how to apply changes to a poorly written essay using the same method that I covered. We will read an essay together, and you and I will make changes for the student who wrote the essay as if we were a group of teachers or newspaper editors. If you need help, I will tell you what kinds of changes to make and where you should try to make them. This activity should help you revise

your own essays because if you can find problems in someone else's paper, you can probably find problems in your own essay as well.

"The last thing you will do each day is make your own revisions on a short essay using the same revision method. You can ask me questions if you like, and I will provide help if you need it. It is important, however, that you can make revisions independently, so I will encourage you to try making changes on your own before asking me for help. Do you have any questions about what we are going to do each day?"

DEVELOP THE STRATEGY AND SELF-REGULATION

 Step 1: **Model *Add* to Essay**

Say, *"I will read this essay out loud and you can follow along. The revising method for this class is to add words, phrases, or sentences to the essay."*

- Read the essay completely, and then go back and talk aloud about where to add information and why.

- Say, *"I need to add information at the beginning of the essay,"* or *"I need to add something here for the whole essay to make sense. There are too few ideas here/in this essay. I will use the caret symbol (^) before each location where I want to add content."*

- Model on the overhead image the way to insert a caret to make the change, and then go on to find other places to make further changes. Say, *"Something is missing here. I need to add another* [word/phrase/idea].*"*

 Step 2: **Collaborative Changes**

Say, *"You did a good job following the way I was adding information to the essay. We will now look at a poorly written essay and make it better using the same method, which for today is to add. First, we need to read the essay. Tell me what you think needs to be changed. You can make the changes directly on the paper or you can tell me what changes to make here. As we read the essay, remember that students don't always write what they intend to say. They may have been thinking of different ideas or different ways to express those ideas than what you actually see now."*

- Read the paper and ask the students to tell or show you what the writer should change. You can write the changes or let the students do the writing. Make sure they make a minimum of two changes.

- If the students need help getting started, say, *"Something does not sound right here. Can you add something to fix this?"* Also, if a student cannot make a change based on knowing where to focus his or her attention, be sure to suggest specific changes, such as adding, so that the essay has at least two revisions. Give constructive feedback to the student (e.g., *"That's fine. You need to make another addition to the essay to make it better"*). You want your students to do more than simply watch you model the revising element, but at the same time, they need your help to ensure that the changes make sense. Say, *"Let me know if this is hard to do."*

- Tell the students that they have one more task for this class.

Step 3: Practice Revising

Say, *"This time, I will show you a short essay and ask you to work on your own. You need to make changes directly on this essay in your own writing, so I cannot do the writing for you. If you have a question about what to do or how to make a change, you can ask me for help."*

- Remind the students to read the essay completely before trying to make any changes and tell them that for this class they should work on adding.

- Give a student whatever help he or she needs after he or she tries to make a change independently. You can and should comment on the accuracy of what the student does. Make sure that he or she makes a minimum of two changes (e.g., spelling, punctuation, single word, sentence). If a student says he or she doesn't think anything needs to be changed, state that this essay has room for improvement and encourage the student to add. If a student maintains that the essay does not need to be revised, point out places to make changes and, if necessary, give the student suggestions, such as in a multiple choice format (e.g., "Should you add this word or that word?") so that he or she is successful.

WRAP-UP

Record notes about the students with limited ability to revise during the last independent activity. Thank the students for working hard and for trying something new.

LESSON OVERVIEW

The students and teachers will review previous steps learned for revising an essay or story. Student tasks and goals for the day of instruction will be established. The teacher will explain that revising can be improved by learning how to delete, move, and rewrite the work of others as well as one's own work. (NOTE: These three lessons repeat the same format as Lesson 1 each day with a different revising task.)

STUDENT OBJECTIVES

The students will revise by deleting, moving, or rewriting essay content.

MATERIALS

• Overhead of an essay for modeling   • Essays previously written by students

---

SET THE CONTEXT FOR STUDENT LEARNING

Review the revising steps taught the previous day. Say, *"We will now practice* [deleting / moving /rewriting] *content in an essay. First, we will practice together and then you will make changes on your own."*

DEVELOP THE STRATEGY AND SELF-REGULATION

Step 1 (Lesson 2): **Model *Delete* from Essay**

Tell the students that that the method for revision for this class is to *delete.* Be sure to read through the essay completely first. Use the same basic procedures as in the *add* model essay. Say something like, "This idea expresses the same information as an earlier idea," "This information is off-topic," "This is redundant," "This doesn't sound like it is needed," "The writer is getting away from the main point," or "This is a weak or incomplete idea." Use a highlighter to highlight the word, phrase, or sentence. Draw a single line through the content to be deleted to make this change more explicit. In other words, highlight the problem and strike through the material that you want to eliminate. Remind the students that you want to be able to see the original material, so they should not cross it out completely.

Step 1 (Lesson 3): **Model *Move* in Essay**

Tell the students that the method of revision for this class is to *move.* Use the same basic procedures as in the previous model essays. Be sure to read through the essay completely first. Say something like, "The order of this [word/phrase/idea/sentence] does not make sense," "Part of the essay isn't in the right order," or "I want to move this [word/phrase/idea/sentence] to a different place." Continue by saying, *"First I will highlight what I want to move. Then I will draw an arrow to show where it should go."* Again, highlight the problem and then demonstrate how to make the revision.

Step 1 (Lesson 4): Model *Rewrite* the Essay

Tell the students that the method for revision for this class is to *rewrite.* Use the same basic procedures as in the previous model essays. Be sure to read through the essay completely first. Say something like, "Something is wrong here. I am not sure the writer meant to write what we are reading on this essay," "This doesn't sound quite right. People may not understand what the writer means," "This is a weak idea," or "I think it would be better to rewrite this [word/phrase/idea/sentence] to make the idea clearer." Continue by saying, *"I will change _____ to _____* [fill in the appropriate content]. *Now that idea makes more sense."* Write the new content either directly above the material that has been highlighted or use an asterisk (*) to show the change somewhere that is legible (e.g., in the margins, below the sample essay).

Step 2: Collaborative Changes

Say, *"You did a good job following how I was adding to the essay. Now we are going to look at a poorly written essay together and make it better using the same method, which for this class is to* [add/delete/move/rewrite]. *We need to read the essay first. What do you think needs to be changed? Either you can make the changes directly on the paper, or you can tell me what changes to make. As we read the essay, remember that students don't always write what they intend to say. They may have been thinking of different ideas or different ways to express those ideas than what you actually see now."*

- Read the essay and ask the students to tell or show you what they would change. You can write the changes or let the students do the writing. Make sure they make a minimum of two changes.

- If the students need help getting started, say, *"Something does not sound right here, can you* [add/delete/move/rewrite] *to fix this?"* Also, if the students cannot make changes based on knowing where to focus their attention, suggest specific changes, such as adding, deleting, moving, or rearranging text, so that the essay has at least two revisions. Give constructive feedback to each student (e.g., "That's fine. You need to make another addition to the essay to make it better," "I know you wanted to delete something, but you really got rid of a point that is really important. The essay won't make sense if you delete that idea"). You want the students to do more than simply watch you model the revising element, but at the same time, they need your help to ensure that the changes make sense. Say, *"Let me know if this is hard to do."*

- Tell the students that they have one more task for today.

Step 3: Practice Revising

Say, *"I will now show you a short essay and ask you to work on your own. You need to make changes directly on this essay in your own writing, so I cannot do the writing for you. If you have a question about what to do or how to make a change, you can ask me for help."*

- Remind the students to read the essay completely before trying to make any changes and tell them that this class has focused on adding, deleting, moving, or revising, if needed.

- Give the students whatever help they need after they try to make changes independently. Comment on the accuracy of the students' work. Make sure they make a minimum of two changes (e.g., spelling, punctuation, single word, sentence). If a student says he or she doesn't think anything needs to be changed, state that this essay has

room for improvement and encourage the student to try to add, delete, move, or rewrite. If the student maintains that the essay does not need to be revised, point out where to make changes and, if necessary, provide suggestions, such as in a multiple choice format (e.g., "Should you delete this word or that word?) so that the student is successful.

WRAP-UP

Be sure to make notes about students with limited ability to revise during independent revising. Thank the students for working with you and for trying something new.

LESSON 5

LESSON OVERVIEW
The teacher will model the REVISE strategy.

STUDENT OBJECTIVES
The students will attend to a teacher-led modeling of revise.

MATERIALS

One copy for each student:
- REVISE mnemonic chart
- Evaluate Cards
- Verbalize Cards
- Self-Check Cards

- REVISE Directions
- Essay previously written by other students (boys and girls in different grade levels)
- Overhead of essay for modeling

SET THE CONTEXT FOR STUDENT LEARNING

Say, *"Today we are going to do something that builds on the work we did together over the last 4 days."* Briefly review with the students what they have learned thus far. *"I will show you a strategy, or several steps, that will help you make better revising decisions. The strategy is called REVISE."* Give each student a mnemonic chart.

DEVELOP THE STRATEGY AND SELF-REGULATION

Step 1: **Describe REVISE**

Say, *"Each letter of the word REVISE tells you to do something specific or a series of specific things"*:

- R *R*ead
- E *E*valuate
- V *V*erbalize
- I *I*mplement
- S *S*elf-Check
- E *E*nd

- Say, *"The word REVISE is a mnemonic (a reminder) for the revising strategy. I will ask you to memorize what each letter represents after we go over it a few times together."*

- Say, *"The first step of the strategy is to read your essay aloud softly. You can remember that first you read because the first letter of the strategy reminder REVISE starts with R. When you read your essay aloud softly, you will to try to find places where your essay needs changes. If you find a place where a change needs to be made, you should highlight the word or words that you want to change. You should also ask yourself if you need more ideas. You will use a caret (^) to show where you want to add something.*

- *"The next step of the strategy is to evaluate what the problems are in your essay. To remember this step, try to remember that the second letter in REVISE is E, which is at the beginning of the word evaluate. To evaluate means to judge or decide something. How can you evaluate the problem? I have a set of Evaluate Cards for you to use as you try to decide what is wrong with the essay."* Read and explain each card.

- *"The third letter in REVISE is V, so we are using a word that starts with V to help you remember the next step of the revising strategy. The third step is to verbalize, or to say what you are going to do to fix the problem. The Verbalize Cards give you some options for making changes, and you will read each of the Verbalize Cards and then decide what you can do to make changes in your essay."*

- *"The fourth letter in REVISE is I, and so the next step in the revising strategy starts with I: Implement. The word* implement *means to carry out or to accomplish something. In this case, it means that you make the changes—add, delete, rewrite, or move something— that you feel are necessary. Basically, in the evaluate step, you are trying to figure out what the problems are; in the verbalize step, you are trying to say what you want to do to fix the problems; and in the implement step you actually make the changes."*

- *"The fifth step is a bit tricky for me to explain, but I think you will understand it after I am through. The S in REVISE stands for self-check your goals and make your changes based on these goals. Here are some goals that would be useful for you to consider."* Show and explain the Self-Check Cards. *"You will actually choose one or two of these goals before you start the REVISE strategy, so at this step, you can check whether or not you are making changes that would meet your goals. This step will help you focus on reasons why you are making revisions."*

- *"The last letter in REVISE is an E and it stands for end by rereading and making any additional changes to your essay. This step is important because you want to check that you are finished with your revisions and that the essay makes sense. Therefore, you will end by rereading the whole essay and making more changes if they are needed."*

Step 2: Model

Say, *"I will now show you how to use the REVISE strategy using the directions chart, which reminds me what the mnemonic means; the evaluate, verbalize, and self-check cards; and an essay that I wrote yesterday. I want to show you how everything fits together before we try to revise an essay as a group."*

- This is where the teacher needs excellent acting skills, a good memory, and some practice. You must be believable when you model the revising strategy, and you must make it look easy. It is a good idea to plan what to say ahead of time because you need to reflect, monitor, and congratulate yourself as you verbally think aloud. Don't forget to set a goal for yourself before you start the actual revisions! This is also a fun part of teaching as long as you are prepared.

- Use any remaining time on this day to practice memorizing the meaning of the mnemonic. The students should be told that they will take a test to see if they have learned what the mnemonic means when you finish working together.

Step 3: Memorization

Each day, until they have memorized the strategy, ask the students to complete a strategy quiz. Take out a sheet of lined notebook paper. Write down the numbers 1 through 6, but be sure to skip two lines between each number so you have plenty of room for your answers. Ask, *"What is the first step in the revising strategy?"* (Answer: Read your essay.) *"What is the next step?"* (Answer: Evaluate the problems.) *"What is the third*

step?" (Answer: Verbalize or say what you will do to fix the problems.) *"What is the fourth step?* (Answer: Implement, make, or do the changes.) *"What is the fifth step?"* (Answer: Self-check your goals.) *"What is the last step?"* (Answer: End by rereading and making more changes if necessary.)

- Say, *"Fine. Let's go back to the first step, which is* [tell the students if they missed it.] *What two things do you do when you read your essay aloud softly?"* (Answer: Highlight places where you want to make changes and use a caret (^) to show where you will add something.)

- Say, *"Go back to the second step. Identify two of the Evaluate cards."* (Answer: This doesn't sound quite right. Part of the essay isn't in the right order. People may not understand what I mean. I'm getting away from my main point. This is a weak or in-complete idea. The problem is _____.)

- Say, *"Go back to the third step and identify the Verbalize Cards."* (Answer: Add, Delete, Rewrite, and Move.) Ask the students what *implement the changes* means if they do not clarify this.

- Say, *"The fifth step was to self-check your goals. Name at least two of the goals."* (An-swer: Make your paper more believable to your reader. Give enough information so that your reader can understand your position. Make sure your changes make sense.)

- Ask, *"Why should we do the last step?* (Answer: So we can see if it all makes sense and to look for any more changes that need to be made.)

- NOTE: Once the students have a good start toward memorizing, you can do this verbally.

WRAP-UP

Be sure to make notes about students with limited ability to revise during independent re-vising. Thank the students for working with you and for trying something new.

LESSON 6

LESSON OVERVIEW

The students will practice the REVISE strategy, first collaboratively with the teacher and then independently. This lesson is repeated until the students have memorized the steps of REVISE and have learned to apply the steps to revising their own essays.

STUDENT OBJECTIVES

The students will revise an essay using the REVISE strategy.

MATERIALS

One copy for each student:
- REVISE mnemonic chart
- Evaluate Cards
- Verbalize Cards
- Self-Check Cards

- REVISE Directions
- Essay previously written by other students (boys and girls in different grade levels)
- Overhead of essay for modeling

SET THE CONTEXT FOR STUDENT LEARNING

Briefly review with the students the REVISE steps. Give each student a copy of the mnemonic chart, the directions chart, and the cue cards.

DEVELOP THE STRATEGY AND SELF-REGULATION

Step 1: Collaborative Practice

After reviewing the REVISE strategy, the students will engage in one collaborative essay. (If you finish this collaborative essay and still have time, go on to the independent practice on the same day.) Basically, you will work together in a similar way as in the previous lessons. The difference is that you will say, "What is the first step?" and so on, in addition to making sure the answer is correct before actually engaging in that step. Be sure to give error corrections that fully state the original content. Say things like, "That's not quite right. *Verbalize* means to say what you are going to do to fix the problems. We need to use the Verbalize Cards to do this step." You can also help the students as much as needed to successfully revise their essays.

Step 2: Independent Practice

Tell the students that you hope they will be able to use the REVISE strategy when you finish working together to help them revise essays in the future. To reach this goal, you want the students to try to use the REVISE strategy on their own and to ask you questions when they get stuck. You will also remind them if they forget any steps or make mistakes in using any of the steps. Finally, you will try to give the students less help as time goes on so they can really do this on their own.

- REMINDER: On the last day, you will have to teach the students to underline text that they highlight because highlighters won't be available on the posttest.

Step 3: Memorization

Practice memorizing the mnemonic for about 5 minutes each day. Use flash cards (the students can make their own to support memorization) for drill and practice if needed. A good time to do this is between essays when you are revising two essays in one day.

WRAP-UP

Be sure to make notes about the students with limited ability to revise during independent revising. Thank the students for working with you and for trying something new.

REVISE

R Read your essay aloud softly. *Highlight* places where you think changes need to be made and ask yourself if you need more ideas (use a caret ^ to show where you will add something).

E Evaluate the problems. Read the Evaluate Cards.

V Verbalize what you are going to do to fix the problems. Read the Verbalize Cards.

I Implement the changes.

S Self-check the one or two goals you set for yourself. Make other revisions based on these goals. Goals are listed on the Self-Check Cards.

E End by rereading and making any additional changes.

Evaluate Cards

Evaluate!

This doesn't sound quite right.

Evaluate!

This is a weak or incomplete idea.

Evaluate!

The problem is _____.

Evaluate!

I'm getting away from my main point.

Verbalize Cards

Verbalize!

Delete: Take something out.

Verbalize!

Move: Rearrange information.

Verbalize!

Add: Include more information, examples, details, etc.

Verbalize!

Rewrite: Say it in a different way.

319

Self-Check Cards

Self-Check!

Did you include enough information so that the reader can understand your position?

Self-Check!

Self-Check!

Is your paper more believable to your reader?

Self-Check!

Did your changes make sense?

REVISE Directions

R   **Read** your essay aloud softly. **Highlight** places where you think changes should be made and ask yourself if you need more ideas. Use a caret ^ to indicate where you will add something.

E   **Evaluate** the problems. Read the Evaluate Cards.
- This doesn't sound quite right.
- Part of the essay isn't in the right order.
- People may not understand what I mean.
- I'm getting away from my main point.
- This is a weak or incomplete idea.
- The problem is _____.

V   **Verbalize** what you are going to do to fix the problems. Use the Verbalize Cards:
- Add: Include more information, examples, details, and so forth.
- Delete: Take something (a word, phrase, sentence) out.
- Rewrite: Say it (a word, phrase, sentence) in a different way.
- Move: Rearrange information (a word, phrase, sentence).

I   **Implement** the changes.

S   **Self-check** the first and second goals you set for yourself. Make other revisions based on these goals. Goals are listed on the Self-Check Cards.
- Make your paper more believable to your reader.
- Give enough information so that your reader can understand your position.
- Make sure your changes make sense.

E   **End** by rereading and making any additional changes.

My Self-Statements

To think of good ideas:

_____
_____
_____
_____
_____
_____

While I work:

_____
_____
_____
_____
_____
_____

To check my work:

_____
_____
_____
_____
_____
_____

Chapter 15

Peer Revising

This chapter is adapted from the Peer Revising lesson plans developed by Charles MacArthur, University of Delaware.

MATERIALS

Transparencies and paper copies:
- The Peer Revising Strategy* Checklist
- Ask Your Partner Sheet

Proofreading Checklist

Peer Revising Strategy Notes

LESSON 1

LESSON OVERVIEW

The teacher will set the purpose for learning a strategy to improve writing. The teacher will describe the steps in peer revision and begin memorization practice.

STUDENT OBJECTIVES

The students will listen to the teacher-led discussion about the peer revision strategy. The students will begin to memorize the peer revision steps.

> ### MATERIALS
> - Transparencies and paper copies (one for each student): The Peer Revising Strategy Checklist (PRS Checklist), Ask Your Partner sheet, Proofreading Checklist

SET THE CONTEXT FOR STUDENT LEARNING

 Begin the lessons by discussing the reasons for learning how to revise essays with a peer. Say, *"I will teach you a new way to revise essays. You should pay attention because at the end of today's lesson, I will test you on what you have learned. First, you should know that good writers often revise with peers when they write."* Give examples of when people share and revise (e.g., the team newsletter). Ask the students to describe times that they have listened to and read the writing of others.

DEVELOP THE STRATEGY AND SELF-REGULATION

Step 1: Describe Part 1. Revising

 Say, *"This is a revising strategy. Most expert writers revise in two ways—they work with a partner or peer to revise and they proofread."*

- Show the PRS Checklist (be sure to keep Part 2 covered while discussing Part 1). Uncover the first step, Listen and READ.

- Say, *"When you revise with a peer, you must first listen and read what has been written. The person who writes the paper is the writer, and the person giving feedback is the listener. We will talk about what the listener does when using the peer revising strategy."*

- Say, *"After you listen and read, you will tell your partner [uncover parts as you describe] what the paper is about. You try to discuss main ideas and important parts. Then you tell the writer what you liked best."*

- Say, *"After telling your partner what you liked best, you will read and make notes. First, you will write a question mark on the page if something is unclear or difficult to understand. Then you will note if details can be added. You will make a least three suggestions for adding more detail by inserting a caret (^) and the suggestions on your partner's paper."*

- Say, *"Once you have finished making revision notes on the paper, you and your partner (the writer) will discuss your suggestions. The writer will make notes about how to make the changes you suggest."*

324

- Say, *"You can also review the Ask Your Partner sheet as well as discuss each sentence on your paper that has a question mark by it to help you decide what to talk about with your partner."*

Step 2: Describe Roles

Say, *"After you have helped your partner with revising, it will be his or her turn to help you. You will switch roles and follow all the steps so that your partner becomes the listener and you the writer."*

Step 3: Describe Revising Papers

Say, *"After you have both listened to, read, recommended changes, and discussed your papers, you each, as the writers, will make revisions."*

Step 4: Describe Proofreading

- Uncover "proofreading" on the PRS Checklist and hand each student a Proofreading Checklist.

Say, *"Revising is not the only thing expert writers do. They also proofread their papers. Before you return your revised paper back to the listener, you will check your paper for complete sentences, capitalization, punctuation, and spelling."*

Step 5: Describe Trading Papers

Say, *"Once you as the writer have made all revisions and proofread your paper, you will give your paper back to the listener, who will also check for errors."*

WRAP-UP

Tell the students that for the next few days, you will be working on revising steps. Practice and test the students' recall of the revising steps.

LESSON 2

LESSON OVERVIEW

The teacher will model the peer revising strategy for revision with a sample paper.

STUDENT OBJECTIVES

The students will attend to the revision modeling lesson. The students will provide feedback on the verbal comments made by the teacher during modeling.

MATERIALS

- Transparencies: PRS Checklist, Ask Your Partner sheet
- Sample essay previously written by students for peer revising

- Paper copies (one for each student): PRS Checklist, Ask Your Partner sheet, Peer Revising Strategy Notes (extra paper to be used only if needed)
- Cue cards (made by the students)

SET THE CONTEXT FOR STUDENT LEARNING

Tell the students that for the next few days, you will be practicing the revision steps of the strategy. Briefly review the PRS Checklist and the Ask Your Partner sheet. Test the students' memory orally as you review.

DEVELOP THE STRATEGY AND SELF-REGULATION

Step 1: Model the Revising Strategy

Say, *"I will now read an essay written by a pretend partner. I will use the revising steps in the PRS Checklist to help me discuss the essay written by my partner. I am the listener and my pretend partner is the writer."*

- Model using the strategy. Use the overheads of the essay, the PRS Checklist, and the Ask Your Partner sheet so that the students can clearly see which step you, the listener, are completing. Be sure to use plenty of positive statements, but include a few negative, inappropriate statements too. Immediately have the students help you correct any inappropriate statements.

- Model how to make and write suggestions on the sample essay.

- Model and write notes for both the questions and opinion statements, pretending at this point to be the writer. Be sure to tell the students that you are now "switching hats."

- Model how the writer writes a revised essay. Be sure to talk the process aloud using the six types of self-statements throughout the process.

Step 2: Evaluate Questions and Opinions

Review and list on the chalkboard or a transparency questions and opinion statements that would be helpful to a peer.

Step 3: **Collaborative Practice with a Sample Essay**

> Say, *"We will work as a class to practice the peer revision strategy with a sample essay."*

- Give each student a PRS Checklist, an Ask Your Partner sheet, and sample essays to use for peer revising.

- Follow the same procedures you had completed during modeling, but this time, let the students take the lead as you and the listener take the role of the writer.

Step 4: **Evaluate Questions and Opinions**

Review and list on the chalkboard or a transparency the new questions and opinion statements that would be helpful to a peer.

WRAP-UP

Practice memorizing the revising steps on the PRS Checklist. Use the student-made cue cards and rapid-fire practice if needed. Repeat the steps of this lesson as many times as necessary to establish good revising questioning and opinion statements from the students.

LESSON 3

NOTE: This lesson is to be repeated until the students can independently complete the peer revising process without teacher assistance.

LESSON OVERVIEW

The teacher will scaffold and guide student pairs in using the peer revising strategy steps.

STUDENT OBJECTIVES

Working independently with a peer, the students will revise an essay using the steps in the peer revising strategy. The students will demonstrate memorization of the revising strategy steps without support materials.

MATERIALS

One copy for each student:
- PRS Checklist
- Ask Your Partner sheet

- The Peer Revising Strategy Notes
- Cue cards (made by students)
- Essays previously written by each student

SET THE CONTEXT FOR STUDENT LEARNING

Briefly review and test the students' recall of the peer revising strategy steps.

DEVELOP THE STRATEGY AND SELF-REGULATION

Step 1: Guided Practice

Say, *"You will work with a partner to read and revise each other's essays. You will use the revising steps in the peer revising strategy to help your partner revise his or her previously written essay. You and your partner will take turns being the listener and the writer. Remember to use helpful questions and opinions like the ones we have used over the past few sessions."*

- Carefully monitor the students as they use the revising steps with their partners.

- Be sure to allot time so that each student and listener gets a similar amount of time.

Step 2: Evaluate Questions and Opinions

Review and list on the chalkboard or a transparency some questions and opinion statements that were helpful to the writers.

WRAP-UP

If lessons continue, practice memorizing the revising steps of the PRS Checklist. Use the Cue Cards and rapid-fire practice if needed. The students should not go on to the next lesson until all of the steps are memorized. Be sure to save the revised essays for the next lesson—proofreading. When the students have mastered the revising steps, congratulate them. Tell them that they are now ready to learn the second part of using the PRS Checklist, which is proofreading.

LESSON 4

Peer Revising

LESSON OVERVIEW
The teacher will model the peer revising strategy for proofreading with a sample essay.

STUDENT OBJECTIVES
The students will attend to the proofreading modeling lesson. The students will provide feedback on teacher comments.

MATERIALS
- Transparencies: PRS Checklist, Proofreading Checklist
- Paper copies (one for each student): PRS Checklist; Proofreading Checklist; student-made cue cards; sample essays to use for peer revising, which should display some proof marks but not be completely proofread

SET THE CONTEXT FOR STUDENT LEARNING

Tell the students that for the next few days, you will be practicing the proofreading steps of the strategy. Briefly review the PRS Checklist and Proofreading Checklist. Test the students' memory orally as you review.

DEVELOP THE STRATEGY AND SELF-REGULATION

Step 1: Model the Proofreading Strategy

Say, *"I will read an essay written by a pretend partner. This essay has already been revised using the revising strategy steps. As you can see, the writer has also made some proofreading corrections. I will use the proofreading steps in the PRS Checklist to help me discuss the essay and the additional edits needed with my partner. I am the listener and my pretend partner is the writer."*

- Use the essay overheads, the PRS Checklist, and the Proofreading Checklist so that the students can clearly see what step you, as the listener, are completing. Be sure to use a lot of positive statements but also include a few negative, inappropriate statements. Immediately have the students help you correct any inappropriate statements.

- Model how to make and write suggestions on the sample essay.

- Tell the students that you are now switching roles. Model how the writer makes proofreading corrections. Be sure to talk through the process aloud using the six types of self-statements throughout the process.

Step 2: Collaborative Practice with a Sample Essay

Say, *"We will work as a class to practice the proofreading strategy steps with a sample essay."*

- Give each student a PRS Checklist, a Proofreading Checklist, and sample essays to use for peer revising.

- Follow the same procedures you used during modeling, but this time let the students take the lead as the listeners and you take the role of the writer.

WRAP-UP

Practice memorizing the proofreading steps of the peer revising strategy. Use the student-made cue cards and rapid-fire practice if needed. Repeat the steps of this lesson as many times as needed to establish good proofreading comments from the students.

LESSON 5

NOTE: This lesson is to be repeated until the students can independently complete the proofreading process without teacher assistance.

LESSON OVERVIEW
The teacher will scaffold and guide student pairs in using the proofreading strategy steps.

STUDENT OBJECTIVES
Working independently with a peer, the students will proofread an essay using the proofreading steps in the PRS Checklist. The students will demonstrate memorization of the proofreading strategy steps without support materials.

MATERIALS
- PRS Checklist
- Proofreading Checklist
- Cue cards (student-made)

- Essays previously written and revised by each student

SET THE CONTEXT FOR STUDENT LEARNING

Briefly review and test the students' recall of the PRS proofreading steps.

DEVELOP THE STRATEGY AND SELF-REGULATION

Step 1: Writers Proofread

Have the students proofread their papers using the Proofeading Checklist.

Step 2: Guided Practice in Peer Proofreading

Say, *"You will work with a partner, reading and proofreading essays. You will use the proofreading steps in the peer revising strategy to help your partner proofread his or her essay. You and your partner will take turns being the listener and the writer. Remember to use helpful comments like the ones we have used over the past few sessions."*

- Carefully monitor the students as they use the proofreading steps with their partners.
- Be sure to allot time so that each student and listener gets a similar amount of time.

WRAP-UP

If lessons continue, practice memorizing the proofreading steps of the peer revising strategy. Use the student-made cue cards and rapid-fire practice if needed. The students should not go on to next lesson until they have all of the steps memorized. When the students have mastered the proofreading steps, congratulate them. Tell them that they are now ready to use all the steps in the peer revising strategy.

LESSON 6

NOTE: This lesson is to be repeated until the students can independently complete the revising proofreading process without teacher assistance.

LESSON OVERVIEW
The teacher will scaffold and guide student pairs in using all peer revising strategy steps.

STUDENT OBJECTIVES
Working independently with a peer, the students will revise and proofread an essay using the revising and proofreading steps in the peer revising strategy. The students will demonstrate memorization of the revising and proofreading strategy steps without support materials.

> ## MATERIALS
> • Essays previously written by each student (ones not used in any prior lesson)

SET THE CONTEXT FOR STUDENT LEARNING

Briefly test the students' recall of the peer revising strategy steps.

DEVELOP THE STRATEGY AND SELF-REGULATION

Step 1: Guided Practice

Say, *"You will work with a partner, reading, revising, and proofreading essays. You will use all steps in the peer revising strategy to help your partner revise and proofread his or her written essay. You and your partner will take turns being the listener and the writer. Remember to use helpful questions, opinions, and comments like the ones we have used over the past few sessions."*

• Carefully monitor the students as they use the revising and proofreading steps with their partners.

• Be sure to allot time so that each student and listener get a similar amount of time.

WRAP-UP

Continue monitoring lessons until the students are able to use the peer revising strategy independently. When the students have mastered all the steps, congratulate them. Tell them that they are now ready to use all the steps in the peer revising strategy any time they write an essay.

The Peer Revising Strategy Checklist

Part 1. Revising

Listen and READ. _____

TELL what the paper is
about. _____

TELL what you liked
best. _____

READ and make NOTES _____
Is everything CLEAR? _____
Can any details be
added? _____

DISCUSS your suggestions _____
with the writer.

Notes

Part 2. Proofreading

CHECK your paper
and correct errors. _____

EXCHANGE papers and check for
errors in:
SENTENCES _____
CAPITALS _____
PUNCTUATION _____
SPELLING _____
DISCUSS corrections.

Ask Your Partner

PARTS?   Does it have a good
                beginning, middle, and
                ending?

ORDER?   Does the paper follow a
                logical sequence?

DETAILS?   Where can more details be
                added?

CLARITY?   Is there any part that is
                hard to understand?

Proofreading Checklist

Sentences

Read each sentence. Is it complete?

Capital Letters

Is the first letter of each sentence capitalized?
Are proper nouns capitalized?

Punctuation

Is correct punctuation at the end of each
    sentence?

Spelling

Circle words you are not sure of.
Check spelling with your word list, spelling
    checker, or dictionary.

Peer Revising Strategy Notes

_____

_____

_____

_____

_____

_____

_____

_____

_____

_____

_____

_____

_____

_____

_____

_____

_____

_____

_____

_____

_____

_____

_____

_____

_____

_____

_____

Section V

Strategy for a Writing Competency Test

Chapter 16

PLAN & WRITE

This chapter is adapted from the PLAN & WRITE lesson plans developed by Susan De La Paz, University of Maryland.

P = Pay attention to the prompt.

L = List main ideas to develop your essay.

A = Add supporting ideas.

N = Number major points in the order you will use them.

W = Work from your plan to develop a thesis statement.

R = Remember your goals.

I = Include transition words for each paragraph.

T = Try to use different kinds of sentences.

E = Exciting, interesting million-dollar words.

MATERIALS

Transparencies and paper copies:
- PLAN & WRITE* Mnemonic Chart
- Brainstorming Sheet
- PLAN & WRITE Planning Sheet
- Goals for Proficient Writing
- Characteristics of Good Essays
- Different Kinds of Sentences
- Exciting, Interesting Million-Dollar Words
- Writing Prompt Worksheet
- Revision Checklist

Essay: Beware of Video Games

Essay: Feeding Wild Animals

Essay: My Favorite Holiday

Essay: The Most Important Things

Essay: My Ideal Saturday

Essay: I Have to Say No

Essay (extra): A Perfect Age to Be (Versions 1 and 2)

Essay (extra): A Special Event (Versions 1 and 2)

Essay (extra): The Most Important Invention (Versions 1 and 2)

PLAN & WRITE Cue Cards

LESSON 1

LESSON OVERVIEW
The teacher will set the purpose for learning a strategy to improve writing. The teacher will describe the steps in PLAN & WRITE and start memorization practice.

STUDENT OBJECTIVES
Students will listen to the teacher-led discussion about using the four planning steps of PLAN and how to continue to plan during composing with WRITE. Students will begin memorizing PLAN & WRITE.

MATERIALS

- Transparencies: PLAN & WRITE mnemonic chart, Brainstorming Sheet, PLAN & WRITE Planning Sheet, Goals for Proficient Writing

- Writing Prompt Worksheet (write prompt on blackboard)
- Notebook paper and pencils

SET THE CONTEXT FOR STUDENT LEARNING

Begin the lessons by discussing the reasons to learn how to plan and compose essays. Say, *"I'm going to teach you a new way to plan and write good essays using the PLAN & WRITE method. You should pay attention because at the end of today's lesson, I will test you on what you have learned. First, you should know that good writers plan before they write, and they continue planning as they compose their essays. Who knows what good writers do?"* Call on a student. *"Here are some reasons why you should learn to write good essays:"*

- First, the basic ideas in essays are found everywhere—on TV, on the radio, in newspapers, in letters to the editor, at home, and so forth.

- Second, people who can write good essays know how to convince other people to agree with their point of view.

- Third, it is important for you to learn how to write good essays because you will need to be able to write good essays for many purposes in school and later in life.

- Say, *"Starting today, I will show you a strategy for planning and then writing good essays and you will learn to use the strategy during the next few weeks."*

DEVELOP THE STRATEGY AND SELF-REGULATION

Step 1: **Describe the First PLAN Step (Pay Attention to the Prompt)**

Say, *"I will now describe this planning strategy. Most expert writers plan before they start to compose. A plan is like a guide, allowing you to think more about the quality of your composition when you are actually writing the essay."*

- Show the mnemonic chart. Uncover the first step. Say, *"Pay attention to the prompt."*

- Say, *"When you write your essay for a writing assessment, it is important to address the prompt. That is why the first step in the planning strategy is to pay attention to the prompt and figure out what you are being asked to write about."*

- Ask the students to describe incidents in which they have written to a prompt.

- Have the students look at the blackboard or an overhead transparency where you have previously written the prompt: This month, your class has an opportunity to take a one-day educational field trip. In an essay, state where you think the class should go, and give reasons explaining why you think this would be a good place for the class to visit.

- Say, *"This prompt tells us two things—the writing situation and the directions for writing. The first part gets you thinking about your writing subject, and the second part gives exact directions for writing."*

  - **Writing Situation**

    This month your class has an opportunity to take a one-day educational field trip.

  - **Directions for Writing**

    In an essay, state where you think the class should go and give reasons explaining why you think this would be a good place for the class to visit.

- Model and say, *"Let's put one line under words in the prompt that tell you what you are supposed to write about."*

- Say, *"Who can tell me what we should write about for this prompt?"* Call on a student. Make sure the students realize that the topic is *where the class should go on a one-day educational trip.* Say, *"What should we do when we identify what we are supposed to write about?"*

- Model and say, *"The prompt also gives you directions that explain how you are to develop your essay. Underline words that tell how to develop your essay twice. Let's look at the first prompt that I have written on the board and find how we are supposed to develop the essay."* Make sure the students realize that they are to give reasons explaining why the class should go on a one-day educational trip to the already-named location.

Step 2: Describe the Second and Third PLAN Steps (List the Main Ideas and Add Supporting Ideas)

 Uncover the second and third steps. Say, *"List the main ideas to develop your essay"* and *"Add supporting ideas* [e.g., details, examples]."

- Model and say, *"The second step of the planning strategy tells you to list, or brainstorm, ideas about the prompt. You will write your ideas on a Brainstorming Sheet."* Show the students the Brainstorming Sheet transparency. Say, *"The third step tells you to brainstorm ideas that support the main ideas. Let's talk about these two steps in more detail."*

- Say, *"Who knows what it means to brainstorm ideas?"* Help the students understand that brainstorming means thinking about what they remember and making notes about their ideas instead of writing complete sentences. Say, *"That's right. Brainstorming is a quick way to make notes about ideas you want to use to answer the prompt."*

- Model and say, *"Here is one way to remember your ideas as you brainstorm. Using this Brainstorming Sheet, brainstorm possible answers to the prompt on the top lines first. After you decide what you will write about, list the main ideas on the long lines and then add supporting details on the short lines."* Show the students where the main ideas and supporting details should be written. *"Supporting ideas can be details that correspond to main ideas, examples, or thoughts that elaborate your main ideas. You can also brainstorm ideas this way on lined notebook paper."*

Step 3: Describe the Fourth PLAN Step (Number the Major Points)

 Put the mnemonic chart transparency back on the overhead projector. Uncover the fourth step. Say, *"Number major points in the order you will use them."*

- Say, *"In the fourth step, you will pick your best ideas and number the major points in the order that you will use them. You must have three major ideas for each of the three body paragraphs of your essay, and you must have at least three supporting ideas, details, or elaborations for each main idea. Try to brainstorm more than three ideas because one idea may not be good."*

- Uncover the next question—How do you plan more as you go?—on the mnemonic chart transparency.

- Say, *"After you make a good plan, you must use it to write your essay. The second essay reminder is WRITE and it tells you how to keep planning as you go."*

Step 4: Describe the First WRITE Step (Work from Your Plan)

- Uncover the statement Work from your plan to develop a thesis statement on the mnemonic chart transparency.

 Say, *"It is easy to write a good essay when you use your plan. In this step, you will reread your major ideas and make up a thesis statement that answers the prompt. You will write your thesis statement on an Essay Sheet."* Show the first page of the PLAN & WRITE Planning Sheet transparency. Say, *"I will tell you more about how to write your thesis statement later on because there are two ways to write a thesis statement. The thesis statement can be the first or last sentence of your introductory paragraph."*

Step 5: Describe the Second WRITE Step (Remember Your Goals)

- Uncover the statement—Remember your goals—on the mnemonic chart transparency.

 Say, *"In this step, you will think about one or more goals for writing a good essay. Let's look at a list of goals for writing proficient essays. Who knows what proficient means?"* Display the Goals for Proficient Writing overhead transparency. Say, *"We will go over the ways to choose goals that are helpful for you on another day."*

Step 6: Describe the Third WRITE Step (Include Transition Words)

- Uncover the statement—Include transition words for each paragraph—on the mnemonic chart transparency.

 Say, *"Transition words help the reader understand how your paper is organized. To perform this step, use transition words for each of your five paragraphs. Later on, I will give you a packet of cards that have different transition words on them, and you can use them until you learn at least one example for each kind of paragraph."*

Step 7: Describe the Fourth WRITE Step (Try to Use Different Kinds of Sentences)

- Uncover the statement—Try to use different kinds of sentences—on the mnemonic chart transparency.

Say, *"You may already know that there are different kinds of sentences. To perform this step, you will use more than one kind of sentence when you write. We will review different kinds of sentences tomorrow."*

Step 8: Describe the Fifth WRITE Step (Exciting, Interesting, Million-Dollar Words)

- Uncover the phrase—Exciting, Interesting Million-Dollar Words—on the mnemonic chart transparency.

Say, *"One of our goals is to use mature, vivid vocabulary. To help you do this, try to use synonyms for words that appear more than once in your essay and use synonyms for common vocabulary words. Who knows what a synonym is?"* Help the students understand that synonyms are words that are similar in meaning to the word they want to use in their essay. Say, *"We will talk about this step in more detail later on."*

WRAP-UP: TEST RECALL OF THE PLAN & WRITE STRATEGY

Say, *"Let's start memorizing PLAN & WRITE. Take out a sheet of paper and write the numbers 1 through 10 on the side."*

1. Say, *"What are two mnemonics, or reminders, that tell you how to plan and write a good essay? Answer this question and explain what each letter in the mnemonic means for numbers 2 through 10. If you cannot answer question number one, raise your hand, and I will explain it to you so you can work on the rest of the quiz."*

2. P =
3. L =
4. A =
5. N =
6. W =
7. R =
8. I =
9. T =
10. E =

LESSON 2

NOTE: This lesson is repeated three times with different student objectives. While these lesson plans indicate that Lesson 2 will take 3 days, you can modify this as appropriate. Extra practice essays are provided if you need them.

LESSON OVERVIEW

In these three lessons, the teacher and students will review the components of good essay writing in PLAN & WRITE.

STUDENT OBJECTIVES

1st day: Students review thesis sentence, transition words, types of sentences, interesting words, and essay parts using a model essay.

2nd day: Students review essay parts and synonyms using a model essay.

3rd day: Students review pronoun and verb agreement and revise an essay.

MATERIALS

- Transparencies: Mnemonic chart; Brainstorming Sheet; PLAN & WRITE Planning Sheet; Goals for Proficient Writing; Characteristics of Good Essays, Different Kinds of Sentences; Exciting, Interesting Million-
- Dollar Words; Essays: *Beware of Video Games* (1st day), *Feeding Wild Animals* (2nd day), *My Favorite Holiday* (3rd day)
- Writing prompt (write on blackboard)
- Notebook paper and pencils

SET THE CONTEXT FOR STUDENT LEARNING: BRIEFLY REVIEW PLAN & WRITE

- Put the mnemonic chart transparency on an overhead projector. Uncover the first half of the sheet to display the mnemonic *PLAN*.

 Say, *"Yesterday, we started learning how to plan a good essay using PLAN. Today, we will review how to use your plan to write the essay out on your paper."* Uncover the second half of the sheet and display the mnemonic *WRITE*. *"When you write your paper, your plan becomes a guide, letting you think more about the quality of your essay. In other words, you need to develop a good thesis statement, remember your goals, include transition words, plan good sentences as you write, and use good vocabulary."*

- Put the Goals for Proficient Writing sheet on the overhead projector. Ask the students questions to make sure they understand what these goals mean, especially the goal for identifying their audience (readers) and mode (expository writing). Be sure to tell the students that if they start writing an expository essay and then switch to narrative (telling a story), their essay will not be proficient and could actually confuse readers.

DEVELOP THE STRATEGY AND SELF-REGULATION

Step 1: Evaluate an Essay (Thesis Statement)

 Say, *"We will now read an essay to find out if the writer has a clear thesis statement and whether he or she has addressed any of our goals for writing proficient essays. We will also look to see if the writer has good sentences and mature vocabulary."*

- Display the following prompt and then place the first essay, *Beware of Video Games*, on the overhead projector.

Prompt:

> *Some people complain that young people today spend too much time playing video games.*
>
> *Write an essay stating whether you believe video games are harmful to young people and give reasons explaining your point of view.*

- Say, *"Read along silently while I read the first paragraph aloud. When I finish reading the first paragraph, we will check to see if the writer has a good introduction with a clear thesis statement that answers the prompt."* Ask the students to identify the thesis statement, to locate it in the first paragraph, and to decide if it has answered the prompt. Ask the students what they would do to improve the thesis statement.

Step 2: Evaluate an Essay (Transition Words)

 Say, *"Read along silently while I read the second paragraph aloud. When I finish reading, we will check to see if the writer includes any transition words."* Make sure they note *the first reason why* as a transition phrase. Without reading the rest of the essay aloud, say, *"Who can tell me what transition words are given to introduce the remaining paragraphs?"*

Step 3: Evaluate an Essay (Different Kinds of Sentences)

 Say, *"I want to review what we mean by different kinds of sentences before we read more paragraphs of the essay."*

- Place the Different Kinds of Sentences transparency on the overhead projector. If you have previously taught students types of sentences, refer to this information now. If not, tell the students that there are at least three kinds of sentences, and it is important for them to use more than one kind of sentence when they write their essays.

- Place the *Beware of Video Games* essay transparency back on the overhead projector.

- Say, *"Read along silently while I read the third and fourth paragraphs of our sample essay aloud. When I finish reading these paragraphs, we will check to see if the writer includes more than one kind of sentence."* Make sure the students see that although there are many complex sentences in these paragraphs, some long sentences are not complex. As an aside, point out additional transition words that are in paragraph four (as an illustration). Ask for suggestions to change one complex sentence into a compound or simple sentence.

Step 4: Evaluate an Essay (Interesting Words)

 Say, *"Read along silently while I read the last paragraph aloud. When I finish reading, we will look back to see whether the writer used any exciting, interesting, million-dollar words."* Find a handful of words on which to focus so that you can finish the lesson. This will be a focal point for the second model essay that will be taught on the following day.

| Step 5: | **Evaluate an Essay (Essay Parts)** |

Say, *"Before you wrote your first essay, I showed you an overhead that described the five paragraphs and what they did."* Review the bottom third of the Characteristics of Good Essays overhead. *"We will now identify the parts of an essay on this paper. The essay parts include an introductory paragraph, three body paragraphs, and a concluding paragraph."* Point out the essay parts on the transparency. *"Who can remember the parts of an essay?"* Call on a student. As an alternative, ask all students to write essay parts on a sheet of paper.

Day 2

Repeat this lesson with the prompt below and the second model essay, *Feeding Wild Animals.* Use the Exciting, Interesting Million-Dollar Words overhead rather than the Different Kinds of Sentences overhead. If students had difficulty with the different parts of the five-paragraph essay, spend the first part of the lesson reviewing them and then focus on synonyms.

Prompt:

> *Wild animals sometimes starve due to overpopulation, natural disasters, and man-made causes.*
>
> *Write an essay stating whether or not you believe people should feed starving wild animals and give reasons explaining your point of view.*

Day 3

Repeat this lesson with the prompt below and the last model essay, *My Favorite Holiday.*

Prompt:

> *Most people have at least one favorite holiday.*
>
> *Write an essay describing your favorite holiday and give reasons explaining why you like it the most.*

First, use the model essay to review pronoun and verb agreement. Then ask the students to revise parts of the essay for 1) essay parts, 2) different kinds of sentences, 3) synonyms, and 4) pronoun and verb agreement.

As you go through this activity, it is important to emphasize both positive aspects of the essay (elaboration of detail) and areas that need improvement (one sentence for the introductory paragraph). It is not important for students to fix every detail; instead, they should look for things that they can fix relatively easily, as if a student had finished his or her essay in 25 minutes and had the remaining 10 minutes to make modest revisions.

WRAP-UP

Day 1 of Lesson 2

Memorize PLAN & WRITE (If you are out of time, assign this as homework or do it during the following class.)

- Quiz the class on the meaning of each letter in the mnemonic PLAN & WRITE. Add an additional question: *What three things do you do when you Pay attention to the prompt?*

- Answer: First you READ it. Then you underline what you are being asked to write about (not the situation) once. Then you underline twice how you develop your essay.

Day 2 of Lesson 2

Memorize PLAN & WRITE

- Quiz the class on the meaning of each letter in PLAN & WRITE. Add an additional question: *What two things do you do when you List main ideas?*

- Answer: You brainstorm possible answers to the prompt and then pick one. Then you brainstorm three main ideas about the topic you picked.

Memorize PLAN & WRITE

- Quiz the class on the meaning of each letter in PLAN & WRITE. Add an additional question: *What are three kinds of supporting ideas?*

- Answer: Details, elaborations, and examples; they can all be used or just one can be used to create a supporting idea.

Additional Activities If Time Permits (Or for Homework, Extra Credit, and So Forth)

1. Write a paragraph on one of the same topics from another point of view. Use at least three different kinds of sentences in the paragraph.

2. Create your own prompt. Be sure it contains a writing situation and the directions for writing the essay. Exchange papers with a friend and practice underlining what you are writing about and how to develop the essay.

3. Write one paragraph using four target words and their synonyms from the Exciting, Interesting Million-Dollar Words overhead.

LESSON 3

LESSON OVERVIEW

The use of a revision checklist to evaluate essays will be introduced in this lesson.

STUDENT OBJECTIVES

The students will learn how to evaluate essays using a revision checklist. The students will use the revision checklist as they evaluate model essays to set goals. They will practice identifying 1) what you are being asked to write about, and 2) how you will develop your essay in several prompts.

MATERIALS

- Transparencies: Mnemonic chart, Brainstorming Sheet, PLAN & WRITE Planning Sheet, Characteristics of Good Essays, Writing Prompt Worksheet, Revision Checklist
- Writing prompt (write on blackboard)

- Essays previously written by students: *The Most Important Things, My Ideal Saturday, I Have to Say No (teacher provided)*
- Notebook paper and pencils

SET THE CONTEXT FOR STUDENT LEARNING

Using overheads from prior lessons, briefly review PLAN & WRITE strategy components.

DEVELOP THE STRATEGY AND SELF-REGULATION

Step 1: Evaluate Sample Essays

 Say, *"Let's look at essays written by students. They were written as practice essays for the same writing assessment. We will make suggestions for improving the essays."*

Display the prompts.

Prompt 1:

> *Think of the most important things you could wish for if given the chance.*
>
> *Write an essay about the wishes you have selected and give reasons explaining why they are the most important.*

Prompt 2:

> *Think about your ideal way to spend a Saturday afternoon.*
>
> *Explain what the day would be like.*

Prompt 3:

> *Think about situations where you should say no to a friend.*
>
> *Write an essay about those situations and give reasons explaining why it is important to say no.*

Go over each of the three sample essays, having the students take turns reading them aloud. As you review each, display and use the Revision Checklist and follow the Rules for Revising for each. Discuss 1) two positive comments, 2) two or three items in need of improvement, and 3) two hypothetical goals for the student writer. Explain to your students that these essays have problems that many students make when writing essays.

Step 2: Practice Paying Attention to the Prompt

Say, *"The last activity for today is to practice paying attention to the prompt. I will hand out a Writing Prompt Worksheet with twelve writing prompts in a list. As you work on this page, you will identify what you are being asked to write about and how you will develop your essay. Underline the first part once and the second part twice. Do not underline the writing situation."*

Show the Characteristics of Good Essays overhead to review the difference between the writing situation and the directions for writing.

After you dissect and underline each prompt, turn your paper over and brainstorm the possible answers to the prompt and at least three main ideas for your answer. Show the students how to do this with the prompt from the Characteristics of Good Essays overhead.

NOTE: Students frequently experience their greatest difficulties in understanding what the prompt is asking them to write about, brainstorming how to respond, and coming up with the main ideas to develop their essay. It is a good idea to review answers on the Writing Prompt Worksheet over the next several days rather than in one session.

WRAP-UP

Review and test recall of the PLAN & WRITE strategy components.

LESSON 4

LESSON OVERVIEW

The teacher will model how to plan and compose an essay.

STUDENT OBJECTIVES

The students will observe the teacher model how to plan and compose an essay.

MATERIALS

- Transparencies: Mnemonic chart, Brainstorming Sheet, PLAN & WRITE Planning Sheet, Characteristics of Good Essays
- PLAN & WRITE Cue Cards

- Writing prompt (write on blackboard or overhead)
- Essays previously written by students
- Chart paper or lined overhead for writing
- Pencils

SET THE CONTEXT FOR STUDENT LEARNING

Using overheads from prior lessons, briefly review PLAN & WRITE strategy components and Writing Prompt Worksheet answers.

DEVELOP THE STRATEGY AND SELF-REGULATION

Step 1: Model the Strategy

- Tell the students that you will show them how to plan and compose an essay.

Say, *"I will now show you how to use PLAN & WRITE together to plan and compose a good essay. I will think aloud as I go. You might be able to help me if I ask you, but what I really want you to do is listen and watch me work. It is my turn to work and your turn to relax!"*

- Model the entire process using the PLAN & WRITE Planning Sheet and the PLAN & WRITE Cue Cards. Read the prompt.

Display the prompt:

> *Think of a person you would like to meet. This person may be from the present or the past.*
>
> *Write an essay about the person you would like to meet and give specific reasons why you want to meet him or her.*

- Use your own words to paraphrase the following script:

Say, *"The first step of my planning strategy is to pay attention to the prompt. That means that I don't start writing yet. I will read the prompt and first decide what I am being asked to write about, and then decide how I will develop my essay. The writing situation is a person I want to meet from either the present or the past. My directions are to write an essay telling whom I would like to meet, so I'll underline these words."*

- Underline the words on the overhead or blackboard.

"I must now identify how I should develop my essay. It says here that I should give specific reasons for wanting to meet him or her, so when I develop my essay, I have to provide specific reasons for wanting to meet this person. I will now underline this twice so that I won't forget what it is."

- Double underline this on the overhead or blackboard.

"Next, I need to list main ideas. The first step is to brainstorm possible answers to my prompt."

- Display the Brainstorming Sheet transparency.

"I will make a list to brainstorm my ideas, using this format, but I will use paper so you can see it later when I write my essay. Right now, I will brainstorm on paper at the blackboard so you can see it when I write the essay later on."

- Make a single long vertical line on the paper.

"Let's see. Whom would I like to meet? The prompt says the person can be from the past or present. I will come up two or three possible answers to the prompt and write notes on the long line at the top of the paper as I go. Well, I think Cleopatra must have been a very interesting person. I'll write her down. Abraham Lincoln is definitely my favorite president. What about people from the present? There are so many people I would like to meet. Maybe Dwayne Wade, my favorite basketball player. Now he's an interesting guy! Of all these people, I think the person I would have the most questions to ask is Dwayne Wade, so I will use him for my essay."

- Circle "Dwayne Wade." Brainstorm at least three main ideas for the development of the essay.

"Now that I have decided to write about meeting Dwayne Wade, I must think of ideas so that I can develop my essay. I must give specific reasons for wanting to meet him. I will list my main ideas first."

- Create three big lines on the paper and three smaller lines for each. Tell the students that they can do this on their own paper if they want.

"What is a good reason to meet Dwayne Wade? Well, I would like to ask him how he got his nickname, Flash, so I guess I'll write for my first main idea: Ask him how he got the nickname Flash.

"Now I need to brainstorm more main ideas. I really want to know how he went from being an almost unknown draft pick to an up-and-coming NBA star. I wonder if his college coach was important to his being discovered, or if a recruiter saw him play. Well, I will make how he went from an almost unknown draft pick to a rising NBA star my main idea, and I can save questions about his coach and recruiters for supporting ideas."

- Put this idea on one of the big lines on the paper.

"Also, another main reason to meet Dwayne Wade is so I could play a little basketball with him."

- Write this idea on a big line on the paper.

  "I would also like to ask him what he thinks about playing with the Miami Heat. I'll add an extra line on my plan for this idea."

- Add this as the fourth main idea.

  "My next step is to add supporting ideas. I will think of details, elaborations, or examples that support my main idea."

- Write supporting ideas on small lines next to each main idea.

  "My first main idea is how he got his nickname Flash. What can I ask about here? Well, I would like to know who gave him this nickname and why."

- Write "Who gave nickname and Why?" on the first two lines.

  "What else could I ask? Oh, yeah, I would like to know if he ever had any other nicknames in college, and if he ever had any nicknames that embarrassed him."

- Write "Other nicknames, embarrassing?" on the third line.

  "I wonder what his teammates think about his nickname Flash. I'll write that down."

- Make an extra line to write, "What teammates think."

  "My second main idea is how he went from being an almost unknown draft pick to an up-and-coming NBA star. I want to know if his college coach was a big help, or if an important recruiter spotted him. I would also like to know how it feels to be a big NBA star now, and I wonder if Shaquille O'Neal helped him."

- Put these ideas on smaller lines of the list, adding a fourth line for Shaquille O'Neal, indicating that they are details.

  "My third main idea is to play basketball with him. I know that I'm not very good, but Wade would be a good teacher. I'll write down some reasons that support this idea. First of all, he should remember what it's like to just be starting out, so he can give me some tips. Also, O'Neal said he was the most phenomenal second-year player he had seen since himself. Finally, he was the youngest player ever to start on opening night for the Heat, when he was 21."

- Write these ideas on smaller lines of the list, indicating that they are details. Quickly review the ideas on the Brainstorming Sheet.

  "Well, it looks like I have some pretty good ideas here. I don't really have any supporting ideas for what it feels like to play with the Miami Heat because I already asked a lot of questions about his teammates, so I will leave that main idea out. I have three and that is fine. These are all good reasons why Dwayne Wade is a person whom I would really like to meet. I guess my next step is to number my ideas. I need to decide which ideas are strong and how to organize them for writing. To help me do this, I have to read my ideas and put a mark by the supporting ideas and examples I will use. Also, I need to number the main ideas in the order that I will use them."

- You should identify at least one idea that is not strong and decide aloud to skip it.

"I have many good ideas here, but I'm not sure if I need them all. I think I'll skip the part about embarrassing nicknames because that might sound silly in my report, and he might not want to answer that."

• Put a dot by the ideas you will use.

"I put dots by all the supporting ideas that I will use. Now I need to organize my ideas in a logical order. I think that I will first write about how Wade became a rising NBA star. Then I will write about how he got the nickname Flash. Finally, saving the best part for last, I will write about why I'd like to play basketball with Dwayne Wade because I think that would be the best part about meeting this basketball player."

• Make sure you order the essays in some way other than numbering 1, 2, 3 vertically to ensure that the students realize they are deciding what makes sense rather than automatically writing paragraphs in the same order that they brainstormed ideas.

"The last step is to continue planning as I compose my essay, thinking about the quality of my essay. I need to remember the mnemonic WRITE. I have some cue cards to help me compose my essay. The cue cards remind me how to write each paragraph, and they also have instructions about using transition words. I will show you how to use these as I write my essay. My PLAN will also help me write because it shows me where to write my ideas as I go."

• Display the PLAN & WRITE Planning Sheet transparency on the overhead. Then hand out cue cards for the students to follow along with you.

"Here are some cue cards for you to use so you can follow along as I go. I will collect these cards at the end of the day, and then you will have them for your use whenever we need them.

"My first step is to work from my plan to develop my thesis statement. I must decide whether I will put my thesis statement first or start with an attention getter. I will show you both ways to write your thesis statement, although I would prefer that you put your thesis statement first until you fully understand what to do."

• Explain that starting with an *attention getter* means starting with something other than the thesis statement and that the cue card shows a series of options.

"What are the two ways to write an introduction for your essay?"

• Students should realize that they can write their topic sentence first or they can place it later in the introduction paragraph by starting with an attention getter.

"You should know how to write a solid introduction by putting your thesis sentence at the beginning of your introductory paragraph. Right now, I will show you how to do this. Later on, I will show you how you start with an attention getter for the introduction to this essay."

• Check off the thesis statement first on the PLAN & WRITE Planning Sheet.

"Take a look a the first cue card. This will help me with my introductory paragraph. Now I'll write my thesis on my essay sheet. Since I have decided to put my thesis statement first, I will write it as the beginning of my introductory paragraph here. That way I

353

won't have to recopy it later. I must be sure that I answer the prompt in my thesis statement."

- Put the following thesis statement on the PLAN & WRITE Planning Sheet transparency.

  "I think I'll write, 'Dwayne Wade, who plays on the Miami Heat basketball team, is a person I would really like to meet.' That seems very straightforward. I have to say more in my introductory paragraph. I think I'll mention my three main reasons why I would really like to meet Dwayne Wade."

- Write down your ideas as you explain them.

  "My first idea is 'If I ever had the chance to meet Dwayne Wade, I would ask him how he went from being an almost unknown college player to a rising NBA star. Also, I would like to find out how he got his nickname Flash.' Good, I used a transition word to indicate my next main idea. Finally, I would ask Dwayne Wade if we could play a game of one-on-one so that I could improve my game by playing with one of my favorite NBA players.

  "My next step in WRITE is to remember my goals."

- Display the Goals for Proficient Writing transparency.

  "My goals are to remain on topic, to show clear organization using frequent transitions, and to use mature, appropriate vocabulary. I will be sure not to forget these as I write."

- Begin writing your first body paragraph using your cue cards for reminders. Also, frequently refer to your finished brainstorming list on the chart paper, blackboard, or transparency.

  "I am off to a good start. My introductory paragraph will guide me through the rest of the paper. Of course, I have to remember all the things from WRITE, especially transition words, different kinds of sentences, and those million-dollar words! I will be sure to use transition words to introduce ideas. My cue cards will be a big help with transitions.

  "I'll start out with a transition to introduce my first main idea."

- Ask the students to look at the first body paragraph cue card.

  "My first reason for wanting to meet Dwayne Wade is to talk about how he became a rising NBA star. I guess I should go on and write about my first supporting idea. 'Dwayne Wade has played a number of strong games and gained a great deal of attention since his days playing with Marquette University. I would like to know how it feels to be a rising star in the NBA. I would also like to know if his college coach helped him become a star and if an important recruiter spotted him. He plays with Shaquille O'Neal for the Miami Heat now, and I wonder if O'Neal has helped him.' Actually, I don't really like the word strong. *I don't think that it describes Wade's best games very well. Perhaps, I can think of a million-dollar word that is more accurate and more interesting. Hmmm, extraordinary. That's it! I'll go back and change* strong *to extraordinary."*

- Erase *strong* and write *extraordinary.*

"Now I can move on to my second idea—how he got his nickname. I have to start this paragraph with a transition word, indicating that I am about to write my second main idea."

• Ask the students to look at the second body paragraph cue card.

"Second, if I met Dwayne Wade, we would discuss how he got his nickname Flash. First of all, I want to know how he got this nickname. I'll write, 'I wonder how he got this nickname and why? Furthermore, I would like to know what his teammates think of this nickname.'

"I REALLY LIKE WHAT I'VE WRITTEN SO FAR! It's interesting and well organized.

"Now I'll move onto my third body paragraph."

• Instruct the students to continue looking at the same cue card because it contains transition words that will be appropriate for the third body paragraph.

"My main idea is that I would like to meet Dwayne Wade so that we could play a game of one-on-one together. This might be a little hard to write about. Luckily, I have brainstormed some good reasons to support this idea. I'll just start writing and I'll try to remember to include different kinds of sentences as I write. 'My third reason for wanting to meet Dwayne Wade is to ask him if we could play a game of one-on-one because I think that he would be a great basketball teacher. I think he would be an excellent teacher for a few reasons. First of all, Wade has not been in the NBA long, and he would probably still remember what it is like to be a player without experience.' Better yet, a novice player.'"

• Erase *player without experience* and write *novice player*.

"I like the word novice. *It looks like this essay is priceless with all of these million-dollar words! Back to the essay, I can support this idea some more. As I move to my next idea, I can include a transition word. I'll use* also. *'Also, Dwayne Wade has played with one of the best players in the world, Shaquille O'Neal.' I think I have used different kinds of sentences in this paragraph so far. Let's see. I have used a simple sentence and more complex sentences."*

• Identify sentence types for your students in your essay.

"Having different kinds of sentences is part of writing a good essay. The final reason, which is another good transition, why I would like Dwayne Wade to teach me how to improve my basketball game is because O'Neal thinks he is one of the best second-year players ever. I will write, 'Shaquille O'Neal said that Wade was the most phenomenal second-year players since himself, and he is the youngest player ever to start on opening night for the Heat. I would like to learn from one of the best!'

"I'm nearly finished. This has been a lot of work, but it really is one of my best essays ever. If I can write a good conclusion, it will be complete. First, I'll review my three body paragraphs to make sure that I summarize this essay accurately."

• Go back and read the three body paragraphs.

"First, I'll pick a transition word to summarize ideas. Let me check my cue card. I'll use 'In summary.' 'In summary, I would be happy . . .' No, not happy. 'I would be overjoyed if

I ever had the chance to meet Dwayne Wade.' *That is much better.* 'I think that he is a very impressive basketball player. If I ever had the opportunity to meet Wade, I would like to ask him about how he became a rising star in the NBA. I would also like to ask him a few questions about his nickname Flash. Finally, I would not let our meeting end without attempting to persuade the great Dwayne Wade to play a game of one-on-one with me so I could learn a little more about the game of basketball from an NBA star!'

"All right! I just wrote a fantastic essay! Thank you for helping me and paying attention to me while I worked."

- NOTE: Following is the script for the second way to introduce a thesis statement.

  "Now I will try to start with an attention getter because I think that is a great way to grab someone's attention and get them excited about reading my essay!"

- Check off *Start with an Attention Getter* on the PLAN & WRITE Planning Sheet.

  "I will show you one way to start with an attention getter and write a new introductory paragraph. I won't redo the other paragraphs, however, because they will be the same.

  "I want to share something important now. If you decide to start with an attention getter, you will write a different kind of thesis statement than if you decide to put your thesis statement first. Let me show you what I mean. I think I'll write, 'Given the opportunity to meet any famous person, I would definitely choose to meet Dwayne Wade so that I could ask him how he became a rising basketball star, discuss his nickname Flash, and invite him to play a game of one-on-one with me.' *The difference between this thesis statement and the other one is that I have put all of my reasons in the same sentence rather than separate sentences. This is because my other sentences in the introductory paragraph will lead up to this one.*

  "Now let's look at the last cue card that reads "How to Start with an Attention Getter." Since I have decided to start with an attention getter, I need to choose one of these ways to pull my readers in."

- Read each method on the cue card aloud.

  "I think I'll start out with a series of questions—I think I can get the reader's attention really well this way. For example, 'Do you know who Shaquille O'Neal thinks is the best ever second- year player for the NBA other than himself? Who earned the nickname Flash, and why do the players call him that?'

  "This is a good place for my thesis statement. It will make the purpose of my essay clearer." Copy the thesis statement from the top of the PLAN & WRITE Planning Sheet. 'Given the opportunity to meet any famous person, I would definitely choose to meet Dwayne Wade so that I could ask him how he became a rising basketball star, discuss his nickname, Flash, and invite him to play a game of one-on-one with me.'"

WRAP-UP

Review and test recall of the PLAN & WRITE strategy.

LESSON 5

NOTE: This lesson usually takes 2 days.

LESSON OVERVIEW
The class and teacher will collaboratively write an essay.

STUDENT OBJECTIVES
The entire class collaboratively sets goals for and composes one essay. The students evaluate the class essay.

MATERIALS

- Transparencies and student copies (one for each student): Mnemonic chart, Brainstorming Sheet, PLAN & WRITE Planning Sheet, Characteristics of Good Essays, Goals for Proficient Writing, Revision Checklist

- PLAN & WRITE Cue Cards
- Writing Prompt (write on blackboard)
- Chart paper or lined overhead for writing notebook paper
- Pencils

SET THE CONTEXT FOR STUDENT LEARNING

Using overheads from prior lessons, briefly review PLAN & WRITE strategy components and Writing Prompt Worksheet answers.

DEVELOP THE STRATEGY AND SELF-REGULATION

Step 1: Goal Setting

- Display the Goals for Proficient Writing transparency

Say, *"We will compose an essay as a class using everything we have learned so far. Before we start on the essay, however, we want to set one or two goals for ourselves. Look at our goals list and tell me which goals we want to work on today."*

Call on students and discuss the goals until they agree.

Step 2: Collaborative Practice

Say, *"For this essay, we will perform planning and composing steps together. You will use the Brainstorming Sheet, PLAN & WRITE Planning Sheet, and the cue cards. I will write on this paper and the transparencies, and you will write the same things on your copies. We have 2 days to plan, write, and compose one essay, so that should be easy for us to do."*

Display the prompt:

> *Think of the most important invention of the last 100 years.*
>
> *Write an essay explaining which invention you have selected and give reasons why you believe it is the most important.*

- Write the plan on the chart paper. Do the thesis statement first. Write the essay on clean PLAN & WRITE Planning Sheet transparencies.

- Say, *"What is the first thing we have to say to ourselves?"* Students should answer, *"Plan the essay."*

- Say, *"Now let's start with the steps. What is step one?"* Students should respond, *"Pay attention to the prompt."*

- Ask, *"How do we pay attention to the prompt?"* Students should respond, *"Underline what you are being asked to write about once, and then underline how you will develop your essay twice."* Get as many students to contribute to the discussion as possible, identifying parts of the prompt.

- Say, *"What is step two?"* Students should respond, *"List main ideas."* Ask the students to help brainstorm possible answers to the prompt and record them on their Brainstorming Sheet as you write it on chart paper. Then decide on one topic and brainstorm at least three main ideas for the development of the essay. Make sure the students are also recording the main ideas on their papers.

- Say, *"What is step three?"* Students should answer, *"Add supporting ideas."* Ask the students to think of details, examples, or elaborations that support the main ideas. Write the ideas down on paper and ask the students to write the ideas on their Brainstorming Sheet.

- Say, *"What is step four?"* Students should respond, *"Number your ideas."* Again, lead the discussion, selecting strong ideas with class consensus and reminding the students to think logically as they do so. Mark the best ideas with dots, eliminating unnecessary details that detract from the remaining content. Ask the students to number the main ideas on their Brainstorming Sheet in the same way.

- Say, *"What should we focus on next?"* Students should answer, *"Plan more as you write."* Review WRITE and tell the students to remember the group goals as they compose. Write each paragraph together, referring to the first cue card and cards with transition words.

Step 3: Evaluate Essay

Say, *"Let's look at our Revision Checklist now."* Go through rating, asking the students how they would evaluate the class essay. Tell the students that the next time they will work in pairs or small groups and they should set goals, plan, compose, and evaluate their performance.

WRAP-UP

Review and test recall of the PLAN & WRITE strategy.

LESSON 6

NOTE: This lesson usually takes 3 days.

LESSON OVERVIEW
Small-group collaborative practice will occur over approximately 3 days.

STUDENT OBJECTIVES
In pairs or small groups, the students will collaboratively set goals for and compose one essay. The teams will share their essays with others and evaluate them with the Revision Checklist.

MATERIALS

- Transparencies: Mnemonic chart, Brainstorming Sheet, PLAN & WRITE Planning Sheet, Characteristics of Good Essays
- PLAN & WRITE Cue Cards

- Writing prompt (write on blackboard)
- Essays
- Notebook paper and pencils

SET THE CONTEXT FOR STUDENT LEARNING

 Say, *"You will have the next 3 days to plan and compose one essay with your team using everything we have learned so far. Before you start on the essay, I will check to make sure you set two or three group goals for yourselves. Look at the goals for proficient essays, decide which goals to focus on today, and write them on your Brainstorming Sheet."* Check whether each group has two or three goals.

DEVELOP THE STRATEGY AND SELF-REGULATION

Step 1: Collaborative Practice

 Say, *"As you work together today and the next 2 days, each person must make his or her own copy of the Brainstorming Sheet and PLAN & WRITE Planning Sheet."*

- Look at the prompt for today. Say, *"Try to complete your PLAN today. Some of you will also write your introductory paragraph."*

Display the prompt:

> *Many young people want part-time jobs.*
>
> *In an essay, state whether you think young people should have part-time jobs and give reasons why you think so.*

- Say, *"Since you have looked at this prompt before, it won't take you long to identify what you are being asked to write about and how you will develop your essay."* Circulate around the classroom and check to ensure that the students are planning. Remind them of the steps they may have omitted and help them with the steps with which they are experiencing difficulty.

- Students should continue writing the essay on the second and third days. Be sure to save time (30 minutes) on the third day for all of the groups to present their essays to the class.

Step 2: Evaluate Essay

Say, *"I would like volunteers to share their essays. Be sure to tell us your goals before you start reading."* Ask the other students look at their Revision Checklist as they listen to their peers. Ask for suggestions for changes. Compliment the students for sharing.

WRAP-UP

Review and test recall of the PLAN & WRITE strategy.

LESSON 7

NOTE: This lesson must be repeated until the students can independently write an essay using *all* PLAN & WRITE procedures. While these lesson plans indicate that Lesson 7 will take 14 days, you can modify this as appropriate.

LESSON OVERVIEW

This lesson involves independent practice in which the students will each plan, write, share, and revise a total of four essays. The students will set goals and receive feedback for each of the four essays written.

STUDENT OBJECTIVES

Students will plan and compose four different essays across 15 days and will work in pairs to share and revise essays.

MATERIALS

- Mnemonic chart
- Brainstorming Sheet
- PLAN & WRITE Planning Sheet
- Characteristics of Good Essays

- PLAN & WRITE Cue Cards
- Writing prompt (write on blackboard)
- Notebook paper and pencils

SET THE CONTEXT FOR STUDENT LEARNING

Using overheads from prior lessons, briefly review PLAN & WRITE strategy components and Writing Prompt Worksheet answers.

DEVELOP THE STRATEGY AND SELF-REGULATION

Look at your calendar to help you plan the students' mastery of the strategy. The first time they write independently, 2 days are allowed to complete the plan. The students also have up to 2 days to write their essays, but they should share with their partners. The goal at this point in the program is to stick to the calendar! Slower students may 1) finish the essay as homework, 2) get additional help (e.g., the teacher allows a student to dictate his or her concluding paragraph), or 3) move on in the program. Do not hold a student back to finish work that was not completed within the time allotted for each essay. Students will have 4 days to plan, write, share, and revise their second and third independently completed essays. The students will have 2 days to plan, write, share, and revise their fourth essay because they must be able to plan and compose fluently.

Days 1 to 4

Students set goals, plan, and compose one essay with teacher help and feedback within two class periods. They can use all support materials.

Display the prompt:

Think about a task you can do well.

Explain how to perform that task.

Days 5 to 8

Students set goals, plan, and compose their second essay with teacher help. They can use all support materials. Prompt the students to do steps they have omitted. Give feedback (or have peers give feedback) to help set new goals.

Display the prompt:

Think about a special event that you will never forget.

Write an essay about what happened, how you felt, and why it is unforgettable.

Days 9 to 12

Students set goals, plan, and compose their third essay with the teacher. Students may use the cue cards, but not the Brainstorming Sheet or the PLAN & WRITE Planning Sheet. Tell the students to use lined paper to plan and compose the day's essay. Show them how to use one sheet of paper to plan and one or two other sheets of paper to write their essays. Prompt the students to do steps they have omitted. Give feedback (or have peers give feedback) to help set new goals.

Display the prompt:

Choose any age you would like to be.

Write an essay explaining why you want to be this age.

Days 13 and 14

Students set goals, plan, and compose their fourth essay with teacher help *within one class period* (or, if you are preparing for a writing competency test, within the amount of time allowed for the test). No cue cards, Brainstorming Sheet, or PLAN & WRITE Planning Sheet can be used, and the students must complete their essays within the class period. Prompt the students to plan before they write and to do steps they have omitted. Give feedback (or have peers give feedback), and tell the students that the next time they write an essay, you won't be able to help them with any steps in the strategy and it will be "like a test."

Display the prompt:

Suppose you could get into a time machine and travel into either the past or the future.

Write an essay about a specific time you would like to visit in the time machine. Explain why you would like to visit this specific time.

WRAP-UP

Wrap-Up Reminders

1. It is critical that the students set goals and receive feedback from you or their peers on their plans and essays.

2. To do this, you must circulate among the students as they work. Make sure the students plan before composing. Provide assistance only when a student skips a step or performs it incorrectly.

3. Fade assistance from you as well as from cue cards, Brainstorming Sheet, and the PLAN & WRITE Planning Sheet, but at the same time, remember that the goal of these lessons is to provide instruction, not to put the students in a testing situation.

4. Students who fall behind should be asked to finish their work as homework.

How do you plan good essays? Follow steps in PLAN:

PLAN

P = Pay attention to the prompt.

L = List main ideas to develop your essay.

A = Add supporting ideas (e.g., details, examples).

N = Number major points in the order you will use them.

How do you plan more as you go? Follow steps in WRITE:

WRITE

W = Work from your plan to develop a thesis statement.

R = Remember your goals.

I = Include transition words for each paragraph.

T = Try to use different kinds of sentences.

E = Exciting, interesting million-dollar words.

Brainstorming Sheet

(a) Possible answers to the prompt:

(b) Main and supporting ideas for the development of your essay:

_____

_____

_____

_____

_____

_____

_____

_____

_____

_____

_____

Thesis statement first _____ or last _____. Write the thesis statement separately if it is going to be the last sentence of the introductory paragraph:

_____

_____

_____

Introductory paragraph:

_____

_____

_____

_____

_____

_____

_____

(continued)

PLAN & WRITE

(continued)

Body paragraph 1:

_____

_____

_____

_____

_____

Body paragraph 2:

_____

_____

_____

_____

_____

Body paragraph 3:

_____

_____

_____

_____

_____

Concluding paragraph:

_____

_____

_____

_____

_____

PLAN & WRITE Planning Sheet

Planning strategy: PLAN	Instructions for each planning step
1. <u>P</u>ay attention to the prompt	Read the prompt. Decide what you are being asked to write about and how you will develop your essay.
2. <u>L</u>ist main ideas	Brainstorm possible responses to the prompt. Decide on one topic and then brainstorm at least three main ideas for the development of your essay.
3. <u>A</u>dd supporting ideas	Think of details, examples, or elaborations that support your main ideas.
4. <u>N</u>umber your ideas	Number major points in the order you will use them.

How to remember to keep planning while composing your essay: WRITE

5. <u>W</u>ork from your plan to develop your thesis statement.*
6. <u>R</u>emember your goals.
7. <u>I</u>nclude transition words for each paragraph.*
8. <u>T</u>ry to use different kinds of sentences.
9. <u>E</u>xciting, interesting million-dollar words.

*NOTE: See PLAN & WRITE Cue Cards for ways to develop the introductory paragraph, as well as for sample transition words and phrases. Brainstorm ideas using a brainstorming sheet or regular notebook paper. Write your essay on a two-page essay sheet or paper.

Goals for Proficient Writing

1. Address the topic (answer all parts of the prompt).

2. Remember to explain, clarify, inform, or instruct (write an expository essay).

3. Remain on topic—keep a central focus.

4. Show clear organization with frequent transitions (connecting words).

5. Include clear supporting facts, examples, details, and definitions that illustrate your main points.

6. Explain your topic so that your reader will know what you are writing about.

7. Use mature, specific vocabulary.

8. Use different kinds of sentences (e.g., simple, compound, complex) that are both short and long.

9. Eliminate as many errors in grammar as possible (e.g., make sure subjects and verbs match).

10. Make your essay lively, engaging, and fun to read.

Characteristics of Good Essays

1. *Expository essays* inform, clarify, explain, define, or instruct by giving information, explaining why or how, clarifying a process, or defining a concept. Be sure to include facts, examples, or definitions; do NOT tell a story.

2. A *prompt* explains the writing situation and the directions for writing.

    Writing Situation: Everyone has jobs or chores.

    Directions for Writing: Before you begin writing, think about one of your jobs or chores. Now explain why you do your job or chore.

3. Our expository essays should have five paragraphs.

    Readers look for an introduction (paragraph 1), a well-developed body (paragraphs 2, 3, 4), and a conclusion (paragraph 5).

    The introductory paragraph should include a thesis statement (a sentence that introduces the topic about which you will write). Paragraphs 2, 3, and 4 should each support the main points of the essay. The last paragraph should summarize or show that you have reached a certain conclusion about the topic.

Powerful Writing Strategies for All Students by K. Harris, S. Graham, L. Mason, & B. Friedlander.

Different Kinds of Sentences

A. Simple sentences

1. The boy ran to the store.

2. The boy and girl ran in a relay race.

3. Kevin went to a party and had fun.

4. Sharee and Kiara are friends and work at the same place.

B. Compound sentences

1. The boy ran to the store, and he bought some apples.

2. Taneesha loves to swim laps; her brother likes to dive.

3. Kevin went to a party, and he got home late.

4. The meeting was over; it was already midnight.

5. We did not see Marshaun at the movie, nor did we see him at the restaurant.

6. You will have to finish the project, or your group will get a failing grade.

C. Complex sentences

1. I like Colleen because she is funny.

2. Trina will be late for dinner because her ride home from work didn't come.

3. The game will end when one team breaks the tie.

4. When I get to California, you will be sleeping.

5. The players went out for a pizza after they practiced.

6. Lucas decided to clean up the house; however, he was not sure if his friends could come over later that night.

Exciting, Interesting Million-Dollar Words

Answer:	reply, respond, acknowledge
Begin:	start, initiate, originate
Decide:	determine, choose, resolve
Sure:	certain, positive, definite
Do:	execute, finish, accomplish
Explain:	elaborate, clarify, define, justify
Idea:	thought, concept, belief, view, opinion
Important:	necessary, vital, critical, essential
Interesting:	fascinating, intriguing, absorbing
Make:	create, invent, construct, execute
New:	fresh, unique, original, unusual
Part:	portion, piece, section, fraction
Plan:	scheme, procedure, method, way
Think:	judge, believe, consider, reflect

Writing Prompt Worksheet

1. Choose a country you would like to visit. Write an essay explaining why you want to go to that country.

2. Think about situations where you should say no to a friend. Write an essay explaining what these situations are and give reasons why it is important to say no.

3. Some people like dogs but other people don't. In an essay, state whether you think dogs should be allowed to roam free and give reasons why you think so.

4. Many young people want to have part-time jobs. Write an essay stating whether you think young people should have part-time jobs and give reasons why you think they should or should not.

5. Think of the most important things you could wish for if you were given the chance. Write an essay about the wishes you have selected and give reasons why they are the most important to you.

6. Think about your ideal way to spend a Saturday afternoon. Explain what the day would be like.

7. Most people have at least one favorite holiday. Write an essay about your favorite holiday and give reasons why you enjoy it so much.

8. Some people believe that boys and girls should be taught in separate classes at school. Write an essay stating whether you think boys and girls should or shouldn't be taught in separate classes and give reasons why you think so.

9. Think of the most important invention of the past 100 years. Write an essay about the invention you have selected and give reasons why you think it is the most important.

10. Think about a task you do well. Explain the best way to perform that task.

11. Think about a special event you will never forget. Write an essay describing what happened, how you felt, and why the event is unforgettable.

12. Choose the age you would like to be. Write an essay explaining why you want to be this age.

Revision Checklist

Place a [+] for each box that describes the essay as it is written now and a [?] for each box where the writer may need to make changes.

Ideas and Development

- ☐ Fully addresses the topic (answers all parts of the prompt)
- ☐ Good development of ideas with many details elaborated and extended
- ☐ Presents details/examples in a way that helps the reader understand the topic
- ☐ Ideas are clear and well illustrated

Organization, Unity, and Coherence

- ☐ Topic is clearly identified
- ☐ Remains on topic
- ☐ Well organized, with a smooth flow from one idea to the next
- ☐ Clear introduction, body paragraphs, and conclusion
- ☐ Uses transitions skillfully to link sentences or paragraphs together

Vocabulary

- ☐ Good word choices that are appropriate, specific, and varied
- ☐ Uses synonyms appropriately
- ☐ The essay is fun to read or tells the reader something about the writer's personality

Sentence Structure, Grammar, and Usage

- ☐ Includes many different kinds of sentences (various lengths and structures)
- ☐ Has few (or no) errors in grammar or word usage and is easy to read

Beware of Video Games

I think video games can be very harmful to young people. In the past several years video games have been a very popular activity among young people. Most towns have video arcades, and many people play video games in their own homes on TV (using Sega or Nintendo) or on a computer. There is no question that many young people have fun playing video games, but that does not mean video games are beneficial.

The first reason why video games are harmful to young people is that they take up too much time. Students already spend several hours a day in school, and as a result, their free time is limited. Given the choice between playing video games, reading, or playing outside with friends, many students choose video games. Consequently, young people today often miss out on a variety of fun activities that benefit their minds and bodies.

Secondly, playing video games too much can have some unhealthy results. If someone spends several hours in front of a video screen on a daily basis, I think that his or her eyesight might weaken. Furthermore, if a student is indoors playing video games, he or she may not be active enough. Playing too video games too much may lead to other health problems such as being overweight.

The final, most important reason why I think video games are harmful to young people is the excessive amount of violence in the more popular video games. The object of many video games is to fight and kill an enemy. As an illustration, in Mortal Kombat, the fighting is very violent and bloody. Even though games such as this one have warning labels on them, many young people have access to these games with or without their parents' permission. Video games encourage violence because they make fighting seem fun and exciting. This is especially troublesome since there is a huge problem with violence among America's youth.

In conclusion, I have decided that although video games can be very fun for many young people, they are actually quite harmful. Many students will choose to waste their valuable free time playing video games. Also, some students may experience health problems such as ruined eyesight and excessive weight gain. Finally, video games are harmful because they are too violent, and they might encourage violence among young people.

Feeding Wild Animals

People should not feed wild animals even if they are starving. In Yellowstone National Park, for example, there are many signs that tell people not to feed animals. People should not feed wild animals for a variety of reasons that affect the environment as a whole, the safety of humans, and the health of individual animals.

First, feeding starving animals interferes with nature's food chain. If a wild animal is starving, that is because the natural food supply for that species of animals is in short supply. When there is a scarcity of food, it is natural for animals to die or stop reproducing. This keeps nature in balance. If a human interferes with this delicate balance by feeding starving animals, that species may overpopulate. This in turn will cause the food chain to become unbalanced, and larger numbers of animals will starve or be preyed upon.

Furthermore, it is not safe to feed wild animals. While some animal lovers feel that it is their moral obligation to feed starving animals, that should not be allowed. Some animals attack people when they are approached. Even though people mean well when they feed starving animals, the animals are not aware that the person does not intend to harm them. In many cases it is better to leave wild animals alone.

Another reason why people should not feed wild animals is for the health and safety of the animals. Very few people know which foods belong in the diets of wild animals. Certain foods make animals sick. Other foods are not appropriate for animals to eat in large amounts such as high protein foods (meats). On occasion, animals die from eating food that people feed them.

Although many people do not like the rule that says, "Do not feed the animals!" it is an important rule that has many reasons to support it. First, feeding starving animals often disrupts the natural balance of the food chain. Also, feeding these animals is not worth risking one's own safety or the safety of other humans. Finally, unless a person knows the proper diet for an animal, it can be very harmful for the animal to eat the wrong type of food.

My Favorite Holidy

My favorite holiday would be Halloween because you get to decorate your house as cool as you want it to be, you get to dress up real scary, and you get a lot of candy.

First of all, Halloween is so fun because you can decorate your house as cool as you choose. Every Halloween my family makes my house real scary looking, inside and out. We put a black light bulb on the porch and play a tape with scary sounds on it. We also make the inside cool too, by putting spider-webs on the corners and picture frames.

Secondly, I like Halloween the best because you get to choose an outfit of your choice. You could choose one from totally wicked-looking to fun and exciting. I have one from this Halloween, I was a big ol' cow. I painted my face with black and white paint. I looked really funny!

Thirdly, I like Halloween because you get a lot of candy. sometimes if you walk around a long time, you can get enough candy to last you to Christmas, that's a long time! Sometimes if you eat too much candy, you will get sick. Also, you have to watch out what you eat, because people will poison them, how sick.

So in conclusion, Halloween is my all time favorite holiday. I enjoy turning my ordinary house into a scary trick-or-treat house. I also like to dress up and have fun. Lastly I love getting the candy.

The Most Important Things

The most important things that I would wish for would have to be no poor people, for a better government. and for me to be in the Navy Seals, and have a two story house.

First, I would want there to be no poverty anywhere in the world because we the U.S.A. are spending our money trying to help other countries we're making ourselves poor.

Secondly, I want a flawless government. I know it won't ever happen, but that's a wish. The government today is o.k., but most people don't like it. I really don't care, but I would like it to be better than it is now when I vote. I want to vote for a good not a bad cause.

Thirdly, I would like to go to the Navy Seals. That has been a life long dream of mine. To fly an F-16 and go on an aircraft carrier.

Finally, another one of my life long dreams is to have a two story house. I don't know why but that's my other wish. I want to walk up the stairs everyday. To look down at my friends when they come over.

In conclusion, the wishes that I picked I think are very reasonable and one day might really happen. I want no poverty, a better government, to be in the Navy Seals, and to have a two story house. Those are my wishes and also my dreams.

My Ideal Saturday

My ideal way to spend a Saturday would be to go to the mall. I also would go to a friend's house. I would go to a movie. That is where I would go or do.

First of all I would go to the mall. I would go to the mall to meet friends and hang out. I also would go to the mall to eat at the food court. I would go to the mall and play video games at the Cyber Station. I also would go to the mall and buy clothes.

Secondly, I would go to a friend's house. I would go to my friend's house play the computer or go out front and play basketball. Also me and my friend would listen to the stereo. I also would go to my friend's house to watch a movie. That's why I would go to my friend's house.

Thirdly, I would go to the movies. I would go to the movies to see a movie that I haven't seen. I would go to the movies to take my girlfriend out. I also would go to the movies when my family goes. I also would go to the movies just so I could do something.

In conclusion, I would go to the mall to meet friends. I would go to my friend's house to play basketball. I would go to the movies to see a movie that I haven't seen. I guess all of these things are fun to me. That is what I would do on a Saturday.

I Have to Say No

Situations where I would say "no" to a friend would be if they asked me to go to a party and I knew there would be drugs or alcohol there. I would say "no" to a friend if they wanted me to take drugs, and I would say "no" to a friend if they wanted to do something that I know I would get in trouble for, like breaking into a house or robbing a store, etc.

I would say "no" to a friend if he/she asked me to go to a party, and I knew there would be drugs or alcohol there. I would say "no" because even if they said I didn't have to do it, I would either be pressured into doing it or someone would get drunk and they would be all over me, like a rapist or something. I don't want to get into things like drugs or alcohol, and I don't want friends who do it, either.

I would say "no" to a friend if he/she asked me to do drugs. I would say "no" because I don't want to harm my body. I wouldn't want to go crazy and hurt any other person either because it's not worth it; therefore, I will never do drugs.

I would say "no" to a friend if he/she asked me to do something stupid like break in a house or rob a store. I would say "no" because you can risk a lot doing that. You can risk getting shot at, or going to jail, etc. I don't think it's worth spending the rest of your life in prison because of something so dumb.

These three or four situations are all examples of times I would say "no" to a friend. Going to a bad party, taking drugs into my body, breaking and entry, etc., are stupid ideas that would just harm myself, harm someone else, or get me into trouble; therefore, I will stay away from people who would like me to do things like that.

A Perfect Age to Be (Version 1)

If you had a chance to drink from the fountain of eternal youth, would you take a sip? Would you like to always be young, vibrant and healthy? Are you scared of growing old? Can you imagine yourself with gray hair, wrinkles and arthritis? While many people would take a sip from that fountain, I think that I would refuse eternal youth because there are some very wonderful things that come with growing old. I think that I would prefer to be 75 years old because I could have a large, loving family, a lifetime of experiences to share with others and a fun, relaxing lifestyle.

First of all, I think that having a caring, extended family would be one of the best parts of being 75 years old. I imagine myself as a happy grandmother surrounded by my children and a bunch of wonderful grandchildren. I think that multi-generational family gatherings are a lot of fun because young people can learn a lot from their elders and older people can be revived in the presence of giggling children and vibrant young adults. Unfortunately, many 75 year olds are not fortunate enough to be surrounded by a large, loving family. If this is the case for me, I will embrace young friends as if they were family, and share good times, knowledge and experiences with them.

A 75 year old has a lot to offer the world in terms of knowledge and experiences. By the time someone is 75 years old, he or she has gained wisdom from three quarters of a century of personal experiences. Furthermore, that person has lived through a part of history. For instance, an American, who is presently 75 years old, has experienced the Great Depression, World War II and has watched as America has moved into the technological age. By the time that I am 75 years old, it will be 2046. I can not imagine the historical and societal changes that I will witness in the next fifty years. I hope that I will be able to share the wisdom that I will gain over years of experiences.

Possibly the most alluring thing about the age 75 is the relaxing and recreational lifestyle that many senior citizens enjoy. I think that I would want to be retired by the time I am 75 years old. I would lead a slow and comfortable lifestyle. I would like to learn how to play golf and go out to lunch with my old friends. It would also be a luxury to be able to go to bed early and get plenty of rest. I think that it is very nice that our government and society encourage a pleasant retirement for the elderly through federal and state benefits and special discounts at the movies, hotels and restaurants. I would like to relax and enjoy the rest of my life as a 75 year old.

Many people hope to never grow old, but I think that 75 years old would be a wonderful age to be. At 75, a warm and loving family can surround a person, including beautiful grandchildren. Also, a 75 year old has a lifetime of experiences to reflect on and share with others. Finally, and perhaps the most attractive part of being a senior citizen is the possibility of enjoying a relaxing and recreational lifestyle.

A Perfect Age to Be (Version 2)

Although I believe that youth is a wonderful thing, I think that the ideal age to be is 75 years old. I imagine 75 as wonderful age because their children and grandchildren love 75 year olds. Also, at 75 a person is shaped by three quarters of a century of experiences, which they can look back on and share with other people. Finally, many 75 year olds are able to enjoy a relaxing and recreational lifestyle.

First of all, I think that having a caring, extended family would be one of the best parts of being 75 years old. I imagine myself as a happy grandmother surrounded by my children and a bunch of wonderful grandchildren. I think that multigenerational family gatherings are a lot of fun because young people can learn a lot from their elders and older people can be revived in the presence of giggling children and vibrant young adults. Unfortunately, many 75 year olds are not fortunate enough to be surrounded by a large, loving family. If this is the case for me, I will embrace young friends as if they were family, and share good times, knowledge and experiences with them.

A 75 year old has a lot to offer the world in terms of knowledge and experiences. By the time someone is 75 years old, he or she has gained wisdom from three quarters of a century of personal experiences. Furthermore, that person has lived through a part of history. For instance, an American, who is presently 75 years old, has experienced the Great Depression, World War II and has watched as America has moved into the technological age. By the time that I am 75 years old, it will be 2046. I can not imagine the historical and societal changes that I will witness in the next fifty years. I hope that I will be able to share the wisdom that I will gain over years of experiences.

Possibly the most alluring thing about the age 75 is the relaxing and recreational lifestyle that many senior citizens enjoy. I think that I would want to be retired by the time I am 75 years old. I would lead a slow and comfortable lifestyle. I would like to learn how to play golf and go out to lunch with my old friends. It would also be a luxury to be able to go to bed early and get plenty of rest. I think that it is very nice that our government and society encourage a pleasant retirement for the elderly through federal and state benefits and special discounts at the movies, hotels and restaurants. I would like to relax and enjoy the rest of my life as a 75 year old.

Many people hope to never grow old, but I think that 75 years old would be a wonderful age to be. At 75, a warm and loving family can surround a person, including beautiful grandchildren. Also, a 75 year old has a lifetime of experiences to reflect on and share with others. Finally, and perhaps the most attractive part of being a senior citizen is the possibility of enjoying a relaxing and recreational lifestyle.

A Special Event (Version 1)

I was reluctant to leave the house one Thursday night because I was addicted to the television show "Friends." This show dictated my life on Thursday nights, preventing me from spending time with my real life friends. Somehow, I was persuaded to miss one episode of the show and go out to a Hollywood restaurant. Missing the T.V. episode of "Friends" turned out to be a pretty good decision. That night at the restaurant I saw real life members from the cast of "Friends," an event that I will always remember.

This memorable event happened on a warm autumn night two years ago. I went out to a new restaurant in Hollywood with my friends, Tehmina and Michelle. Michelle is a woman who is very involved in the film and television star social life of Hollywood. Therefore, she liked to take us to the coolest and trendiest places in town. On this night, Michelle took us to a new club called "Jones'" that was a swanky, guest list-only type of establishment. I was impressed to be able to get inside such a place, and I could not believe my eyes when I saw four of the members from the cast of "Friends" standing by the stage. I immediately went over to the stage to get a closer look. Yes, they were my television friends. Then, while I was standing next to the stage, three of the actors started walking back to their table. As they walked, each of the actors brushed by me, mumbling "excuse me."

My feelings about this special event are barely describable. At first I experienced feelings of disbelief. I thought, this can't really be the cast of "Friends," I must be seeing things! When I had confirmed the identities of the actors, I felt so excited. I also felt extremely nervous as Tehmina encouraged me to go and meet the actors. Finally, I was thrilled when the three men walked past me.

The reason why I will never forget this event is because contact with the actors from "Friends" was a union of fantasy and reality for me. I no longer watch this television show, but at the time I thought the characters from the show were indeed my own personal friends. Back in those days, I stayed home every Thursday night to watch the show on T.V. I laughed at their jokes and listened to their problems. That is why seeing the actors face to face turned my Thursday evening fantasy into a reality, and permanently etched the events of the evening into my memory.

Encountering the cast of "Friends" in a trendy Hollywood restaurant is an event that I will never forget. As I look back on this experience, I can remember precise details of what happened that night. Furthermore, I can recall how I felt that night to the extent that I can almost re experience those actual feelings. Finally, as I re counted the events of that special evening, I realized that I will probably never forget this event because it brought a touch of reality to my Thursday evening fantasy.

A Special Event (Version 2)

One of the most unforgettable events of my life was when I saw members from the cast of the T.V. show "Friends" in a Hollywood restaurant. This happened two years ago when I was living in Los Angeles, but I can still remember it as if it happened yesterday. I can remember all the details of the encounter, including my exact feelings. I can even remember thinking that I would never forget that moment.

This memorable event happened on a warm autumn night two years ago. I went out to a new restaurant in Hollywood with my friends, Tehmina and Michelle. Michelle is a woman who is very involved in the film and television star social life of Hollywood. Therefore, she liked to take us to the coolest and trendiest places in town. On this night, Michelle took us to a new club called "Jones'" that was a swanky, guest list-only type of establishment. I was impressed to be able to get inside such a place, and I could not believe my eyes when I saw four of the members from the cast of "Friends" standing by the stage. I immediately went over to the stage to get a closer look. Yes, they were my television friends. Then, while I was standing next to the stage, three of the actors started walking back to their table. As they walked, each of the actors brushed by me, mumbling "excuse me."

My feelings about this special event are barely describable. At first I experienced feelings of disbelief. I thought, this can't really be the cast of "Friends," I must be seeing things! When I had confirmed the identities of the actors, I felt so excited. I also felt extremely nervous as Tehmina encouraged me to go and meet the actors. Finally, I was thrilled when the three men walked past me.

The reason why I will never forget this event is because contact with the actors from "Friends" was a union of fantasy and reality for me. I no longer watch this television show, but at the time I thought the characters from the show were indeed my own personal friends. Back in those days, I stayed home every Thursday night to watch the show on T.V. I laughed at their jokes and listened to their problems. That is why seeing the actors face to face turned my Thursday evening fantasy into a reality, and permanently etched the events of the evening into my memory.

Encountering the cast of "Friends" in a trendy Hollywood restaurant is an event that I will never forget. As I look back on this experience, I can remember precise details of what happened that night. Furthermore, I can recall how I felt that night to the extent that I can almost re experience those actual feelings. Finally, as I recounted the events of that special evening, I realized that I will probably never forget this event because it brought a touch of reality to my Thursday evening fantasy.

The Most Important Invention (Version 1)

Have you ever enjoyed fresh fruits and vegetables from South America? Have you ever marveled at our nation's military might? Is there someone or someplace very far away that you would like to visit? These things are all possible due to an invention by two brothers named Orville and Wilbur Wright. The Wright brothers invented the first engine driven air flying machine. This invention has led to the creation of better airplanes, which allow people to transport cargo, fight wars, and visit far off places in relatively short periods of time. The airplane is truly the most important invention of the last 100 years.

The first way that the invention of airplanes has changed the world is by providing a faster way for cargo to be shipped. The airplane has changed the way mail, food and other goods are sent around the world. Air mail allows everything from important documents to personal letters to be transported anywhere in the world in as quick as a day. Before the airplane, long distance, written communication would sometimes take several months. Also, cargo airplanes can deliver perishable goods, such as fresh fruit, vegetables, flowers or meat. This allows people to enjoy fresh products from distant parts of the world. Furthermore, the quick delivery of food products has helped improve world trade. World trade has also benefited from the import and export of other goods, such as expensive, lightweight products like electronic equipment and machine parts.

Also, the invention of airplanes has changed the way that war is waged. With airplanes wars can be fought on land, sea and in the air. There are many special airplanes designed for the armed forces that have changed the way wars are fought. For example, there are long distance and short range bombers that can fly in the day or at night. There are fighter planes that can fly at very fast speeds. Also, there are planes with radar on them that helps find enemy aircraft. In addition to supplying new types of fighting machines, airplanes provide more efficient ways for military transport. Carrier planes allow materials and troops to be moved in very short periods of time. This lets materials and troops enter and leave dangerous areas in no time at all.

The final way that the invention of airplanes has had an important effect on the world is by the way it has made travel to other parts of the world much easier. Commercial airlines provide a fast, safe and comfortable way for people to go to distant places. Passengers can travel almost anywhere in the world in less than a day. This allows people a chance to visit friends and family who live in far-off places. Also, airplanes provide a pleasant way for people to travel all around the world and visit places that before they had only been able to read about.

In conclusion, the airplane is the most important invention in the past 100 years. Efficient cargo planes have improved communication and world trade and given people the chance to enjoy products from all around the world. Also, the development of military planes has had a major impact on the way wars are waged. Finally, commercial airplanes provide a fast, safe and comfortable way to visit far away people and places. As a whole, the invention of airplanes, as well as the development of bigger and better airplanes, has changed the world forever.

The Most Important Invention (Version 2)

The invention of the first powered, controllable airplane is the most important invention of the last 100 years. First of all, the airplane has drastically increased the speed at which cargo can be transported. Second, airplanes have forever changed the way in which wars are fought. Third, the invention of the engine driven airplane has made traveling to far-off places very safe and easy.

The first way that the invention of airplanes has changed the world is by providing a faster way for cargo to be shipped. The airplane has changed the way mail, food and other goods are sent around the world. Air mail allows everything from important documents to personal letters to be transported anywhere in the world in as quick as a day. Before the airplane, long distance, written communication would sometimes take several months. Also, cargo airplanes can deliver perishable goods, such as fresh fruit, vegetables, flowers or meat. This allows people to enjoy fresh products from distant parts of the world. Furthermore, the quick delivery of food products has helped improve world trade. World trade has also benefited from the import and export of other goods, such as expensive, lightweight products like electronic equipment and machine parts.

Also, the invention of airplanes has changed the way that war is waged. With airplanes wars can be fought on land, sea and in the air. There are many special airplanes designed for the armed forces that have changed the way wars are fought. For example, there are long distance and short range bombers that can fly in the day or at night. There are fighter planes that can fly at very fast speeds. Also, there are planes with radar on them that helps find enemy aircraft. In addition to supplying new types of fighting machines, airplanes provide more efficient ways for military transport. Carrier planes allow materials and troops to be moved in very short periods of time. This lets materials and troops enter and leave dangerous areas in no time at all.

The final way that the invention of airplanes has had an important effect on the world is by the way it has made travel to other parts of the world much easier. Commercial airlines provide a fast, safe and comfortable way for people to go to distant places. Passengers can travel almost anywhere in the world in less than a day. This allows people a chance to visit friends and family who live in far-off places. Also, airplanes provide a pleasant way for people to travel all around the world and visit places that before they had only been able to read about.

In conclusion, the airplane is the most important invention in the past 100 years. Efficient cargo planes have improved communication and world trade and given people the chance to enjoy products from all around the world. Also, the development of military planes has had a major impact on the way wars are waged. Finally, commercial airplanes provide a fast, safe and comfortable way to visit far away people and places. As a whole, the invention of airplanes, as well as the development of bigger and better airplanes, has changed the world forever.

PLAN & WRITE Cue Cards

Introductory Paragraph: Thesis Statement First

- Answer the prompt in the first sentence.
- Write your first main idea as the second sentence.
- Write your second main idea as the third sentence.
- Write your third main idea as the last sentence.

Second and Third Body Paragraphs: Transitions to Connect

- Second/Third,
- My final (reason/example) is
- Furthermore,
- Another (reason) to support this is
- What is more,
- The next step

First Body Paragraph: Transitions to Introduce Ideas

- First,
- My first (reason/example) is
- One (reason why/example is)
- To begin with,
- In the first step,
- To explain,

Concluding Paragraph: Transitions to Summarize

- In conclusion/To conclude,
- In summary/To sum up,
- As one can see/As a result,
- In short/All in all,
- It follows that
- For these reasons,

PLAN & WRITE Cue Cards

How to Start with an Attention Getter
- Use a series of questions.
- Use a series of statements.
- Use a brief or funny story.
- Use a mean or angry statement.
- Start with the opposite opinion from what you believe.

Introductory Paragraph: Thesis Statement Last
- Start with an attention getter (see cue card) and lead up to the thesis statement.
- Answer the prompt in your last sentence.
- Include your first, second, and third main ideas in a series.

Section VI

Strategy for Reading and Writing Informational Text

Chapter 17

TWA + PLANS

This chapter is adapted from the TWA + PLANS lesson plans developed by Linda Mason, Pennsylvania State University.

T = **T**hink Before Reading

W = Think **W**hile Reading

A = Think **A**fter Reading

P = Pick Goals

L = List Ways to Meet Goals

A = And

N = Make Notes

S = Sequence Notes

MATERIALS
TWA* Mnemonic Chart
TWA Learning Contract
TWA Checklist
My Self-Statements
TWA Outline
TWA + PLANS Mnemonic Chart
TWA + PLANS Goals Suggestion Sheet

LESSON 1

LESSON OVERVIEW

The purpose of this first lesson is to discuss the TWA strategy as a good strategy for getting information from social studies and science text for the purpose of writing about what is learned. The teacher will explain and discuss how to use the TWA strategy before, during, and after reading. The teacher will explain and discuss why using the TWA strategy will help with reading and writing.

STUDENT OBJECTIVES

The students will commit to learning and applying the TWA strategy when reading and writing about text they've read. The students will orally state how the nine steps of TWA are used before, during, and after reading.

MATERIALS

One copy for each student:
- TWA mnemonic chart

- TWA Learning Contract
- Student folders, scratch paper, pencils

SET THE CONTEXT FOR STUDENT LEARNING

- Tell the students that they will be learning about reading and writing from social studies and science readings. Tell them that before you can write about text, you need to learn how to read the text for information. Discuss briefly what good readers do while reading passages that inform and share knowledge about people, places, and things (e.g., they reread a part if they do not understand it, look for the main idea, summarize information).

- Tell the students that you are going to teach them a strategy or "trick" for reading. Tell them that this trick will help them understand more about what they have read, help them remember the things they have read, and help them write about the things they have read.

DEVELOP THE STRATEGY AND SELF-REGULATION

Step 1: | **Introduce TWA**

Put out one copy of the TWA mnemonic chart so that only the heading "TWA" shows. Uncover each part of the strategy as you introduce and discuss it. Be sure to emphasize that TWA is a strategy that good readers often use before, during, and after reading. Use the analogy of an airplane taking off. Say, *"With TWA we can take off with reading! Just like a pilot of a plane, we are the pilots and in control of our reading. Just like a pilot who does specific things before, during, and after a plane trip, we need to do things before, during, and after reading."*

Step 2: | **Introduce Think Before Reading**

Tell the students that there are three steps to complete when you are Thinking Before Reading. The first step is to Think about: The Author's Purpose (uncover this). Use the pilot analogy again. Say *"A pilot thinks about his or her purpose and then has an understanding of where he or she is to go. Thinking about the author's purpose works in the*

same way. It lets you know where you are going." Ask the students what they know about this step. Be sure to include that authors write to inform, to persuade, and for personal expression. Say, *"When we know the author's purpose, it helps us understand what we are about to read."* Describe and discuss together how this helps reading. *"For example, if the author has written for personal expression, we know to look for certain things. The author may have written a story or personal narrative (e.g., about a personal event). We know to look for characters, places, times, and so forth. If the author has written to inform, we know to look for information about things such as real people, places, and events."*

- Uncover Think about: What You Know. Use the pilot analogy. Say, *"The pilot of a plane knows a lot about flying. When pilots know where they are going, they begin to think about what they know—the flight path, the airport, and so forth. When reading, thinking about what you know also helps you understand what you are reading. Like a pilot, you create a map in your head about the topic."*

- Uncover Think about: What You Want to Know. Use the pilot analogy. Say, *"A pilot wants to know if there are storms in the flight path, other planes in the flight path, and so forth. This helps him or her look for things while flying, making the trip easier. Thinking about what you want to know helps you look for things while reading, therefore making reading easier."*

Step 3: Introduce Think While Reading

- Tell the students that there are three things good readers do while reading.

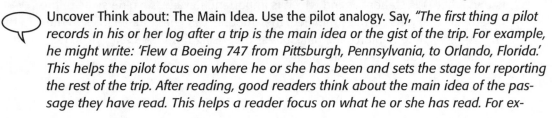 Uncover Think about: Reading Speed. Use the pilot analogy. Say, *"A pilot must constantly check his or her speed. Going too fast or too slow can have disastrous results. When reading, checking reading speed or pace is something good readers do as well. Reading speed is important because reading too fast or too slow can make it harder for you to understand and remember what was read."*

- Uncover Think about: Linking Knowledge. Use the pilot analogy. Say, *"Pilots link what they know about a new situation with what they already know about flying. For example, if a pilot comes upon a storm, he or she links how to fly in stormy weather with his or her experience in flying in stormy weather before. Linking knowledge is something good readers do as well. It is easier to understand and remember something that is linked to what you already know.* Provide another example. *If I am reading about football, I will link all new information about football with what I know and that's a lot!"*

- Uncover Think about: Rereading Parts. Use the pilot analogy. Say, *"A pilot must constantly check his or her instruments. If a pilot does not understand what the instruments say, he or she keeps reading, or rereads, them. Good readers also check their understanding. When they do not understand, they reread."*

Step 4: Introduce Think After Reading

- Tell the students that there are three things good readers do after reading.

Uncover Think about: The Main Idea. Use the pilot analogy. Say, *"The first thing a pilot records in his or her log after a trip is the main idea or the gist of the trip. For example, he might write: 'Flew a Boeing 747 from Pittsburgh, Pennsylvania, to Orlando, Florida.' This helps the pilot focus on where he or she has been and sets the stage for reporting the rest of the trip. After reading, good readers think about the main idea of the passage they have read. This helps a reader focus on what he or she has read. For ex-*

ample, if you have read a passage about your school's gym, your main idea might be 'Our school gym has a lot of great sporting equipment.'"

- Uncover Think about: Summarizing Information. Use the pilot analogy. Say, *"A pilot will also write details on his or her trip logs. For example, if a pilot ran into a storm, he or she would write a statement about the storm and then add details such as where the storm occurred, what kind of storm it was, how long the storm lasted, and how the plane handled the storm. These details are important to the pilot. A pilot will not include trivial details in summaries. He will not include what he had for lunch because this does not have anything to do with flying! Good readers also think about summarizing what they have read in a passage. The details of a passage make it more interesting and help with understanding the author's message. Using the 'gym' example again, you might add details to the summary about the type of equipment in the gym, about the locker room, and so forth. You would probably not talk about the bulletin board in the class next to the gym. Good readers and writers know how to skip trivial details—details that are not important—when summarizing."*

- Uncover Think about: What You Learned. Use the pilot analogy. Say, *"After finishing a trip, a pilot shares details of the trip with other pilots or with his or her family. The pilot may write about his trip for his boss or company. The pilot starts at the beginning and tells what happened with some details included. Using only what has actually hap-pened during the flight, the pilot retells the events of his or her flight. Good readers can tell what they have learned from reading a passage. Retelling what you have learned in reading helps you understand and remember the information."*

Step 5: Commitment to Learn the Strategy

Ask the students to "sign up" to learn the strategy. Introduce the TWA Learning Contract. Give each student a learning contract and have them complete it and sign it. After they have signed the contract, you sign it. Be sure to tell the students that you are committing to doing your best in teaching them the TWA strategy. These will be kept in their folders.

WRAP-UP

- Practice TWA. Have the students write out the mnemonic for TWA with spaces for the three steps on scratch paper. Ask the students to orally state the steps and check off spaces.

The students write only the following:

T _____ _____ _____

W _____ _____ _____

A _____ _____ _____

- Ask the students to explain what TWA stands for and why it is important to use TWA be-fore, while, and after reading. Help the students as needed to ensure that each student knows what TWA stands for and why it is important. Review the nine steps of the TWA mnemonic orally. As each is identified, the students can check the blank spot next to the "T," "W," and "A" to reinforce learning. Stress that using the TWA strategy can help read-ing and writing about text material.

- Tell the students that they will need to come to the next class and write out the TWA mnemonic (like above) and say what it means from memory. Have each student take the scratch paper with TWA and the spaces with them to study.

- Give each student a folder and copy of the mnemonic chart. Have the students put everything except the scratch paper in the folder. Thank them for working hard. Collect the students' folders.

LESSON 2

LESSON OVERVIEW

The teacher will model the TWA strategy before, during, and after reading. The teacher will model using self-statements throughout strategy use.

STUDENT OBJECTIVES

The students will develop a list of self-statements for using TWA.

MATERIALS

- TWA mnemonic chart
- Expository passage sample ("Gum")
- TWA Checklist
- TWA Self-Statements sheet

- Student folders
- Scratch paper; pencils; yellow, blue/green, and pink highlighters

---

SET THE CONTEXT FOR STUDENT LEARNING

- Test to see if the students remember TWA. Give the students scratch paper and ask them to write out the strategy reminder—TWA—with spaces. Then ask them what each letter stands for. Be sure they take turns so that all have a chance to share.

  T _____   _____   _____

  W _____   _____   _____

  A _____   _____   _____

- Orally practice the nine steps of TWA. It is essential that each student memorize the mnemonic. If some students are having trouble with this, spend a few minutes practicing it. Tell the students that you will test them on it each day to make sure they have it. Remind the students that they can practice memorizing it. If the students are having trouble with the parts, give them a few minutes to practice together in pairs. Ask the students if they remember why it is important to use TWA. Let them (or you) give examples of how TWA can help in reading and writing.

DEVELOP THE STRATEGY AND SELF-REGULATION

Step 1: Model TWA

- Tell the students that you will show them how TWA works when reading a passage. Tell them that TWA works especially well for passages that are nonfiction—passages that have information about people, places, and things, but could be used for anything they read. Tell them that you will go through all the steps of TWA with the passage "Gum." Let them know that you will be reading out loud so that they can see all the steps. Tell the students that you will also say out loud the things you say to yourself when reading. The students can assist you when appropriate, but remember: YOU ARE IN CHARGE!

- Introduce the TWA Checklist. Show the students the TWA Checklist that you will use when reading "Gum." Tell the students that you will be showing them how to use a checklist and also that you will be talking out loud again so they can hear the things you say to yourself when thinking about the nine steps in TWA. Give each student a TWA Checklist and ask him or her to check off steps as you model.

- Model the whole reading process using TWA with self-statements to guide you. Be sure to use all kinds of self-statements. Tell the students that in the next lesson you are going to show them how to do each of the steps in a special way and that they will be getting a lot of practice in each step. For now, you will be showing them how using the TWA strategy works after all the parts are learned. Be sure to check each step off as it is completed. A model script follows:

- Say, *"I have a passage to read. It will be easy to understand because I know the steps in TWA that will help me understand and remember the passage. What is the first thing I should do? The first thing I need to do is to think about three things before reading. First, I need to think about the author's purpose. Well, I can do this. The title is 'Gum.' I should read the first sentence to be sure."* Read the first sentence. *"I'm still not sure. I'll read the second sentence."* Read the second sentence. *"Okay. The author is writing about gum. His purpose is to inform. I know that when an author writes to inform, he will be writing information with details."* Check off the first step on the TWA Checklist. *"The next thing I need to do is to think about what I know. I know a lot about gum."* Share some information. Check off the second step on the TWA Checklist. *"Next, I need to think about what I want to learn."* Share some information. Check off the third step on the checklist. *"I have checked the three steps to Think Before Reading. I am ready to read."*

- Start reading at a normal speed and then speed up. Say, *"Whoa—slow down—this is not making sense. I see on my TWA Checklist that I need to think about Reading Speed. I will slow down so I can understand what I am reading."* Note that stopping at punctuation is a good way to monitor this. Read at an acceptable speed and stop when you come to something to link knowledge. Read and then come to something you do not understand. Say, *"This doesn't make sense."* Reread. *"Oh, I understand now."* Finish reading the passage, modeling each of the steps again. Do this recursively while reading the entire passage. Check off the three steps on the TWA Checklist after you have read the entire passage.

- Say, *"I really think I know a lot more about gum now. What do I need to do next? After reading, think about . . . . Well, the first step is the main idea. I want to know the main idea of each paragraph. The main idea or the gist of the first paragraph is . . . . This was simple to do in this first paragraph because the main idea was in the first two sentences."* Introduce the highlighters. *"I will use these highlighters to help me find the main ideas and details."* Highlight the main idea in yellow. Then model how to state the main idea out loud in your own words. Check off the TWA Checklist. *"I see that my next step is to summarize. I know that part of the summary is the main idea. I have a good start because I have the main idea in this paragraph. What do I need to do? I need to add two or three details that tell me something about the main idea. I also need to take out any information that is not important."* Highlight details to keep in blue/green and details to eliminate in pink. Model how to state the summary in your own words. Check off the TWA Checklist. Tell the students that you will make a check mark for each paragraph read. Count the number of paragraphs; write the total number of check marks on the TWA Checklist needed for main ideas and summary.

- Say, *"Am I finished? Well, there are more paragraphs in this passage about gum. I think there were some other main ideas with details in the passage. The next paragraph talks about how . . . ."* Model main idea and summary with each paragraph. Check off the TWA Checklist for each paragraph. *"WOW! I came up with a lot of main ideas and summaries."* Note that you will have check marks for each paragraph on your TWA Checklist.

• Say, *"I am almost finished! I have really learned a lot about gum. And that is a good thing because the last thing I need to do is to think about What You Learned."* Model orally retelling what you learned. Tell the students that later they will be writing retells. Check off the TWA Checklist.

Step 2: Reinforce Performance

Show the students that after reading, you will check your TWA Checklist to see if you have completed all the steps. If you have done this you will get to make a star, a smiling face, and so forth on the TWA Checklist.

Step 3: Introduce Self-Statements

• Give each student a TWA Self-Statements sheet. Explain that they will use this sheet to record some things they can say to themselves when reading with TWA. Ask them if they remember some things you said to yourself when thinking before, while, and after reading. Stress that the things you said to yourself helped you remember the TWA strategy and how to use it.

• Have the students record one or two things they could say when thinking before, while, and after reading. Be sure to do each section one at a time and be sure to tell the students that these are things they can say inside their head. If the students resist, they can always write down some of the things you said.

WRAP-UP

• Practice TWA. Ask each student to explain what TWA stands for and why it is important to use TWA before, during, and after reading. Help each student as needed to ensure that they understand what TWA stands for and why it is important. Stress that using TWA helps when reading and give some examples. Remind the students that they will need to come to the next session and write out TWA and say what it means from memory.

• Give each student his or her folder. Have the students put everything except the scratch paper in their folders. Collect the students' folders and thank them for working hard.

Gum

Sometimes things are discovered by accident. For example, chewing gum was accidentally discovered in the 1860s by workers in the United States. A company was searching for materials to use as rubber when they found chicle. The basic material used for the first chewing gum was chicle. Chicle comes from a tree that grows in Central America. Because chicle was expensive and hard to get, a substitute gum was invented.

The new man-made gum is made in the same way as the chicle chewing gum. Once the mixture is made, it is heated and then cooled. Then the gum mixture is put on a large belt, rolled to the right thickness, cut, wrapped, and packaged. Bubble gum is made the same way. The difference is that rubber latex is added to the mixture to give it more strength. This helps the gum stretch when making bubbles.

The first bubble gum was accidentally created by W.E. Diemer in 1928. He discovered how to make bubble gum while testing gum recipes. After he made the first bubble gum, "Dubble Bubble," he taught others how to blow bubbles. He invited kids into his home to talk about his invention. His wife told a New York newspaper, "He would say to me, 'I've done something with my life. I've made kids happy around the world.'"

LESSON 3

LESSON OVERVIEW

The class will collaboratively practice before and while reading. The teacher will introduce and discuss the main idea and summarization strategies. The group will collaboratively practice main idea and summarization strategies. The group will collaboratively retell orally what they have learned.

STUDENT OBJECTIVES

The students will practice, with their peers and the teacher, using TWA to read a passage.

MATERIALS

- TWA mnemonic chart
- Expository passage sample ("States of Matter")
- TWA Checklist

- TWA Self-Statements sheet
- Scratch paper; pencils; yellow, blue/green, and pink highlighters; student folders

---

SET THE CONTEXT FOR STUDENT LEARNING

- Test TWA. Give the students scratch paper and ask them to write out the strategy reminder TWA. Then ask them as a group what each letter stands for. Be sure they take turns so that all have a chance to share.

T _____ _____ _____

W _____ _____ _____

A _____ _____ _____

- Orally practice the nine steps of TWA. Discuss and give examples of how TWA helps with reading assignments. If the students are having trouble with the parts, give them a few minutes to practice together in pairs.

DEVELOP THE STRATEGY AND SELF-REGULATION

Step 1: Collaboratively Complete the Think Before Reading and Think While Reading Steps

- Give each student a copy of the passage "States of Matter" and a TWA Checklist. Ask the students to get their TWA Self-Statements out of their folders and remind the students to refer to them, especially when they have difficulty with one of the steps. Tell the students that you will complete the steps of TWA together. Tell the students that you expect them to help monitor using the strategy by checking their own TWA Checklist for each step.

- Collaboratively decide the author's purpose. The author's purpose is to inform. Ask the students what kinds of things should be looked for in informational writing. Check off the TWA Checklist.

- Collaboratively complete the What You Know and What You Want to Learn steps. Check off the TWA Checklist.

Step 2: Collaboratively Read the Passage

Read the passage "States of Matter" together, taking turns in the group. Remind the students to refer to the TWA Self-Statements sheet. Discuss reading speed (note that stopping at punctuation is a good way to monitor this), linking knowledge, and rereading parts throughout. Check off the TWA Checklist.

Step 3: Introduce and Model Main Idea Strategy and Summary for Each Paragraph

- Tell the students that you know a trick for developing main idea statements and summaries. Explain that for TWA, you want the main idea to give you the gist of each paragraph. Explain that this will help when developing the paragraph summaries and retelling what you learned.

- Give each student a yellow highlighter. Read the first paragraph in "States of Matter." Together, find the sentence in the paragraph that tells the gist of the paragraph. Highlight this sentence in yellow. Look at the other sentences in the paragraph: Are any others important for the gist? Highlight these in yellow.

- Examine what is highlighted. Is there a list of words that can be titled as one word? If so, write that word on top of the list. For example, "wood," "nails," and "ice" should be refered to as solids. You would not give these as a list of words in a main idea statement.

- Develop a main idea statement. Tell the students that these are best if they are in their own words. Check off the TWA Checklist for each paragraph.

- Give each student a blue/green and a pink highlighter. Tell the students that the pink and blue/green markers serve a special purpose. The markers will help identify which sentences are important details and which are not so important details. Discuss each sentence and decide as a group if the sentence is an important detail—if so, highlight it in blue/green. If not, highlight it in pink.

- Tell the students that you are now ready to develop the summary together. Model how to develop a summary for the first paragraph. Be sure to note that the main idea is the first part of the summary. Tell the students that summaries are best and easiest to understand and remember if they are in the students' own words. Check off the TWA Checklist.

- Collaboratively develop a main idea statement and a summary for each paragraph. Check off the TWA Checklist as you do this.

Step 4: Collaboratively Think About What You Learned

- Collaboratively tell orally "what you learned" in the passage.

 Say, *"We will learn how to retell orally, and later we will retell in writing."* Tell the students that you all are going to give in your own words a retell of the passage—just as though the person listening knows nothing about "States of Matter." Collaboratively retell. Be sure to include your self-statements to help you with retelling. Note that a good way to remember is to think of the main ideas and then think about the important details for each main idea. Spend time talking about your thought process in doing a retell. Check off the TWA Checklist.

Step 5: Add to Self-Statements Sheet

Now that the students have had an opportunity to try the strategy, have them look over their TWA Self-Statements sheets and add any other statements that may help them in using the strategy.

Step 6: Reinforce Performance

Ask the students to look at the TWA Checklist. Did they complete all parts? If so, they may write a star, check mark and so forth.

WRAP-UP

- Remind the students that they will need to come to the next session and write out TWA and tell what it means from memory. Give each student his or her folder. Have them put everything except the scratch paper in their folders. Collect the students' folders and thank them for working hard.

NOTE: If the students need another day or two of group collaborative practice, repeat the lesson with a new passage.

CHAPTER 17

LESSON 3

TWA + PLANS

States of Matter

Matter comes in different forms and sizes. Matter can be a solid, a liquid, or a gas. These three forms are called the states of matter.

A solid is one state of matter. Solids have a definite shape and a definite volume. Wood, nails, pencils, coins, and ice are all solids. They all have a definite shape and a definite volume.

A liquid is another state of matter. Water, milk, vinegar, and vegetable oil are liquids. Liquids do not have a definite shape. But liquids do have a definite volume. For example, fifty milliliters of orange juice will take up fifty milliliters of space whether you pour it into a glass or spill it onto the floor.

The third state of matter is gas. Oxygen, carbon dioxide, and helium are gases. Think about the shape of balloons. If you take the same gas and blow it into a differently shaped balloon, the gas will take the shape of the new balloon. Like liquids, gases do not have shapes of their own. They take the shapes of their containers.

The volume of a gas can also change. If the gas inside a balloon escapes into the room, it will spread out until it takes up all the space it can. Its volume would then be much greater than its volume in the balloon. A gas always fills its container completely. If you push on a balloon filled with a gas, you may be able to squeeze the gas into a smaller space. A gas has no definite volume and no definite shape.

LESSON 4

LESSON OVERVIEW

The students will begin to practice using TWA to read a passage. The teacher will monitor pairs of students to determine if additional individual instruction is needed.

STUDENT OBJECTIVES

Pairs of students will collaboratively practice TWA.

MATERIALS

- TWA mnemonic chart
- Expository passage sample ("The Constitution")
- TWA Self-Statements sheet

- TWA Checklist
- Student folders, scratch paper, pencils, highlighters

SET THE CONTEXT FOR STUDENT LEARNING

- Test TWA. Give the students scratch paper and ask them to write out the strategy reminder TWA. Then ask them, as a group, what each letter stands for. Be sure they take turns so that all have a chance to share.

  T _____   _____   _____

  W _____   _____   _____

  A _____   _____   _____

- Orally practice the nine steps of TWA. Discuss and give examples of how TWA helps with reading assignments. If the students are having trouble with the parts, give them a few minutes to practice together in pairs.

DEVELOP THE STRATEGY AND SELF-REGULATION

Step 1: Pair Practice

Tell the students that they will try the steps of TWA with a partner. Let them know that you will be listening carefully to each thing they do and that you want them to report back when they finish each step. Stress that you will assist them as much as necessary.

Step 2: Complete Think Before Reading Steps

- Give each student a copy of the passage "The Constitution" and a TWA Checklist. Tell the students to get out their TWA Self-Statements sheet and remind them to refer to the sheet when needed. Tell the students that you want them to complete the first three steps of TWA with their partner. When they finish these steps, they will need to report back to you.

- Have each pair develop the author's purpose and report back to you. Be sure that the students check off their TWA Checklist.

- Have each pair complete the Think about What You Know and What You Want to Learn steps, reporting back to you and checking off the TWA Checklist as they complete each step.

Step 3: Pair Practice Think While Reading

Let the students work in pairs to read the passage. Tell them that you want them to take turns: One will practice the three steps for Think While Reading with the first paragraph and the other will practice the three steps for Think While Reading with the next paragraph, and so on. Stress that they will need to consider the three steps of Think While Reading, and that they should check off the TWA Checklist when they have finished reading. Carefully monitor what the students do while reading.

Step 4: Pair Practice Main Idea and Summaries for Each Paragraph

Let the students work in pairs to develop main idea statements and summaries for each paragraph and report back to you. Tell them that you want them to take turns: One will practice the strategy with the first paragraph, and the other will practice the strategy with the next paragraph, and so on. They should check off the main idea and summary as it is completed.

Step 5: Pair Practice Think About What You Learned

Let the students work in pairs for Think about What You Learned and report back to you. Be sure to help them by giving examples of how you can use the main ideas, details, and summaries to develop a great retell.

Step 6: Reinforce Performance

Ask the students to look at their TWA Checklist. Did they complete all parts? If so, they may write a star and so forth.

WRAP-UP

- Ask the students if they need/want to add or change anything on their self-statements sheet.

- Remind the students that they will need to come to the next session and write out TWA and tell what it means from memory.

- Give each student his or her folder. Have them put everything except the scratch paper in the folder. Collect the students' folders and thank them for working hard.

NOTE: Repeat this lesson until the students have demonstrated that they can complete the steps of the strategy independently.

The Constitution

The American Revolution was won in 1783. The United States became an independent country with 13 states. The new country needed new laws. A constitution is a group of laws.

The leaders of the United States decided to write laws, or a constitution, for their new country. In 1787, leaders from 12 of the states went to Philadelphia, Pennsylvania. In Philadelphia, the leaders of the 12 states wrote the Constitution of the United States.

Before the American Revolution, England made laws for the American colonies. Americans always wanted to make their own laws. The Constitution says that the American people can help write their own laws. How do Americans do this? The Constitution says that Americans should choose, or vote, for people to work for them in their government.

Laws in the United States are made in the Capitol building in Washington, D.C. The Senate and the House of Representatives are both in the Capitol building. Men and women who write laws are called senators and representatives. The Constitution says that Americans should vote for people to be their senators and representatives. Every state sends two senators to work in the Senate. Representatives are sent based on the number of people in a state. States with many people send many representatives to work in the House of Representatives. States with fewer people send fewer representatives to work in the House of Representatives.

Americans vote for a president every four years. The president is the leader of the United States government. The president helps make our laws. Americans help write their own laws by voting for their senators, representatives, and president.

LESSON 5

LESSON OVERVIEW
The teacher will model writing notes after using TWA before, while, and after reading.

STUDENT OBJECTIVES
The students will complete a TWA Outline while following the teacher-led modeling lesson.

MATERIALS

- TWA mnemonic chart
- Expository passage sample ("Yellowstone")
- TWA Self-Statements sheet
- TWA Checklist
- TWA Outline
- Student folders, scratch paper, pencils

SET THE CONTEXT FOR STUDENT LEARNING

Test TWA. Give the students scratch paper and ask them to write out the strategy reminder—TWA—with spaces. Review each letter briefly.

T _____ _____ _____

W _____ _____ _____

A _____ _____ _____

Orally practice the nine steps of TWA only if needed at this time. Ask the students if they remember why it is important to use TWA. Let them (or you) give examples of how TWA can help in reading.

DEVELOP THE STRATEGY AND SELF-REGULATION

Step 1: Model Writing Notes with TWA

- Tell the students that you will show them how to write notes with TWA while reading a passage. Tell them that you will go through all the steps of TWA with the passage "Yellowstone." Let them know that you will be reading out loud so that they can see all the steps. Tell the students that you will also say out loud the things you say to yourself while reading. The students can assist you when appropriate.

- Model the whole reading process using TWA. Tell the students that they will not use the highlighters but will write notes on the TWA Outline to help them with main ideas and summaries.

Say, *"I have a passage to read. It will be easy to understand because I know the steps in TWA that will help me understand and remember the passage. What is the first thing I should do? I need to check off the three steps in Think Before Reading. The first step is Think about: The Author's Purpose. Well, I can do this. The title of the passage is 'Yellowstone.'"* Check off that step on the TWA Checklist. *"The next step is Think about: What You Know."* Check off the second step on the TWA Checklist. *"The third step is Think about: What You Want to Learn."* Check off the third step on the TWA Checklist. *"I have checked off the three steps to Think Before Reading. I am ready to read."*

Start reading at a normal speed and then speed up. *"Whoa–slow down–this is not making sense. I see on my TWA Checklist under Think While Reading that I need to think about Reading Speed. I will slow down so I can understand what I am reading."* Read at an acceptable speed and stop when you come to something that will link knowledge. Continue reading and then come to something you do not understand. *"Hmmm . . . This doesn't make sense."* Reread. *"Oh, I understand now."* Finish reading the passage, modeling each of the steps again. Do this recursively while reading the entire passage. Check off the three steps on the TWA Checklist after you have read the entire passage.

 Say, *"I really think I know a lot more about Yellowstone now. What do I need to do next? The first step in After Reading is Think about: The Main Idea, I need to think about the main idea of the first paragraph. Today, instead of highlighting, I am going to write on the TWA Outline. You can write along with me.* Hand each student a TWA Outline. *"Well, the first step is Think about: The Main Idea. The main idea or the gist of the passage is. . . . This was simple to do in this passage because the main idea was in the first sentence."* Model how to state the main idea out loud in your own words. Model how to write notes for the main idea in outline format. Check off the TWA Checklist. *"I see that the next step in After Reading is Think about: Summarizing Information. I know that part of the summary is the main idea. I have a good start because I have the main idea in this paragraph. What do I need to do? I need to add at least two details that tell me something about the main idea."* Model how to write notes for details. Model how to state the summary in your own words. Check off the TWA Checklist.

Use the TWA Outline. The following is an example of a complete outline. Remember to orally produce a summary for each paragraph:

1. YELLOWSTONE NATIONAL PARK

    a. Located in Montana, Idaho, and Wyoming

    b. Declared first national park in 1872

2. SETTLERS FIRST MOVED INTO AREA

    a. Settlers killed animals

    b. Settlers cleared the land

    c. Park established to protect the land and animals

3. YELLOWSTONE POPULAR TOURIST DESTINATION

    a. Geysers and hot springs

    b. Many natural wonders

    c. Visitors never disappointed

 Say, *"Am I finished? Well, there are two more paragraphs in this passage about Yellowstone. I think there were some other main ideas with details in the passage. The next paragraph talks about how. . . ."* Model main idea and summary with each paragraph/ check off TWA Checklist for each paragraph. *"WOW! I came up with a lot of main ideas and summaries."* [NOTE: You will have check marks—three for each paragraph on your checklist.]

"I am almost finished! I have really learned a lot about Yellowstone. And that is a good thing because the final After Reading reminder is Think about: What I Learned." Discuss this. Next, model how you will use the outline to help you with the retell. Look over the TWA Outline and then model retelling. Check off the TWA Checklist.

Step 2: Reinforce Performance

Ask the students to look at the TWA Checklist. Did they complete all parts? If so, they may write a star, and so forth.

Step 3: Self-Instruction Sheet

Ask the students to add to their self-statements to help them with writing the outline.

WRAP-UP

Practice TWA. Ask each student to explain what TWA stands for and why it is important to use TWA before, during, and after reading. Stress that using TWA helps when reading and writing notes and give some examples. Remind the students that they will need to come to the next session and write out TWA and tell what it means from memory.

Give each student his or her folder. Have them put everything except the scratch paper in the folder. Collect the students' folders and thank them for working hard.

Yellowstone

Yellowstone was the first national park named by the United States government. In 1872, more than two million acres were set aside for the park. The new park covered land in the states of Montana, Idaho, and Wyoming.

Before Yellowstone became a park, settlers pushed into the wilderness near the Yellowstone area. They killed off many of the animals. They cleared the land for farming. More people followed. More animals, grasslands, and trees were destroyed. The park was established to keep the land in its natural condition.

People love to visit this fun place. Yellowstone has a variety of attractions such as geysers and hot springs. This is the only place on earth with so many of these natural wonders. One of the most famous sights is a geyser that erupts every 30 to 60 minutes. It spits boiling water and steam about 150 feet into the air. Yellowstone National Park has so many things to see. Visitors are never disappointed.

LESSON 6

LESSON OVERVIEW
The teacher will monitor students' collaborative practice of using TWA and outlining.

STUDENT OBJECTIVES
Students will collaboratively practice in pairs writing an outline with TWA.

MATERIALS
- TWA mnemonic chart
- Expository passage sample from class readings [Note: it is best to start with a passage with three to four paragraphs for this lesson]
- TWA Checklist
- TWA Outline
- TWA Self-Statements sheet
- Highlighters, student folders, scratch paper, pencils, stickers

SET THE CONTEXT FOR STUDENT LEARNING

Test TWA. Give each student scratch paper and ask him or her to write out the strategy reminder TWA. Then ask the students what each letter stands for. Be sure they take turns so that all have a chance to share.

T _____ _____ _____

W _____ _____ _____

A _____ _____ _____

Orally practice the nine steps of TWA if needed. Discuss and give examples of how TWA helps with reading and writing assignments.

DEVELOP THE STRATEGY AND SELF-REGULATION

Step 1: Complete Think Before Reading and Think While Reading Steps

- Give each student a copy of the passage you have copied from class readings, a TWA Checklist, and a TWA Outline.

- Ask the students to get their TWA Self-Statements out of their folders and remind the students to refer to them, especially when they have difficulty with one of the steps. Ask the students to add statements as needed to help with writing an outline. Tell the students that they will complete the steps of the TWA Outline with their partner.

- Have the students complete the steps for Think Before Reading and Think While Reading. Check off the TWA Checklist.

Step 2: Complete The Main Idea Strategy and Summary

Ask student pairs to highlight and write main idea notes for the first paragraph. Develop main idea statements. Tell the students that these are best if they are in their own words and that it is easier to do when using the outline. Check off the TWA Checklist.

- Ask student pairs to highlight and write notes for the details in the first paragraph. Tell the students that you are now ready to develop the summary. Develop the summary for the first paragraph. Be sure to note that the main idea is the first part of the summary. Tell the students that summaries are best and will be easier to understand and remember if they are in their own words. This will be easier to do in their own words if they look at the outline. Check off the TWA Checklist.

- Ask student pairs to highlight, develop notes, main idea statements, and summaries for each paragraph. Have them check off the TWA Checklist as they do this. Be sure to tell the students that they should have a check mark for each paragraph for the main idea and summary. Say, *"How many check marks should we have for each main idea and summary in [passage title]? Yes, we should have _____ check marks for each because there are _____ paragraphs."* Note the number of paragraphs in the passage you selected.

Step 3: Complete Think About What You Learned

Ask peers to discuss What You Learned. Tell them to use the TWA Outline to help them. Note that a good way to remember is to think about the notes they made about the main ideas and then think about the important details for each main idea. Check off the TWA Checklist.

WRAP-UP

Remind the students that they will need to come to the next session and write out TWA and tell what it means from memory. Give each student his or her folder. Have the students put everything except the scratch paper in the folder. Collect the students' folders and thank them for working hard.

NOTE: Repeat this lesson as needed.

LESSON 7

LESSON OVERVIEW

Pairs of students will practice TWA and outlining. Highlighters and the TWA Checklist are faded in this lesson.

STUDENT OBJECTIVES

Pairs of students will collaboratively practice TWA and outlining without highlighters and the TWA Checklist.

MATERIALS

- TWA mnemonic chart
- TWA Outline
- TWA Self-Statements sheet

- Passage sample selected from class materials
- Student folders, scratch paper, pencils

SET THE CONTEXT FOR STUDENT LEARNING

Test TWA. Give the students scratch paper and ask them to write out the **strategy reminder** TWA. Then ask them what each letter stands for.

T _____ _____ _____

W _____ _____ _____

A _____ _____ _____

Tell the students that today they will use their strategy reminders for checking off parts.

DEVELOP THE STRATEGY AND SELF-REGULATION

Step 1: Pair Practice

- Tell the students that you can still use TWA even when you do not have a checklist or highlighters. Show them how to use the **strategy reminder (the one they have been writing each day as a checklist—see above)**. Show them how you can lightly write "MI" for main idea sentences and "D" for sentences with important details.

- Tell the students that they will practice all the steps of TWA using pencils for identifying main ideas and details with a partner. Let them know that you will be carefully observing each thing they do and that you want them to report back when they finish each step. Stress that you will assist them as much as necessary.

Step 2: Complete Think Before Reading Steps

- Give each student a copy of the passage you have selected from class readings. Tell the students to get out their TWA Self-Statements sheet and remind them to refer to the sheet when needed. Tell the students that you want them to complete the first three steps of TWA with their partner. When they finish these steps, they will need to report back to you.

- Have each student write the **strategy reminder** TWA on top of the passage paper. Have each pair complete the Think Before Reading steps. The students should place check marks in the space by "T," "W," and "A" as they finish the steps.

Step 3: Pair Practice Think While Reading

Let the students work in pairs to read the passage. Tell them that you want them to take turns: One will practice the three steps for Think While Reading with the first paragraph, and then the other will practice the three steps for Think While Reading with the next paragraph, and so on. Stress that they will need to consider the three steps of Think While Reading, and that they should check off the space by the "W" on their **strategy reminder** Checklist when they have finished reading. Carefully monitor what the students do while reading.

Step 4: Pair Practice Main Idea and Summaries for Each Paragraph

Let the students work in pairs to develop notes, main idea statements, and summaries for each paragraph. Tell them that instead of highlighting they can write "MI" for main ideas or "D" for details. Show them how to do this until they can easily do it on their own. Tell them that you want them to take turns: One will practice the strategy with the first paragraph, and then the other will practice the strategy with the next paragraph, and so on. They should check off The Main Idea and Summarizing Information spaces by "A" as they are completed.

Step 5: Pair Practice Think About What You Learned

Let the students work together for Think about What You Learned and retelling the passage. Check off space on their **strategy reminder**.

Step 6: Reinforce Performance

Ask the students to look at their **strategy reminder**. Did they complete all parts? If so, they can make a star, and so forth.

WRAP-UP

NOTE: Remind the students that they will need to come to the next session and write out TWA and tell what it means from memory. Give each student his or her folder. Have the students put everything except the scratch paper in their folder. Collect the students' folders and thank them for working hard.

LESSON 8

LESSON OVERVIEW

In this lesson, writing an essay is introduced. A strategy such as the PLANS strategy in this book works especially well. [Note: Refer to the section on PLANS for an expanded version of lesson plans and materials.] A TWA + PLANS Goals Suggestion Sheet is provided; however, you should develop goals to meet the needs of your students and classroom objectives. If using the provided sheet, we recommend that the students work toward meeting all goals!

STUDENT OBJECTIVES

Students will commit to learning a new strategy for writing an essay: PLANS.

MATERIALS

- TWA + PLANS mnemonic chart
- TWA + PLANS Goals Suggestion Sheet
- TWA Learning Contract
- Student folders, pencils, paper

SET THE CONTEXT FOR STUDENT LEARNING

Test for student knowledge of the TWA steps. Do this orally and very briefly.

DEVELOP THE STRATEGY AND SELF-REGULATION

Step 1: PLANS

Ask the students if they know the meaning of the word *plan*. Discuss how planning helps improve writing (e.g, helps to organize writing, helps to make an essay longer). Say, *"I am going to teach you a three-step plan for writing essays about something you have read. The three steps can also be used for other types of writing. For example, you could use the three steps to help you write stories or reports that you do in class.*

P *Pick Goals*

- Give each student a TWA + PLANS Mnemonic Chart. Tell them that they will need to look at each step on the chart as you talk about them.

- Cover your paper so that only the first step shows. Say, *"The first thing that you need to do when you write a paper is to figure out what you want to do. In other words, you should pick goals for what you want your paper to say. The goals you set for your paper should direct what you do.*

  For example, if you read a passage about whales and needed to write a paper or an essay about the passage, the first thing you should do is set some goals for what you would like you paper to accomplish. For instance, a goal might be to write a paper that includes the main idea and important details about the passage. Can you think of any other types of goals I might set?"

- Brainstorm ideas for goals.

Then say, *"As you can see, there are many types of goals I can pick that will help me write my paper. I can set goals for how much I want to say, for the types of things I*

415

want to include, for the types of words I use, and so on. Also, the type of goals that I pick will depend on the type of paper I am writing. Some of my goals for an essay will be different from my goals for a story. To help you pick your goals for your paper [point to "Pick Goals" on the mnemonic chart], *I am going to give you a chart with goals on it."* Hand each student a TWA + PLANS Goals Suggestion Sheet. Say, *"We can add goals as needed to help us with our writing. Please keep this TWA + PLANS Goals Suggestion Sheet in your folder; you can use it when you are asked to write a paper. Good writers use all the goals on this sheet."*

• Review each of the goals on the TWA + PLANS Goals Suggestion Sheet. Read each goal to the students and have them repeat it.

Say, *"When using the goals sheet, we pick the goals we want to focus on. Of course, we do not want to totally ignore any of the goals . . . good writers use them all!*

Now let's return to our TWA + PLANS 3-Steps Mnemonic Chart. If I had to write a paper about what I read about whales, my first step would be to "Pick my Goals." Point to this. "I would do this by looking at my TWA + PLANS Goals Suggestion Sheet and pick at least three goals. For instance, I would pick . . . ." Select three goals and explain why you picked each. *"Next, I would put a check mark next to each of my goals on my TWA + PLANS Goals Suggestion Sheet so that I will remember them. Also, I would put a star by the most important one (i.e., to include all the main ideas)."*

L *List Ways to Meet Goals*

• Uncover the second step on the TWA + PLANS: List Ways to Meet Goals mnemonic Chart. Say, *"Once I have checked my goals, I need to think about how I will meet or accomplish the goals. In other words, next to each goal I have chosen, I will list one or more things that I can do to help me meet that goal. For example, if I were writing a paper about what I read about whales* (point to goal on goals sheet), *one way I might be able to successfully meet the goal is by looking at the outline that I made with TWA. If I wanted to add more adjectives to my paper, I might read the passage and write adjectives on my TWA Outline. If I want to make sure my paper has capitalization and punctuation, I will read each sentence and check for that."* Model/write these on your goals sheet.

A

   • Point out that the "A" in PLANS doesn't do anything—it is just a filler letter that means "and."

N *Make Notes*

Say, *"Once I have finished picking my goals and listing ways to meet those goals, I would make notes about the kinds of things that I might use in my paper."* Uncover "N." Say, *"Because I made some notes on an outline when reading with TWA, I can use these. This part is easy because of the work I did with TWA. I can also add to the notes to help me meet my goals."*

S *Sequence Notes*

Say, *'When I finished making all of my notes, I would think about what I wanted to come first in my paper, then second, third, and so forth.'* Uncover "S." *"I would put a '1' by what I wanted first, a '2' by what I wanted second, a '3' by what would go third, and so forth. This will help me when I write my paper."*

Step 2: Write and Say More

 Say, *"Once I have finished PLANS, I will be ready to write."* Uncover Step 2 on the TWA + PLANS Mnemonic Chart. *"My notes would be my plan and would guide what I write. However, as I write, I may think of other things to say, and I want to be sure to include them as well. To help me do this, I will remind myself to say more as I write, and to remember my goals."*

Step 3: Test Goals

Say, *"The last step in the TWA + PLANS Mnemonic Chart [uncover step 3] is to Test Goals to see if I met my goals. To do this, I would read my paper again and check to see if I met each goal that I set. For example, if I set a goal to write a paragraph for each main idea, I would count the number of paragraphs written and write that next to my goal. I would put Yes if I met my goal and No if I did not. If I did not meet any of my goals, I would think about how I might meet them on my next writing assignment."*

Step 4: Revise TWA Learning Contract

Ask the students to revise the TWA Learning Contract by committing to learn PLANS. Ask them to revise ways in which they will use TWA + PLANS.

Step 5: Practice PLANS

- Work with the students on identifying writing goals on the TWA + PLANS Goals Suggestion Sheet. They can paraphrase. It is important that students learn what each goal is and that they can say it in their own words.

- If time permits, tell the students that you are going to work on memorizing the 3 steps for planning and writing.

WRAP-UP

Have the students put all materials in folders. Remind them that you will check next time to see if they remember TWA + PLANS and the 3-steps and the goals on the goals suggestion sheet.

LESSON 9

LESSON OVERVIEW
The students will be provided guided practice in using TWA + PLANS for reading and writing about a passage.

STUDENT OBJECTIVES
The students will practice using the TWA + PLANS strategy until they can independently write an essay about a passage they have read.

MATERIALS
- TWA + PLANS mnemonic chart
- TWA + PLANS Goals Suggestion Sheet
- TWA Outline

- Passage selected from class readings, student folders, pencil, paper

SET THE CONTEXT FOR STUDENT LEARNING

Test for student knowledge of steps of TWA + PLANS.

DEVELOP THE STRATEGY AND SELF-REGULATION

Step 1: TWA

Have the students complete the nine steps of the TWA Outline for a passage you have selected from class materials.

Step 2: PLANS

P *Pick* Goals

- Give each student the TWA + PLANS Goals Suggestion Sheet.

- Review each of the goals on the goal chart. Ask the students to pick goals for their paper. Add goals to goals suggestion sheet if needed to meet your classroom objectives and students' needs.

L *List* Ways to Meet Goals

- Ask the students to list ways to meet their goals.

A

- Point out that the "A" in PLANS doesn't do anything—it is just a filler letter for "and."

N Make *Notes*

- Ask the students to review notes on the TWA Outline and make revisions and additions.

S *Sequence* Notes

- Ask the students to review notes on the TWA Outline and sequence if needed.

Step 3: Write and Say More

Remind the students to say more as they write and to remember their goals as they write their essay.

Step 4: Test Goals

Ask the students to check to see if they met all of their goals.

Step 5: Practice PLANS

If time permits, tell the students you are going to work on memorizing TWA, PLANS, and the 3 steps.

WRAP-UP

Have the students put all materials in folders. Repeat this lesson again until the students have demonstrated that they understand and can apply the concept of TWA + PLANS. It may take a couple of lessons for them to expand from selecting a few simple goals to trying more complex ones. Once they have mastered the strategy steps in TWA + PLANS, fade support materials. For example, be sure to teach students to write a TWA Outline on their own without the outline provided in the materials. In fact, this can be added as a goal.

TWA

Think Before Reading

Think about:

The Author's Purpose

What You Know

What You Want to Learn

Think **W**hile Reading

Think about:

Reading Speed

Linking Knowledge

Rereading Parts

Think **A**fter Reading

Think about:

The Main Idea

Summarizing Information

What You Learned

TWA Learning Contract

STRATEGY _____

Student _____ Date _____

Teacher _____

Target Completion Date _____

Goal_____

_____

_____

_____

How to meet this goal_____

_____

_____

_____

Signatures:

Student _____

Teacher _____

- -

_____ has successfully completed

instructions in the _____ Strategy and

agrees to use it in _____

_____

_____

Date _____

Student _____

Teacher _____

TWA Checklist

T   Think Before Reading

Think about:

     The Author's Purpose   _____

     What You Know   _____

     What You Want to Learn   _____

W   Think While Reading

Think About:

     Reading Speed   _____

     Linking What You Know   _____

     Rereading Parts   _____

A   Think After Reading

Think About:

     The Main Idea   _____

     Summarizing Information   _____

     What You Learned   _____

My Self-Statements

Think Before Reading:

_____
_____
_____
_____
_____
_____

Think While Reading:

_____
_____
_____
_____
_____
_____

Think After Reading:

_____
_____
_____
_____
_____
_____

TWA Outline

Main Idea	
Detail	
Detail	
Detail	

Main Idea	
Detail	
Detail	
Detail	

Main Idea	
Detail	
Detail	
Detail	

TWA

Think Before Reading

   Think about:

      The Author's Purpose

      What You Know

      What You Want to Learn

Think **W**hile Reading

   Think about:

      Reading Speed

      Linking Knowledge

      Rereading Parts

Think **A**fter Reading

   Think about:

      The Main Idea

      Summarizing Information

      What You Learned

PLANS

1. Do **P**ick Goals

     List Ways to Meet Goals

     And

   Make **N**otes

     Sequence Notes

2. Write and Say More

3. Test Goals

TWA + PLANS Goals Suggestion Sheet

1. Goals for Starting My Essay

_____ Write a paper that has a paragraph for each main idea in the passage read.

_____ Write a paper that uses the main idea as a topic sentence in each paragraph.

_____ Write a paper that has details that support the main idea in each paragraph.

2. Goals for Writing My Essay

_____ Write a paper that includes adjectives (words that describe).

_____ Write a paper that includes adverbs (action word helpers).

_____ Write a paper that includes a combined sentence (one sentence for two sentences + uses a connecting word).

3. Goals for Revising My Essay

_____ Check for punctuation and capitalization!

_____ Check my spelling!

_____ Read my paper out loud to myself. Does it make sense?

Note: Use the Vocabulary Strategy for teaching adjectives and adverbs or one of the revising strategies if your students are unable to complete goals 2 and 3 sections independently.

Index

Page numbers followed by *f* indicate figures; those followed by *t* indicate tables.